BORDER CROSSINGS

ISBN 0-13-530155-6

0 57812 30155 9

BORDER CROSSINGS
Doing Business in the US

Wendy Evans • Henry Lane • Shawna O'Grady
with the contribution of Terry Hildebrand, PhD

Prentice Hall Canada, Inc.
Scarborough, Ontario

Canadian Cataloguing in Publication Data

Evans, Wendy
    Border crossings : doing business in the United States

ISBN 0-13-530155-6

1. Business failures – United States. 2. Success
in business – United States. 3. Success in
business – Canada. I. Lane, Henry W.
II. O'Grady, Shawna. III. Title.

HF5386.E85   1992   658'.00973   C92-094955-X

Prentice-Hall Inc., Englewood Cliffs, *New Jersey*
Prentice-Hall International, Inc., *London*
Prentice-Hall of Australia, Pty., *Sydney*
Prentice-Hall of India Pvt. Ltd., *New Delhi*
Prentice-Hall of Japan, Inc., *Tokyo*
Prentice-Hall of Southeast Asia (Pte.) Ltd., *Singapore*
Editora Prentice-Hall do Brasil Ltda., *Rio de Janeiro*
Prentice-Hall Hispanoamericana, S.A., *Mexico*

Design: Alex Li
Manufacturing buyer: Lisa Kreuch/Anita Boyle
Composition: Jaytype Inc.

ISBN: 0-13-530155-6

Printed and bound in Canada by WEBCOM

1 2 3 4 5   W   96 95 94 93 92

CONTENTS

ACKNOWLEDGEMENTS

This book is the outcome of a project that can trace its roots and inspiration to people and events in the Fall of 1987. First C. B. (Bud) Johnston, then Dean of the Western Business School, was continually perplexed by reports of failures of Canadian retailers in the United States. He was the first to ask why it was that some of Canada's biggest and best retailers were having so much difficulty in the United States. It was an intriguing question, and one that we believed would be interesting to try to answer. The National Centre for Management Research and Development (NCMRD), under the direction of David S. R. Leighton, held a workshop on the topic "Doing Business in the United States." A number of senior Canadian business executives with experience in the United States met with academic researchers to share experiences and to identify areas of research that would help firms improve their performance. There was general agreement among the executives that doing business in the United States was very different than in Canada.

The Plan for Excellence at the Western Business School provided funding to Henry Lane, Shawna O'Grady, and Terry Hildebrand for the first phase of the project. Shawna O'Grady and Terry Hildebrand focussed their energies on developing the project over the initial two-year period. Shawna O'Grady continued her involvement until the book's completion with her major survey of cultural differences between Canadian and American chief executive officers. Over this period generous assistance and excellent advice were provided by Professors Michael Pearce, Jim Rush, Mitch Rothstein, and Rod White of the Western Business School. Professor Lane's appointment to the Donald F. Hunter Professorship in International Business, a Maclean Hunter endowment, and as Program Manager for the Doing Business in the United States program at the NCMRD provided him the time necessary to pursue the project in depth. He is grateful to Maclean Hunter for this opportunity.

It was fortuitous that as the first phase was ending, Wendy Evans of Evans and Company and Ryerson Polytechnical Institute became interested in the same issue and applied to the National Centre for Management Research and Development for funding. Wendy graciously modified her proposed research plan to complement and to extend the scope of the ongoing research. Her membership on the project team provided essential specialist and practitioner viewpoints that were important contributions to the success of the project. In addition to the support she received from the NCMRD, she is grateful for the support she received from the Office of Research and Innovation at Ryerson and for the research assistance of Steven Cox on the Loblaws and Lenscrafters cases.

The NCMRD provided the financial support necessary to complete phases two and three of the project, to document the research, and to prepare the manuscript for publication. All the authors very much appreciate the continued support of David Leighton and Jim Hatch, past and current Directors of the NCMRD, in this regard. We would like to express our appreciation to all the company executives who participated and made this research possible. Their goodwill and insights will serve to guide the future success of other companies who wish to do business in the United States.

Finally, we are grateful to our publisher Prentice Hall Canada for their enthusiastic response and for the excellent guidance of Managing Editor Tanya Long.

FOREWORD

The National Centre for Management Research and Development located at the Western Business School was formed in 1986. Its mandate is to conduct rigorous applied research which makes a positive contribution to the practice of management. The Centre has six broad research programs at present, one of which is "Doing Business in the United States" (DBUS).

In 1990 Henry Lane was appointed the Donald F. Hunter Professor of International Business and took on leadership of the newly created DBUS program. His goal was to undertake his own research and to facilitate research by others in this important area. The result has been a number of research projects and a wide array of output of which this book is an example.

This book is very timely and should strike a responsive chord with Canadian retailers and consumers. For years the press has reported on the largely unsuccessful attempts of Canadian retailers to enter the United States market. In contrast it often appears that US retailers are entering the Canadian market with relative ease. This book makes an important contribution toward the understanding of these phenomena. It also enhances our understanding of competitiveness within the retail and other industries.

There are a number of reasons why the book will be a valuable addition to the book shelf. Readers who want to know more about some of the major retailers in Canada and the United States will find the in-depth case studies very informative. Firms contemplating entry into the United States market, or indeed any foreign market, will find the authors' insights and practical suggestions very valuable. Those who are interested in the characteristics of Canadian managers in contrast with their American cousins will find the book fascinating and provocative.

Perhaps the most important feature of the book is that all of the authors' conclusions are based on one of the most thorough research projects ever conducted in this area. As a result it will be a seminal work upon which others will build.

Jim Hatch
Director
National Centre for Management
Research and Development

PART 1

·

THE STORIES

INTRODUCTION

Over the past two decades, a number of Canadian retailers have entered the United States with mixed results. Until recently, the reasons for their success or failure had not been investigated. This had led to myths, rumours and speculation about the keys to success in the United States market. With the American retail market worth nearly $1.5 trillion, there is a very powerful incentive for Canadian retailers to expand south; however, the road to success has been difficult.

This book is the culmination of over three years of research that began with an observation and a set of questions. The observation was that many Canadian retailers had entered the United States and, one after another, most withdrew. Of the approximately 32 major Canadian retailers to have entered the United States that the authors identified, only 11 are still operating there, and of these, only 7 are in holding steady or growth modes, a success rate of just over 20 percent. This situation had been exacerbated by the recession. Prior to the economic downturn, the success rate stood at approximately 30 percent. As the companies were withdrawing, the newspapers and business magazines in Canada were filled with the stories of how much money had been lost. Although some of Canada's largest and most successful retailers were among the casualties, other Canadian retailers seemed to be succeeding. These experiences were intriguing because the companies were successful retailers in Canada and the executives understood their business. These were not examples in which companies attempted to diversify out of one industry and into retailing such as was the case with Robert Campeau's purchase of Allied and Federated Stores.

The questions were: "Why can't some of Canada's biggest and best retailers succeed in the United States?", "What explained the performance differentials?", and "How could the potential for success be increased for future entries?"

At about the same time that we were asking these questions and the numerous newspaper articles about the retail failures were appearing, the possibility of a Free Trade Agreement (FTA) between Canada and the United States was being debated and this focussed even more attention on doing business with and in the United States. The uproar in Canada surrounding the FTA obscured an important reality, however; Canadian companies had been investing and operating in the United States for years. Regardless of whether or not the FTA was passed by Parliament, Canadian companies would continue to invest and operate in this extremely large and important market.

According to the federal government, Canada–United States trade was worth $176.2 billion in 1991, an increase of 35 percent over 1987. The combined U.S.–Canada market is the world's biggest single market, worth approximately $5 trillion a year. Canada and the United States already share the largest bilateral trading relationship in the world, and the free trade agreement has increased access within this market. The American retail industry represents approximately 30 percent of this $5 trillion market.

The implications of the FTA on the supply side for the Canadian retail industry are generally positive as duties are gradually eliminated on American manufactured products. A reduction of psychological barriers may encourage the movement of Canadian retailers south and American retailers north. New American entrants will provide "fresh faces" in an all too repetitive tenant mix in the Canadian shopping centres, thus providing the consumer with more choice.

Although the above effects are positive, the entry of American retailers into Canada is increasing the competition for market share in an already crowded marketplace. It is thus important that Canadian retailers both look to the United States for expansion and prepare for American competition in Canada. The findings of our research indicate that American retailers are generally more competitive and market driven, more price oriented with lower cost structures, and are very well managed. To maintain and gain market share in either country will necessitate extensive learning and adaptation on the part of Canadian retailers.

CANADIAN AND AMERICAN RETAILERS: COMPARATIVE PERFORMANCES IN EACH OTHER'S MARKET

There has been some border hopping between Canada and the United States by retailers from both countries. However, the success rate of American companies that have moved to Canada has been greater than that of Canadian companies that have moved to the United States as shown in Table 1. The specific companies that make up the broad categories in Table 1 are shown in Tables 2 and 3. This is not an exhaustive list, but is representative of the major Canadian and American retailers that have crossed the border. In addition, many smaller retailers now also seem to be joining in such as Timothy's Coffees of the World, Moneysworth and Best, Soapberry, and Magicuts.

Table 1   Comparative Performance

Canadian Retailers Entering the United States	American Retailers Entering Canada
• Entries – 32	• Entries – 23
• Presently operating in the United States – 11 (of which 7 are in a hold or growth mode and 4 are contracting)	• Presently operating in Canada – 23
• Profitable withdrawals – 2	
• Withdrawals – 17	
• Results unknown – 2	

Table 2 Canadian Companies

Presently operating in the United States*	Withdrawals
• Loblaw	• Mark's Work Wearhouse
• Provigo (Cost Less and Petrini's)	• Canadian Tire (White's)
• Swiss Chalet	• Reitmans
• Scott's Hospitality (Manchu Wok)	• Signor Angelo
• Canadian Tire (Auto Source)	• Cotton Ginny
• Dylex (Wet Seal, NBO, Harry Rosen, Club Monaco)	• The Brick
	• Dylex (Foxmoor, Brooks)
• Jean Coutu	• Dalmys
• Birks (US operation for sale)	• Consumers Distributing
• Peoples Jewellers	• Shoppers Drug Mart
• Grafton Group (Seifert's)	• Coles Book Stores
• Le Chateau	• Shirley K
	• The Panhandler
	• Pennington's
	• St. Clair Paint
	• Colour Your World
	• Scott's Hospitality (Black's Photography)

Profitable withdrawals	Results unknown
• Scott's Hospitality (KFC)	• Mother Tucker's
• Mmmuffins	• Au Coton

* Of the companies that were operating in the United States at the time of writing, the first seven were in a hold or growth mode while the last four were contracting.

Table 3   American Companies

• Toys R Us	• Woolworth Corporation (2)**
• Pier 1	Department stores:
	- Woolco
• Eddie Bauer	Specialty stores:
• Ethan Allen	- Kinney Canada
• Sears	- Northern Reflections
• K Mart	- Kinney Shoes
• Color Tile*	- Footlocker/Lady Footlocker
• Price Club*	- Randy River
• T. J. Maxx*	- Willow River/Raglan
• The Gap*	- Canary Island
• Lenscrafters*	- Afterthoughts/Reflections
• Radio Shack	- Champs Sports
• A&P (now German controlled)	- Karuba
• Talbot's* (now Japanese owned)	- Silk and Satin
• Eyemasters*	
• Tiffany's*	
• Cole Hahn*	
• Costco*	
• The Nature Company*	
• The Bombay Company	
• The Disney Store*	

New entrants
**Woolworth is only counted as 2 entries: department store and specialty stores.*

There are no known withdrawals of major American retailers from the Canadian market.

THE RESEARCH STUDY: AN OVERVIEW

Little information existed on Canadian retailers' experiences in the United States when this research began. Since entry and adaptation to another country are complex processes that involve implementation and operating problems, it was necessary to understand the progression of events and the impact of a potentially different competitive and cultural environment in the United States. Therefore, interviews and case studies were chosen as the primary vehicle for developing and documenting the experiences of Canadian retailers.

The first challenge was to develop a list of Canadian companies that had entered the United States. Some companies were obvious from newspaper accounts, but the only comprehensive list had been developed by Statistics Canada which claimed it was protected by the Secrecy Act and, therefore, not available to the public. Statistics Canada did agree to confirm the names of companies on a list compiled from various sources.

The companies chosen had to be successful in Canada to rule out the argument that poor management skills and/or problems in Canada were responsible for failure in the United States.

Once companies had been identified and verified, an attempt was made to match companies with differing performance levels while controlling for size and retail category. It became obvious that this would be difficult since there were many more withdrawals than successes. After matching the companies as best as possible, the next barrier appeared: gaining entry and obtaining permission to study the companies chosen in the research design.

Owing to the relatively small number of retailers that crossed the border, and the sensitivity of the information required, the number of potential participants was limited. As CEOs of the companies were contacted and were asked to participate in the study, many key companies agreed to participate. Out of those approached, ten agreed to case studies, and another five agreed to interviews.

The case study companies were Mark's Work Wearhouse, Canadian Tire, Peoples Jewellers, Grafton Group, Coles Bookstores, Loblaw Companies, Provigo, Dylex, Lenscrafters, and The Price Company (Price Club). Interviews were held with the CEOs from Shopper's Drug

Mart, The Panhandler, Le Chateau, The Gap, and The Bombay Company. The companies studied account for approximately half of all the Canadian retail companies which have entered the United States. Case studies and interviews with the American firms constitute approximately 20 percent of the American entrants into Canada.

Information was also obtained from conferences which included presentations from executives from John Labatt Ltd., Canadair, Royal Trust, Scott's Hospitality, Mmmuffins, Canadian Rogers Cable Systems Inc., Audits and Surveys Inc. (New York City), Solomon Brothers Inc. (New York City), Cadillac Fairview Corporation, and Saffer Advertising. In addition, interviews were held with Jim Dion, a retail consultant, and Allan Gotlieb, former Canadian ambassador to the United States.

The project had four main components. Cases were written first on the experiences of Canadian retailers in the United States and then of American retailers in Canada. For each of the cases, in-depth interviews were held with senior management involved with the United States operation. Internal company documents, annual reports, investment analyses, and newspaper and magazine articles were used as additional sources of data. Completed cases were sent to the CEOs for comments and to ensure accuracy of the contents. The third component of the study used a survey research methodology to compare the values and attitudes of chief executive officers (CEOs) of Canadian and American retail companies. Finally, the cases were updated just prior to writing this book.

A list of the executives interviewed for the cases and a brief summary of the companies studied in this project is provided below. The individuals listed shared their experiences, both good and not so good, and insights into doing business in the United States. Their goodwill made this research possible, and the authors thank them for their participation. Their experiences and the lessons they learned will help other Canadian businesses.

CANADIAN RETAILERS IN THE AMERICAN MARKET

1) *Mark's Work Wearhouse* is a 150-store specialty retail chain which started by catering to the workwear needs of the "blue collar" working person and evolved into a store that also sold leisure wear. 1991 sales were just under $250 million, with earnings of $4.3 million. Mark's entered the United States in 1981 by opening two stores. It expanded to ten stores and, in 1987, the United States operation filed for bankruptcy.

Executives interviewed: Mark Blumes, Past President and
Chief Executive Officer
Moe Blumes, Executive Vice-President and
Chief Financial Officer
Craig Fetzer, Vice-President of Marketing
Bruce Libin, Legal Counsel and
Executive Team Member

2) *Canadian Tire Corporation* is one of Canada's largest hard goods specialty retailers with over 420 stores in Canada selling automotive equipment, lawn and garden tools, hardware, and leisure goods. Sales in 1991 were just under $3.0 billion and earnings were $215 million. Canadian Tire acquired White Stores Inc. based in Wichita Falls, Texas in 1981. After sustaining heavy losses for years, White's was sold in 1986. In 1991, Canadian Tire re-entered the United States to test its Auto Source concept.

Executives interviewed: Dean Groussman, Past President, now President of
Zale Corporation
Alan Goddard, Vice-President, Public Relations
Dean Muncaster, Past President
John Kron, Past Executive Vice-President

3) *Peoples Jewellers Limited* is Canada's largest jewellery chain with 1991 sales of $212 million and income of $17.2 million. It had 270 stores in Canada. Peoples entered the United States twice. The first time it acquired a small chain in Utah and Montana which it sold in 1982. The second entry occurred in two stages. In 1981, Peoples purchased 15 percent of the Zale Corporation, the largest jeweller in the United States and the world, with 1991 sales of $1.34 billion. In 1986, the company, in a joint venture arrangement, purchased the remaining stock of Zale. It

took over the management of the company and improved its performance. In 1992, due largely to the ravages of recession and heavy debt, Zale was required to seek protection under Chapter 11.

Executives interviewed: Irving Gerstein, President
Charles Gill, Senior Vice-President, Finance
Nick White (Zale), Senior Vice-President, Merchandising
Merrill Wertheimer (Zale), Senior Vice-President, Finance
Jerry Dawes (Zale), Senior Vice-President, Store Operations
Randy Lively (Zale), Senior Vice-President, Administration

4) *The Grafton Group* was among Canada's top seven clothing retailers with sales of $561 million in 1991. In 1979, Grafton acquired Seifert's, a chain of 51 clothing stores in the United States midwest. By 1987, Seifert's had expanded to 147 women's specialty stores in 23 states. It also purchased a shoe chain, Oak Bay, in 1979. In 1987, Oak Bay operated 47 outlets in nine states. A combination of the recession and debt proved too much for Grafton. In May 1992, it sold its bankrupt shoe chain, Maher's, to Bata; and creditors approved the sale of 90 percent of Grafton-Fraser to Cadillac Fairview, leaving Grafton with 10 percent of Grafton-Fraser and 45 percent of Seifert's. The remainder of Seifert's had been previously sold to its creditors.

Executives interviewed: William Heaslip, Chairman and CEO
James Seifert, President, Seifert's Inc.

5) *Coles Bookstores Limited* is one of Canada's top two book chains with 1991 sales of $179.9 million and income of $5.0 million. Coles opened its first store in the United States in 1965, and grew to a chain of 58 stores in 24 states. Both the Canadian and United States divisions were incurring heavy losses in the early 1980s. By 1984–85 the Canadian company was profitable, and Coles decided to sell the American operation to the retail giant, Walden Books, in 1987.

Executives interviewed: Bill Ardell, Past President
Jack Cole, Past President
Deborah Lewington, Buyer

6) *Loblaw Companies Limited* is the largest Canadian food distributor with 1991 sales of $8.5 billion and operating income of $219 million. It operates at both the retail and wholesale level. Loblaw entered the United States through the acquisition of several American companies beginning in 1947. The United States operation consisted of the National Tea retail chain which focussed on markets in New Orleans, Louisiana, and St. Louis, Missouri, as well as a wholesale division. The unprofitable operation was restructured and downsized from 892 stores in 1975 to 102 stores in 1989. Profits were now healthy and operating income increased by over 20 percent between 1989 and 1991.

Executives interviewed: Richard Currie, President

7) *Provigo Incorporated* is Canada's second largest food retailer and wholesaler with 1991 sales of $6.5 billion and operating income of $700,000 (after a $60 million write-off associated with discontinued operations). Provigo entered the United States in 1977 with the purchase of a Canadian food distributor, Loeb Ltd., whose subsidiaries included a wholesaler in the United States. In 1988, Provigo bought 11 Petrini and 15 Lucky–Alpha Beta supermarkets in the San Francisco Bay area and, shortly thereafter, opened five discount food stores in the same area. In 1989–90 ten of the supermarkets were sold or closed and the company declared a loss for the 1990 fiscal year. By 1992, despite severe economic recession in the U.S., Provigo had succeeded in turning around the U.S. operation with all divisions showing a positive operating income.

Executives interviewed: Yvan Bussières, President

8) *Chateau Stores* is a vertically integrated manufacturer, retailer and importer of clothing for men and women, with more than 160 stores and sales of over $150 million in 1991. In 1984, it expanded into the U.S. market opening over 20 stores during the next few years. By 1991, losses were mounting in the United States and Chateau made the decision to close a quarter of its American stores. More unprofitable United States stores were closed in 1992.

Executives interviewed: Herschel Segal, President and Chairman

9) *Dylex Limited* is Canada's largest specialty apparel retailer, with sales of $1.84 billion and operating profit of $43 million resulting in net earnings of $3.2 million in 1991. During the 1980s, Dylex entered the United States market through the acquisition of apparel manufacturer Tobias Kotzin and the NBO stores, Brooks Fashion Stores, the Wet Seal chain, and Foxmoor. It also opened the Club International chain, Harry Rosen and Club Monaco in the U.S. In 1987, Brooks filed for bankruptcy followed by the sale of the Foxmoor chain. Club International was sold in 1991. Wet Seal and the NBO stores are flourishing, and the Club Monaco chain is being tested and refined before embarking on any expansion.

Executives interviewed: David Posluns, Chief Financial Officer

10) *Shoppers Drug Mart* is Canada's largest drug store chain with approximately 640 stores, sales of $2.9 billion and earnings of $87.9 million in 1991. It entered the United States in 1972 opening its first drug store in Florida. The chain expanded to 38 stores in that state and was profitable during the first seven years, after which it started to lose money. It was sold to Shoppers' parent company Imasco (actually to People's Drug Stores which had been purchased by Imasco) in 1984.

Executives interviewed: David Bloom, President, Chairman and CEO

AMERICAN COMPANIES OPERATING IN CANADA

1) *The Bombay Company Inc.* is a specialty retailer of home decor products with over 300 stores. It began in the United States as a mail order firm in 1976. The American company was purchased by Tandy Brands in 1980 and the Canadian rights were bought by a Canadian, Robert Nourse, in 1979. By 1983 there were 36 stores in the United States and 13 in Canada. The Canadian operation was profitable; however the United States was losing money. Nourse was asked to take over the American operation and the company grew to over 300 stores with sales of $139 million by 1991. It was profitable in both markets.

Executives interviewed: Robert Nourse, President and CEO
                        Steven King, Vice-President Real Estate.

2) *The Price Club* is a membership warehouse club with 69 warehouses and sales of $6.6 billion by 1991. The Price Company was started in California in 1976 and expanded across the United States. In 1986, it entered the Canadian market through a joint venture with Steinbergs. Within two and a half years, the Canadian operation had turned a profit. By 1991 it had opened 12 warehouses with sales of approximately $1.1 billion. In October 1990, the Price Company increased its ownership in Price Club Canada from 50 percent to 100 percent.

Executives interviewed: Pierre Mignault, President, Price Club Canada

3) *Lenscrafters International Inc.* is a super-optical store selling eyeglasses made on site with one-hour delivery. This 100 percent owned subsidiary of United States Shoe Corporation grew from three stores in 1984 to 446 stores by 1991 with sales of almost $600 million. In 1987 it entered the Canadian market and, by 1991, had become profitable and was the largest optical superstore chain in Canada with 30 stores.

Executives interviewed: John McArthur, President, Lenscrafters Canada

4) *The Gap* is a specialty retailer which operates stores selling casual and activewear for men, women and children under the trade names of Gap, Banana Republic, GapKids and BabyGap. The company operates over 1,000 stores across the United States with sales of approximately $2.0 billion. It opened its first store in Canada in March 1989, grew to 24 stores by 1990, and was continuing to expand aggressively in the Canadian market.

Executives interviewed: William Fisher, Vice-President, Gap Canada

CHAPTER 1

STARTING AT SQUARE ONE: PLANS MEET REALITY

In Part 1 the stories of numerous and varied Canadian retailers that entered markets in the United States are described. Most of these forays took place years before the Free Trade Agreement and, in some cases, decades before it was implemented. To us, this fact underscores the reality that Canadian companies have always operated in the United States and most likely always will, with or without free trade agreements.

The reasons for venturing into the United States were much the same for all the companies. The limits to growth had been reached in Canada and the only way executives saw continued growth was to expand into the United States. If Canadian companies are to grow to the size necessary to develop the financial muscle and economies of scale necessary to compete from their base in a small open economy in the global marketplace of the 1990s, they need to look outside their borders at the large markets to the south. Global competition in the 1990s includes fighting to maintain market share in one's home market. The difficulty in defending successfully against competitors who are bigger and better in many areas has been witnessed dramatically in the past decade in the automobile industry in Canada and in the United States. Canadian retailers are facing their version of this story as powerful, rich and sophisticated American retail giants enter the Canadian marketplace and provide Canadians with what they want: better service, more choice and lower prices. The inside view of some of these American firms and how they operate is provided in a later part of the book.

In many industries, such as retailing, it is not possible to export the product or service and a market presence is required to serve a firm's customers. Therefore, learning to live in and operate in a new environment is critical for success. In most, but not all, of the situations to be described in this part of the book, executives perceived the United States to be a natural extension of the Canadian market, their own backyard so to speak. The United States was thought to be very similar to Canada, only larger. And American consumers were assumed to have tastes and buying habits like Canadians. That these assumptions were inaccurate was a major revelation for most of the people involved.

These stories also tell of how difficult it is to succeed in the United States. We think that they help to chart the "commercial waters" in the United States. Such a chart is necessary for executives who are considering setting up operations in the United States and who think that they already know those waters which, on the surface, look so familiar. We trust that the descriptions and analyses of what happened will help other retailers, as well as executives in other industries, navigate the tricky and potentially dangerous "waters" awaiting them in the United States.

MARK'S WORK WEARHOUSE

Background

Mark's Work Wearhouse was created as a one-stop shopping place that would meet all the workwear needs of the working man and his family. It evolved to eventually include all their informal apparel needs.

The first store opened in 1977 in Calgary, Alberta and was an immediate success. This early success led to an expansion program by forming joint venture stores and by 1980, the company had 33 stores. The large number of joint ventures became difficult to manage and control. It was decided to roll all the joint ventures into one company and issue stock publicly which would rationalize the organizational structure and provide capital for continued expansion. The huge success of the public stock offering gave the company a feeling of "we can do anything." This confidence was compounded by the boom atmosphere in Alberta at the time. The company seemed invincible and embarked on another rapid expansion program. By the end of 1981, the number of stores doubled to 66 throughout Canada. In that one year, sales also increased from $40.7 million to $81.7 million and every store was operating at a profit.

The company had found a market niche and it became the largest Levi jeans supplier in Canada. This gave it an advantage because jeans suppliers considered Work Wearhouse to be very important. Its products fit well with Canada's climate. The company also concentrated on providing superior customer service. One of the key personnel evaluation criteria for raises and bonuses was quality of customer service.

Entry into the United States

In 1980 Work Wearhouse was approached to expand into the United States by an American who owned an advertising firm that specialized in developing retail concepts, site selection, and store design, as well as marketing and advertising campaigns. At the time Mark Blumes, the founder of Mark's Work Wearhouse, was not interested because the Canadian operation was taking all his time. After the stock offering in 1981 his attitude changed. He thought, "Why not go into the United States, we can't be beaten." The company had the idea that bigger is better. It was caught on a wave and had a mentality of who cares.

In addition to this euphoria, Canadian competitors were beginning to copy the Work Wearhouse concept. Mark thought expanding into the United States might help him "protect the concept." Since the advertising consultant had told him that nothing like it existed in the western United States and that it should work well, Mark believed he could operate there without any direct competition.

The consultant was hired to conduct market studies for potential sites. Mark established the following criteria for the site selection process:

1. Only cities with a population of 50,000 or less should be considered. Mark was very concerned about protecting his concept. He wanted to open quietly and learn about the market before any major expansion

took place. By entering small, remote areas, the company could test the retail concept without attracting the attention of much larger competitors.

2. The areas had to have a concentration of energy related industries that employed blue collar workers. Mark knew that the concept worked in areas like Calgary so he wanted to start in an area with similar characteristics.

The consultant investigated nine cities in five states that met the criteria. Research included an examination of the competition in the area; site availability for stores 8,000 to 10,000 square feet; population surveys; work force studies; and an examination of growth trends. The consultant also met with developers to find out what they were developing and why. The analysis revealed that retailers in the area were more specialized than Work Wearhouse's Canadian competition. Stores tended to be relatively small (3,000 – 4,000 square feet) and carried a narrower product mix. In addition, sales prices and profit margins were much lower in the United States, especially for jeans. The analysis also showed that the workwear concept was unique to those areas. Management's conclusion was that the concept was powerful enough to overcome the lower prices with volume sales.

The first choice was Casper, Wyoming which had an oil related economy (like Alberta) and large growth was expected. However, no suitable sites could be found. The second choice was Rock Springs which was similar to Casper, but had a smaller population of 35,000. A developer had a site available, but he would not let Work Wearhouse have it unless the company also took a site in Pocatello, Idaho where he needed a retailer to anchor the mall he was building. The consultant advised against entering the Pocatello area because it was a farming community with slow population growth. However, in Calgary the executive committee decided that it was a good idea to test the concept in an agriculturally based economy while still remaining unobtrusive to competitors. It was decided to gamble on Pocatello. The reasoning, according to a company executive, was that, "It was going to be so easy in Rock Springs that we wouldn't learn anything. We decided we had better open in mid-America so we would learn something about the concept in the United States."

Start-Up

The first two stores were opened in November and December 1981. A Canadian was sent to manage the Rock Springs store and a local person was recruited to run the store in Pocatello. However, the Canadian was quite junior within the company; he had been an assistant store manager. A more senior and experienced manager was not sent because the remote locations caused recruiting problems since no one wanted to live there. In retrospect the consultant commented, "The Canadian was far too junior in position to be sent to the United States. I was to work with him so I could learn more about Work Wearhouse...so I could help them market the concept further. I knew very little about it at this time since we entered the United States only months after the first meeting with Mark."

The consultant continued working with the United States operation and had responsibility for designing and opening stores, leasing the store outlets, hiring the local manager for the Pocatello location, and for coordinating the activities of the two United States stores since he was located in Salt Lake City and was much closer to them. Although he had no prior retail experience in clothing, he was excited to work with Work Wearhouse because he knew that "nothing like the concept existed in the western United States."

All key strategic, marketing and administrative decisions were made in Calgary. In addition, since the consultant was in the process of learning about the Work Wearhouse concept, the Canadian executives made most of the operational decisions that would normally have been made by regional managers. It was decided to transfer the Canadian concept, without any modifications, including the Canadian marketing campaign to the United States. Canadian management seldom visited the operation in the United States. To keep the executive committee informed, the consultant travelled monthly to Calgary to report on activities.

It did not take long for operating problems to appear. The first problems that arose were with the product line. It was imperative that products be sourced from United States suppliers. In most cases, high production costs made Canadian products too expensive compared to American products. In addition, the transportation costs from Canada made this an even more expensive alternative. However, sourcing in the United States was far more difficult than anyone ever expected. In

Canada, Work Wearhouse had very good relations with its suppliers and had no trouble obtaining products when needed. In the United States, the situation was completely different. With only two stores, Work Wearhouse did not have the buying leverage it had in Canada, and therefore, was put low on American suppliers' list of priorities. Canadian buyers purchasing for the United States stores had trouble obtaining the desired product lines in the sizes they wanted and at the times they wanted them. This made it impossible to truly reproduce the Canadian concept, and the stores took on a 'sort of' Work Wearhouse look because certain product lines could not be duplicated. As the consultant commented, "It was difficult to operate two stores in the United States mainly because you are not big enough to be somebody to your suppliers. One of the real successes Work Wearhouse had in Canada was being important to suppliers because to succeed they have to become a partner with you."

The Canadian Operation Experiences Its First Set-Back

In August 1981, the National Energy Program was introduced by the Canadian Federal government. This program had a dramatic effect on the economy of Alberta, due to the province's dependence on oil and gas. The effects of the NEP were being felt in Alberta by late 1981 and in early 1982. The province went into a recession that affected the majority of businesses in the economy. Mark Blumes stated, "When Alberta crashed, so did we."

Thirty-three percent of the company's sales (in 1981) and 65 percent of the company's profits were from stores located in Alberta. At the time, Alberta was the only province where Work Wearhouse was well known and was considered established. The costs associated with entering and gaining recognition in other provinces had lowered profits in these areas. Although in 1982 the company's sales grew to $90.7 million, it suffered a loss of $3.1 million dollars. For the first time Work Wearhouse was faced with surviving in difficult economic times. The company discovered that it did not have adequate systems to control and monitor costs. In fact, Moe Blumes, Vice-President and Chief Financial Officer, stated that when he joined the company, systems were almost non-existent. At the time, there were no systems for accounts payable, inventory, budgeting or cost control. All of the company's energy and talent had been focussed on expansion.

The company was also experiencing difficulties in marketing and merchandising. After touring a few stores, Mark realized that "the stores were in a mess. They looked unkempt and they conveyed inconsistent messages." Rapid expansion, without adequate controls, had allowed stores to be opened that did not accurately reflect the Workwear concept.

Corrective action was taken. Control and accounting systems were installed but the design and implementation took longer than expected, and it was not until 1985 that Moe felt that adequate systems were in place. The business was also downsized. During 1982, eight of the worst performing stores were closed and the management group was rationalized. Thirty-one of the 109 member management group were asked to leave the company. Steps were taken to ensure consistency of image and merchandising across Work Wearhouse stores. Staff training courses were instituted and a presentation manual was written that detailed such things as how to fold jeans.

The biggest move, however, was to change the marketing strategy. The company could not survive difficult economic times by focussing on discounting jeans because the margins were too low. The strategy of selling more jeans than anyone else was no longer working. The company repositioned itself from a discount retailer to a specialty retailer. The off-price promotional portion of sales was reduced. Instead, the company concentrated on consistent low prices and good quality. The product line was expanded to include fashionable, casual wear (i.e. rugby shirts, sweat suits, cotton sweaters, etc.) which had higher margins. By 1988, pure workwear made up only 20–25 percent of the Mark's Work Wearhouse product line.

The serious operating problems in Canada from 1982 to 1985 meant the majority of Work Wearhouse's resources (financial, management time and energy) were directed to saving the Canadian operation. This led to the United States operation being "orphaned in 1982 and 1983." The consultant was still visiting Canada monthly to report on United States operations and the executive committee was still involved in all major decisions, but now the United States operation clearly was second in importance. The two senior executives, Mark and Moe Blumes, spent very little time in the United States. They did try to implement financial control systems, but had difficulty attracting talented accountants. Since no one in the United States operation had "bottom-line", profit center experience there was no commitment to following an effective accounting/budget system. Moe Blumes commented, "Financial statements and budgets were prepared but they were not very believable. There was no commitment to them. The data base was weak and messy, so the budgeting process was basically futile. We tried endless fixes but nothing worked. We never knew what we lost until we actually left the country."

Results in the United States

Initially, Rock Springs experienced good sales volume, but no profit due to higher than expected overhead expenses. Problems with suppliers had constantly hindered the business. The Pocatello store was struggling since farmers were having problems with their crops and the one factory in the town had laid off one-third of its workers.

The solution was to expand and to grow out of the problems. With more stores, Mark's Work Wearhouse would be more important to suppliers and a network of stores would create a bigger base to absorb overhead expenses. Stores were added, sales volume increased to satisfactory levels, but still there were no profits. One reason that profits were elusive was the competition.

Although no competitor had the total workwear concept, each of the company's products had competition from at least one retailer. As Mark exclaimed, "It wasn't just competitive, it was a war! Those boys play for keeps. Their arsenal was impressive." After Work Wearhouse implemented their low price strategy, the competition lowered their prices and increased their promotions. The company had to work extremely hard to compete, even in the area of providing customer service, which was one of the Canadian organization's key success factors. Mark commented that, "Service in the United States is superior. In Canada, it is easy to provide exemplary service. It's easy to make a difference through incentives and training programs. Not in the United States. We really had to work at providing good service."

The company's response to the competition was to face them head on within the range of its concept. It advertised heavily, priced products competitively with the market and provided some products, sourced from Canadian suppliers, that were not available in the United States. The results were impressive. All stores had the highest sales volume per square foot within each of the malls they occupied. But as the consultant explained, "We had tremendous sales volume, but those sales came at a heavy price. You just don't walk into a marketplace and take over. They don't just roll over and die. In Canada they built their business by becoming a giant in the jeans industry by off-pricing and selling tremendous volumes of jeans. They did this in a relatively short time. Well, I can tell you there are already a few giants in the jeans industry in the United States [i.e. the Gap, K Mart, J.C. Penny]. We learned early on that we could sell a tremendous amount of jeans, but only at a low profit. We would never win the jeans business in the United States unless we got to be a very large operation."

In Canada, off-pricing meant that instead of allowing for a profit margin of 35 percent, you allowed for 20 percent. In the United States, profit margins started in the 20 percent range because of stiffer price competition. Moe Blumes compared jeans in the United States to a commodity. There were high sales volumes, but extensive advertising was necessary to get the sales. Also, there was no customer loyalty and consumers were price sensitive. Therefore, although the company had high sales volumes, it was not making sufficient margins to cover the cost of operating a store.

The solution to the difficulties once more seemed to be expansion — this time into a metropolitan area. Even in Canada, the company was learning that it could manage the metropolitan markets better than the rural area markets. Also, it was no longer necessary to protect the concept because all the competitors knew Work Wearhouse was there.

Salt Lake City was chosen because the economy was reported to be strong although no market or demographic research was completed, and the consultant was located there and knew developers in the areas. A senior Canadian was sent to help manage the United States operation because everyone (including the consultant) realized that the consultant did not have the merchandising skills necessary to effectively manage the operation alone. Sales volume increased by about 30 percent, but profits were still not achieved as the promotional expenses, including planned markdowns, were excessive.

The business of promoting discounted jeans, and other low priced items, was not producing a profit for the company. Margins were too low and stiff competition prevented this from changing. To increase profits, the company decided to go back to the basics of workwear, such as overalls. These products did not sell nearly as fast as jeans. However, the margins were far superior. Concentrating on workwear meant that the company had to give up its goal of fast expansion and attainment of significant market share, since the strategy was now a longer term approach with slower sales growth and the establishment of long term customer relationships.

To complement this longer term strategy, the company hired an American merchandiser to take over the management of the United States operation. The consultant joined the Canadian operation as Vice-President of Marketing, while the senior Canadian representative remained in the United States as a principal buyer. The new executive had over 20 years experience in United States retailing and had just left a job as Vice-President of a major retail manufacturer in Texas. He came into the company with "visions" of how he could turn the company around, but realized this was not a short term proposition. He moved the company further into a long term strategy and focussed on improving buying strategies and profit margins by concentrating even less on jeans sales. However, he was faced with a parent company whose resources were seriously constrained.

The parent company, in an attempt to improve the profit situation in the United States, opened a distribution centre in Salt Lake City early in 1986. Moe Blumes explained why: "We learned [in Vancouver] that the big truck crossing the Rockies cost a fortune to use to deliver directly to stores. So we got the big truck to deliver to a distribution centre and had little trucks deliver to the stores. That worked so well in Vancouver that it was immediately implemented everywhere. And because we were doing it in Canada, we also did it in Salt Lake City."

The warehouse was established, despite the fact that it really required 15 to 20 stores to make it economical. The logic was that if Calgary, which had a population of between 600,000 and 700,000 people, had 7 stores at the time, then Salt Lake, which had a population of 1 million (including surrounding areas), could sustain 8 or 9 stores.

In retrospect, head office realized this was not a good move. As it turned out, the warehouse and the truck were underutilized in their nine months of operation. Since the United States managers were not involved in the decision, they had not bought into the idea. They did not understand what the warehouse was for and never tried to make it work. In addition, the warehouse added significantly to the already high overhead costs.

Business in Utah was not nearly as good as expected. Work Wearhouse had failed to take into consideration that Salt Lake was a traditional Mormon community. The majority of families were supported by one income which was very different than most of North America. As a result, family disposable incomes were, on average, lower in the area and shoppers tended to be very frugal. This led to serious competition and the need for sale prices, which resulted in low profit margins. The pure size of the Salt Lake market meant that high advertising costs were required to obtain sales. The United States operation was losing more money than ever.

The Beginning of the End

Even as early as 1984, people associated with the Canadian company were not interested in being involved with the United States operation. It became known, but not spoken, that the United States would not succeed. A board member commented, "This ended up becoming a self-fulfilling prophecy because the company could not get people to go to the United States. It was viewed as a corporate dead-end. Nobody wanted their hands soiled by being associated with it." These attitudes became even stronger by 1986.

The American executive who was hired to turn the company around was different. He had clear ideas of how to operate in the United States and was prepared to make a long term investment. However, soon after he arrived the economic conditions seriously hindered sales. All of the stores were located in "dying towns," and the Canadian company simply did not have the financial resources to weather the economic downturn. It appeared that he had been brought in too late. It was decided in Calgary, by the executive committee, that resources being used in the United States would be put to better use in Canada. Work Wearhouse decided to close the United States operation. On January 14, 1987, the

United States division of Mark's Work Wearhouse filed for bankruptcy in the United States ending four and one-half years of operation there.

Reflecting on the Experience

This section presents an analytic summary of events in the Mark's Work Wearhouse case using categories the authors believe to be important and that will be used again in later cases to provide comparisons between the different entry experiences in the United States. It also incorporates comments offered by executives interviewed during the research about some lessons they learned from their experience.

Reason for entry and approach

Entry into the United States was essentially *reactive*. The company was approached by an American advertising consultant who believed that the Work Wearhouse concept could be duplicated in the United States since, in his opinion, nothing like it existed there. Competitors were starting to appear in Canada and were copying the concept, and management believed that they could protect the concept by expanding into the United States where there would not be any direct competition.

Dates of operation in the United States

The first stores were opened in November and December 1981. The company filed for bankruptcy in January 1987 ending approximately five years of operations.

Attitude toward entry

Mark Blumes' comments in the case suggest an attitude that could be considered over confident or cavalier. However, regardless of how one chooses to characterize this attitude, it suggests that entry into the United States was not thoroughly considered strategically, carefully planned, or executed with the sober intent that management eventually realized such a move deserved.

An important lesson learned was that a company's management has to want to be in the United States and has to be willing to put into its venture whatever is necessary to make it succeed. A corollary is that the venture has to be big enough to be important to senior management, rather than a curious sideline to see what develops.

Entry mode and rationale

A greenfield mode (ie, expanding store by store) was chosen and remote areas were selected that resembled some of the company's locations in Canada. Concern for protecting the retail concept influenced this choice of entry mode along with the fact that, presumably, there were no acquisition candidates. It was felt that the company could start small and almost "hide" in these locations to test its retail concept, to learn about the market, and to avoid being noticed by competitors before any expansion took place.

Management underestimated the length of time and the amount of financial resources that were required to "grow" a greenfield operation to the size that was necessary to be competitive in the United States. Realizing that the company was too small to be successful, the response was to expand. This required more investment and more management time, but neither were available in the quantities sufficient to reach the breakthrough point to significantly influence product and administrative costs that contributed to the company's higher cost structure. It also was difficult to "hide" from the competition while the company was growing. Even though the United States was a large and populous country, news travelled fast and it was difficult to keep a secret.

Research prior to entry

Areas with concentrations of energy related industries employing blue collar workers and cities with populations of less than 50,000 people were considered. In the cities meeting these criteria, the competition was identified along with their product mix, store images and pricing strategies. Population and workforce surveys were conducted and growth trends examined. Management met with real estate developers to learn what they were developing and why. The competitive analysis revealed that competitors had relatively smaller stores, were more specialized and carried a narrower product mix, and had lower prices and lower margins. No one had the same retail concept as Mark's.

Transfer of retail concept

The conclusion drawn from the competitive analysis was that the Mark's Work Wearhouse concept was unique and powerful enough to overcome the lower prices and margins in the United States. Management attempted to transfer the concept, as it existed in Canada, to the United States without modification. Management was able to create the store image it wanted and to staff its stores with friendly people. However, it was not able to replicate its product mix or to provide a higher level of service than its competitors.

The inability to identify a direct competitor can be interpreted as a void in the market and a great opportunity, or as a signal to spend more time and effort considering the retail concept since a niche may not exist.

Geographic operating area

The operating area was relatively *dispersed*. Nine stores were spread through Wyoming, Idaho and Utah with the only real concentration being the few stores in the Salt Lake City metropolitan area. Salt Lake City had been chosen primarily because that was where the American consultant working with Mark's was located and it was between Wyoming and Utah so management felt it would contribute to the development of a network of stores. No demographic or market research was done on this area prior to expansion into it. A distribution facility was established in Salt Lake City but it was underutilized.

Store locations

Suitable locations were difficult to find or even impossible as in Casper, Wyoming which was the company's first choice. Even second choices often had conditions attached. Securing the desired site in Rock Springs meant agreeing to take an additional site in Pocatello. When suitable sites were found, rents often were expensive due to competitive bidding pressures.

The important tenet of retailing is location, location, location!

Canadian management

Knowledge and qualifications   Since the first stores were opened in rather remote locations, the company could not recruit any of its senior managers to transfer to the United States since they were not interested in living in those locations. The first Canadian to go to the United States was sent to manage one of the stores and to help the American consultant learn about the Workwear concept and how to market it. However, he was an assistant store manager and really too junior for the designated task. Senior management had no first hand knowledge or experience in the market the company was entering. Also, they only visited the American operations sporadically.

An important lesson was that the American retail environment was too competitive, and potentially too costly, for a company not to send is first string players. A company has to be prepared to send its best talent to the United States or have them devote their attention to the operations there in collaboration with qualified American executives.

Experienced managers who understand the market differences, have knowledge of the distribution system and suppliers, and who understand the American consumer are critical for success. This is particularly true for buyers. The American consumer was found to differ from Canadians. Americans were more price sensitive and were sophisticated comparison shoppers. Tastes were different and styles that sold well in Canada did not necessarily sell well in the United States.

Commitment   Management was not strongly committed to the United States company. When problems developed in the Canadian company, the stores in the United States were forgotten until the problems at home were solved. The consultant in the United States did not have a significant investment in the venture. Someone has to have ownership of the project.

Decision-making   Key strategic, marketing and administrative decisions were made in Calgary. Even many of the operating decisions that might normally be made by regional executives were made at Canadian headquarters because the experience and knowledge base did not exist in

27

the United States company.

American management

The principal management figure in the United States for the first few years, the advertising and marketing consultant, had strengths in advertising and store design, but had no retail experience and no merchandising experience. He probably did not fully understand the Workwear concept for almost a year after it was initially transferred to the United States. In 1986, a senior American executive with the requisite retail experience who was considered to be a talented merchandiser was hired. His idea of how to turn the situation around, however, was a long term vision and he faced a deteriorating situation and a parent company whose resources were constrained.

Suppliers

It was necessary to source products in the United States because Canadian products were more expensive. However, sourcing goods in the United States was much more difficult than anticipated. Two stores did not provide the buying leverage Mark's Work Wearhouse was accustomed to in Canada and Mark's was therefore low on suppliers' priority lists. Buyers could not get the products they wanted, in the sizes they wanted, at the times they wanted or at the prices they needed to be competitive. Mark's was important to their suppliers in Canada but not in the United States. One executive commented, "You have to be big enough to be 'somebody' to your suppliers."

Systems

When Alberta went into a recession in 1981 and 1982, Mark's Work Wearhouse followed. At that time management came to realize that they had not developed the systems necessary to manage and control the company's expansion in Canada, let alone in the United States. The company did not have adequate systems for inventory, accounts payable, budgeting, or cost control. Without these systems firmly established in Canada, they could not be transferred to the United States company which made it impossible to monitor and understand the situation there.

Competition

The competitive reaction and intensity of competition were a real eye-opener for Mark's management. Although no American retailer had the same workwear concept, each of Mark's products had competition from at least one retailer. When Mark's implemented its low price strategy, the competition reduced their prices and increased their advertising. Mark's higher overhead costs made it impossible to compete. Without higher margins, Mark's could not be profitable. Management also discovered it had to work much harder to deliver the level of service provided by its competition and demanded by the American consumer.

Competitive retaliation seemed to be a matter of principle in the market share war. A new retailer was not going to walk in and take share without a fierce battle. American competitors were discovered to be numerous, smart, sophisticated, experienced and tough.

CHATEAU STORES OF CANADA

Background

Chateau Stores' entry into the United States was consistent with the experiences of, and lessons learned by, other Canadian retailers. The Chateau Stores story parallels many elements found in the Mark's Work Wearhouse case and helps to develop a more accurate picture of the retail environment in the United States.

Chateau Stores of Canada Ltd. was a vertically integrated retailer, manufacturer and importer of affordable, fashion-forward clothing and footwear geared to "young-at-heart" men and women of all ages. Chateau Stores of Canada was founded in 1959 and grew to 148 stores across the country by 1990. In 1984, it expanded into the United States opening more than 20 stores over the next few years. By 1991, losses were mounting in the United States and Chateau closed a quarter of its United States locations and focussed on its core business in Canada.

Entry into the United States

1983 was an excellent year for sales and the company began looking for expansion opportunities. At the time it had 73 stores and, although there were still expansion opportunities in Canada, management had been watching other companies such as Dylex, which had recently made several major acquisitions in the United States. It seemed that expansion into the American market was the natural route to take.

Although management considered various alternatives, such as finding a partner with which to move into the United States, ultimately they decided on a greenfield entry. No formal market research was undertaken. A decision was made to hire an American to develop and operate a United States division. This individual had been the president of an American retail firm and had many years of experience. As Chateau President, Herschel Segal stated, "We didn't know the ten major areas in the states, we didn't know the difference between Washington and Boston and the cornfields of Illinois and Detroit." In quick succession an office was opened in Boston, a design office was launched in New York, and six store locations were found. Segal noted that it was at the height of the retail boom in the United States and that Chateau paid top dollar for their locations which had meant high occupancy costs ever since that time.

Shortly after the first stores were opened, problems developed and the Canadian company began to lose money. That, combined with the fact that the American hired to run the United States division was not felt to be good enough, led to major problems in the United States. Despite mixed results and an uncertain management team, sixteen more stores were opened in the northeast over the next few years. Though they were regionally concentrated, they were spread among several markets with five around Washington and Baltimore, five in Chicago, three in Detroit, and three in Boston. Chateau's management, distracted by the continuing poor performance in Canada, did not do well in choosing these locations or supplying the United States stores with products. As Segal related, "The new division lacked attention and things fell apart."

In hindsight, Segal noted that "you cannot go into a very competitive and driving market like that, with an unproven person and a team that has not been working together." He felt that when a company has a concept and a corporate culture, it knows what it wants and how to do it. But, when they hire an American, "though you speak the same language and you think everything is understood, the execution is different."

The offices were closed in Boston and New York. A new organization was created in Canada for purchasing and operations. Whereas previously the United States had been treated as a region, it was later separated in terms of reporting, buying and distribution, making it easier to control. Three unprofitable stores were closed.

In 1991, the company continued to suffer heavy losses in the United States, and the Canadian company lost money during the first six months ($1.6 million), more than triple the loss for the comparable period in 1990. In mid 1991, Segal had come to the conclusion that he was going to hire a "first class president" to run the United States operation. He had sent "one talented vice-president after another" to turn around the United States but it had not worked, and he felt it was key to hire an American. Short of moving to the United States himself, which he did not think feasible, he was left with no other option. When the interim figures were released in September 1991 showing increased losses, the decision was made to close more stores that were unprofitable in the United States. The recession had exacerbated an already major problem.

Segal observed that success in the United States is essentially having the product mix and the people who deliver the product. The United States retailers "have the drive and the confidence to put in the product. We send in six of something, sell out the mediums (sizes) and we're out of business. They send in 36 with back-up, hype and cappers, promotion, and contests for the sales people. It's a very competitive business." He felt that American management were extremely hard working and highly professional.

American consumers were much more price conscious than Canadians. They always expected quick service and a deal. Segal felt that the United States was a faster moving market in terms of all the players, both buyers and sellers. Not only do Americans buy different products than Canadians do, but often there were cultural differences. For various reasons, Americans were ready for some styles before Canadians, while for others they were behind the Canadian market. Part of the challenge was handling the diverse demands of the different regions. Canada was not necessarily more uniform, but "if you're Canadian you understand the differences and you know how to react. In the United States you are caught unaware, and you don't know what to do."

COLES BOOKSTORES LIMITED

Background

Coles was one of the early entrants into the United States, having opened its first store in 1965. Led by management who believed in a natural north-south economic flow, southward expansion was a logical extension of the Canadian operation. In 1978, Southam Inc. purchased Coles Book stores. During the early 1980s, heavy losses were incurred in both the United States and Canadian companies. New management turned the Canadian company around by 1984–85. Attention was then turned to the stores in the United States. Various remedies were considered, but Southam finally decided to minimize its losses by selling the ailing United States operation.

In the early years Coles concentrated on used text books, but later added school stationery and a selection of new books. In 1939, it published its first Coles Notes and 1940 saw the opening of the Yonge and Charles Street store in Toronto, not far from the present location of the "World's Biggest Bookstore" at Yonge and Edward Street. In 1956, it opened its first store in a shopping centre and from there followed a string of others. Suburban shopping centres sprang up across the country in the latter half of the 1950s through the mid 1970s providing Coles, and many other retailers, with a vehicle for expansion from coast to coast. Early on, Coles made the decision to become market-dominant by locating in virtually any shopping centre location.

The expansion was described as the "cookie cutter approach" where set assortments of books were slotted into predetermined fixturing and store configurations. As many as three stores were opened in a week. Expansion was efficient and sales were growing quickly. Little attention was paid to regional differences. Though these differences were not considered to be very significant, there were some obvious problems, when, for example, waterskiing books were included in Prairie store assortments.

The product mix, consisting of well-priced books over a wide range of subjects, school texts, Coles Notes for students, and a range of its own published titles and reprints, was right for the market. This expansion occurred at the height of the baby boom. Not only did Coles have the vehicle for expansion across the country in the shopping centres, but it had an expanding young market.

Most books purchased for the Canadian company came from the United States. Canadian indigenous publishing was limited and made up only a small proportion of the total assortment in Canadian bookstores. As is still the case, in order to make a profit most Canadian publishers represented a number of United States publishers and acted as their agent/distributor. Coles large size meant that, in many cases, it alone was buying more of a title than was the Canadian agent. Because of its large buying power, United States publishers were prepared to deal directly with Coles, circumventing the Canadian agent. As such, Coles developed good relationships with numerous American publishers, many of whom were very interested in having Coles locate in the United States.

When competition between shopping centre developers resulted in excessive mall duplication and fragmentation of the market place, Coles focussed its attention on locations previously considered to be secondary, i.e. areas with populations of 25,000 or less. Eventually, it ran out of locations. By the mid 1960s, Coles had approximately 150 stores and had "used all the Canadian locations that were viable."

Entry into the United States

In 1965 Coles opened its first store in New York State. It had been advised that a new shopping centre was being built. The location was deemed satisfactory and Coles proceeded with the new store in the same fashion as with any new store in Canada using the "cookie cutter" approach with identical fixtures and, for the most part, the same mix of merchandise and book selections.

With the exception of some regional differences, Coles' management perceived the United States market to be "very similar, although much larger than that in Canada." Management reasoned that as new stores were opened, they could be added to the appropriate Canadian district manager's territory based on north-south proximity. Coles management believed that business should naturally flow north and south. The American market was viewed as a southern extension of the Canadian market. Since the head office already dealt with United States suppliers, there was no perceived need to duplicate the very expensive purchasing operation. Hence, all the purchasing remained in Canada.

Store Locations

Competing for locations was a major problem. Coles was an unknown company in the United States market and during this same period Walden's and Dalton's, presently the two largest book retailers in the United States, were embarking on major expansion programs.

The B. Dalton Company Inc. was a wholly owned subsidiary of the Dayton Hudson Corporation, a large company with extensive retail holdings encompassing department stores and many specialty chains. Dalton's began in 1966, and by 1985 operated 746 Dalton Bookseller, 38 Pickwick Discount Book and 14 B. Dalton Software Stores. It eventually was sold to Barnes and Noble, another sizeable United States retail book chain. Walden's, the other major book retailer, was owned by Carter Hawley Hale, which, like Dayton Hudson, was a large and well established United States retailer owning the May Department stores, Target Discount stores and many others. Walden Book Company operated four book chains with approximately 940 stores. Both companies operated from coast to coast, Walden's being represented in all 50 states and Dalton's in all but three states. Walden's was subsequently purchased in 1984 by another retail giant, K Mart Corporation. Thus, both book retailers had a significant advantage over Coles with major backing from their respective parent companies and preferred status and clout with the shopping centre developers. Frequent parallel leasing between the Walden and Dalton group effectively shut Coles out of the majority of good malls and led to Coles accepting some extremely questionable locations.

Coles used the same expansion tactic in the United States as it did in Canada. When a site became available which, in the eyes of the retained real estate expert and Canadian management, was suitable, they took it. Guidelines did not exist as to which types of locations would be acceptable provided they fulfilled certain demographic conditions. Between 45 percent and 50 percent of the stores were in super regional centres, 22 percent and 24 percent respectively were in regional and local malls, five percent in strip centres, and one store was located in Manhattan on Water Street. There was no preference given to one region over another, and by 1986, 58 stores existed in 24 states. Within the states, stores were generally spread across a variety of markets with little or no concentration in any one.

Jack Cole stated that "rents in the United States were generally comparable or lower," depending, of course, on the individual market. It was generally cheaper to build in the United States especially in the south, thus the rents were lower. In later years the favourable differences have decreased.

In terms of the layout and general decor, the United States stores were virtually the same as they were in Canada. The same black and yellow signs, style of fixturing and layout was used. The promotional nature of the stores was carried through into the United States with books piled on cube fixtures and signed by price near the front of the store.

Labour

It was Coles' experience throughout the time in the United States that the labour market was as good as or better than that of Canada. Management felt that the American business environment and all the people in it were competitively motivated without the benefit of government subsidies, preferential tariffs and benevolent marketing boards enjoyed by many Canadian industries. They found the workers more willing and dedicated, and labour shortage was not a problem.

In terms of costs, United States labour was cheaper than in Canada, both in terms of salary and benefits. Coles chose to pay the same rates as they paid to their Canadian staff as they felt it was only equitable. The United States staff had the same bonus program and social benefits, and were consequently better off than other comparable United States retail employees.

Product Mix

The product mix in the United States was very similar to that of the Canadian stores although, obviously, the United States stores carried fewer Canadian titles. Coles' own publishing efforts were expanding in Canada. These books carried high margins and covered a wide range of subjects, not just Canadian content. Thus, they were shipped to the United States as well. Some were quite British in flavour, which resulted in poor sales south of the border. Generally the stores stocked a broad range of books across a wide number of subjects and the selection compared favourably with that of the competition.

Remainders were a substantial part of Coles' business both in Canada and the United States. Remainders occur in the book trade when publishers sell off the excess portion of a print run. This excess might be a combination of simply having over-estimated the market and printed too many books and/or returns from booksellers. Almost all books are purchased on a returnable basis by the booksellers which means they can return any overstock generally after three months and before one year from the date of invoice. Normally publishers issue lists of "remaindered" books and the various booksellers bid for them. This is extremely lucrative for the retailers since the cost might be as low as $.10 on the dollar and they might markup the title to half the original price and make a large margin.

Hence, Coles pursued this profitable mix in the United States as well, and according to Jack Cole, their margins were higher than those of W.H. Smith in Canada and Dalton in the United States. Over the past ten years or so, remainders had dropped as a percentage of Coles total assortment in Canada which was a very successful move in that it has virtually exchanged places with W.H. Smith (its major competitor) in terms of remainder to regular stock mix.

Text books were also part of the United States product mix. Next to last editions of texts were purchased very cheaply when a new edition was released. They were then put on sale at a fraction of the price of the new edition while still making a good margin.

Regional Differences

Because the stores were spread across a large number of states and management spent insufficient time in the United States, very little was known about each individual market. An example was the store in Brownsville, Texas, where Coles had difficulty due to the very high proportion of Spanish speaking people in the area. Regional differences were not sufficiently taken into consideration in the buying. Downhill skiing books were sent to Florida, European cooking books with different weights, measures and spelling were sent to the United States, and the Water Street store in Manhattan had a large section of nature books.

A New Owner for the Canadian Operation

Southam Inc., a large Canadian-owned company in the communications and information industries, bought Coles in 1978. By the early 1980s sales and profits were flagging both in Canada and the United States. Jack Cole stayed on with the company until 1981 at which time he retired. The former President of Avon Canada became President for a short period of time during which sales and profits did not improve. Bill Ardell was hired as President in 1982.

The United States company was losing between $1.3 and $2.0 million per year, and the total loss for the Canadian and United States divisions was approximately $10 million post interest. Under the leadership of Ardell, the Canadian company was turned around by 1984–85. The emphasis was changed from that of highly promotional stores carrying a large proportion of remainders to stores promoting selection, quality and value. Between the period from 1965 to 1985, the Canadian company had added about 50 stores to the chain bringing the total number to 185.

In Canada, the book retail market had been dominated by three major chains, Coles, Classics and W.H. Smith along with the department stores. W.H. Smith (then a subsidiary of W.H. Smith U.K.) subsequently purchased Classics to create a chain larger than Coles. Despite the increased competitive threat created by this union, Coles maintained and, in fact, strengthened its position in the Canadian market. Coles focus changed to reflect changing market conditions; systems were refined; and two new retail concepts, Active Minds and the Book Company, were launched to appeal to more specialized segments of the market. With the turnaround of the Canadian operation, attention turned to the United States.

Management of the United States Operation

As noted earlier, Canadian management knew very little about the United States market. Regional differences and tastes were not accounted for in purchasing which was done by one person from the head office in Toronto. The company was still emphasizing remainders which require a specialized method of presentation, unlike a regular book store format, in order to be successful. According to Deborah Lewington, who later performed the purchasing function for the United States during the last year of operation, the American managers did not understand how to present the remainders.

Long distance management made negotiations more difficult with stores and suppliers. Inventory control was very poor in the United States stores. Unlike the Canadian operation, the United States stores had to supply invoice numbers and obtain permission from suppliers in order to take advantage of publishers' returns policies. Although this was the norm for the industry in both markets, due to its size and buying power in Canada Coles had been able to negotiate a virtually "open" returns privilege with Canadian suppliers. They were not prepared for the paper work required to return books in the United States and hence, suffered major overstocks.

In the early days of the United States operation, as new stores were opened, they were added to Canadian district managers' territories based on north/south proximity. When there were only a few stores, this method worked reasonably well. As the number of United States stores grew and locations were spread across the country, the territories of the district managers became far too large and varied to be effectively managed.

American district managers were eventually hired and the country was divided into five regions: East Central, Southeast, Northeast, Mid-West, and Water Street . Although this was an improvement over the previous situation, the districts were still very large and diverse, and the stores were far apart.

All store hiring and firing was the responsibility of the United States district managers. The Canadian company was not involved and Ardell felt that they (in Canada) were "so poorly connected to the market that the Canadian operation didn't know whether they were getting good or bad staff."

On examining the United States operation, management realized that they needed American management to run it. Bill Ardell subsequently hired an American who had been working with W.H. Smith in the United States to be Vice-President of the United States stores. She reported directly to Ardell and controlled the whole operation with the exception of finance which was handled in Canada. A Canadian buyer was sent to the United States office and a second buyer was hired from Barnes and Noble, a United States discount bookstore chain with over one hundred stores. In addition, an advertising manager was hired, also from W.H. Smith United States.

The United States office was located in New York City where there was only one Coles store located in the central business district on Water Street. All the other stores were located in shopping malls in different markets across the country. It is very important for any buyer to have close access to the stores for which he/she is buying. In this case, the only store to which they had quick access was the one serving a market that was not representative of the rest of the chain. Although the office was close to the sources of supply, the lack of easy access to the retail stores was a definite drawback.

Rather than the situation improving with the opening of the New York office, it deteriorated further. Bill Ardell stated that the United States office suffered from "excessive zealousness." They put in the wrong merchandise and did not control the quantities of Canadian product. "The problems were enhanced by the individual in charge." The inventory situation worsened and Ardell felt that there was inadequate expertise in running the United States business.

Although not as large as Dalton's or Walden's, with 58 stores in the United States, Coles business was still meaningful to the publishers and distributors. The publishers offered substantial advertising allowances to the majors of which Coles was considered one. Dalton's, Walden's, and the others made good use of these funds, but Coles was so spread out geographically that they could not advertise efficiently. Thus, this source of funds went largely untapped except for in-store advertising and point-of-sale promotion.

Competition

By the mid 1980s, the competition had become far more intense than it was 20 years earlier when Coles entered the market. As previously noted, Dalton's and Walden's were the major competition in the early years, both undergoing rapid expansion programs and vying for new locations at the same time as Coles. They had grown into book chain giants.

Until the 1980s, both chains were selling books largely at regular prices. In 1981, Dalton's started a new chain called Pickwick Discount Book Stores to appeal to the price-conscious customer. By 1985 Pickwick had grown to 38 stores. This strategy was initiated largely as a competitive response to a relatively new discount bookseller called Crown Books. Walden was not far behind, opening their first discount bookstore, Reader's Market, in 1984. Within a year they had opened four more stores.

Crown was started in 1977 and, after several changes in ownership, was spun off from Dart Drugs as a separate company in 1983. By 1984 it had grown to 183 stores selling discounted books including best-sellers, remainders, and large selections within popular genres such as cooking and art. All titles from the *New York Times* best-seller list were discounted by 35 percent, and many other titles by 50 percent. Deborah Lewington explained that they bought huge quantities and received better discounts than Coles — "Even paperbacks were sold at 30 percent off."

The Crown stores, unlike Coles, were located largely in free-standing, strip centres and central business district locations, but their low prices, combined with heavy promotional advertising, large selection and physical store space provided formidable competition in the low end market which was originally Coles' domain. Dart Drug, the parent company until 1983, had also included sections of fast moving books in many of its stores adding more competitive pressure within the market.

Along with Crown, "Book Warehouses" were a major source of competition. A book warehouse is a wholesaler who buys a large number of books at low prices, and "opens up shop for two weeks, a month, or possibly permanently. It is like a no-frills store with the books in boxes." Coles discounts were not as deep as either Crown or the book wholesalers.

Barnes and Noble was another low priced competitive force in the United States market. It sold popular-priced books and college texts through discount outlets and college bookstores. Although prices were not as low as those of Crown and the book wholesalers, Barnes and Noble provided yet another popular priced alternative to customers.

The growth of the competition over the years left Coles in a middle position, with the full selection, regular-priced chains on one side and the lower-priced competition on the other.

Selling the United States Operation

With the financial and inventory situation worsening in the United States, Coles Canada decided to hire a consultant to give them an assessment of the market position, performance, prospects and recommendations for the United States operation.

The report concluded that "answers to long term problems are not found in the current store environment or in the measurement of, or improvement in, any one particular variable." Short term fixes would still mean that factors such as "location, merchandising superiority, pricing latitude, supporting structures and other aspects would continue to be problematic." It suggested a variety of strategic options such as closing the United States operation, selling or franchising to employees, leasing in other retail locations, buying an existing chain, and creating a "mega store" with smaller satellite stores in surrounding towns. Other than closing or selling the operation, the consultants felt that "none of the options alone could solve all of Coles concerns without a very large investment."

Bill Ardell recalled that when he asked the consultant how Coles could set up a book store chain in the United States, and whether it could be a success, their reply was that it was not possible to set up a greenfield operation. Coles would have to acquire a United States company since the major national competitors, Dalton's and Walden's, as well as the strong regional chains, would make it impossible to find locations.

At this point, with the situation deteriorating, Coles made the decision to close the United States office which had been in operation for only 18 months. In mid 1986, the purchasing was brought back to Toronto and divided among four buyers. Advertising came under the marketing department. However, very little was done in the United States market.

As Deborah Lewington stated, when she began buying for the American stores from the Canadian office "management was starting to get rid of the United States operation." The Canadian operations function was also taxed heavily since the five United States district managers all reported to the Vice-President of Operations in Canada. Inventory control was manual and hence even more difficult to manage from a distance. She related that there was a lack of support to do anything in the United States during this time and a lack of commitment to the American operation as a whole.

The corporate group, Southam, was deliberating whether or not to remain in the United States market. Bill Ardell said that it "took six to nine months to persuade the corporate group to get out. It was taking too much management time and financial resources." Finally, in early 1987, the decision was made to sell the United States operation. Within four to five months the sale to Walden had been finalized.

Bill Ardell stated that he would not enter the United States again using the greenfield sites. The only way he would ever consider entering the United States would be through an acquisition — "the time frame is too long for a greenfield operation." He added that Coles had "re-examined the Canadian market and they see lots of opportunities here. There is no easy road to doing business in the United States — it's lots of tough slugging."

Reflecting on the Experience

This section presents an analytic summary of events in the Coles Bookstores case using the same categories selected to reflect on the

Mark's Work Wearhouse entry into the United States. The Coles' story echoes many similar features found in the Mark's Work Wearhouse and Chateau Stores experiences. A significant difference was that Coles was predominantly ordering from American publishers prior to entering the United States and, therefore, already had a supplier base established and relationships formed. This difference alone, however, was not enough to ensure success and to keep Coles from having to withdraw.

Reason for entry and approach

Coles had reached the limits of growth in primary locations in Canada and sought to sustain growth by expanding into the United States. The company essentially followed the same policy as in Canada which was to let the real estate opportunities determine store locations.

Dates of operation in the United States

Coles operated in the United States from 1965 until 1987.

Attitude toward entry

Management perceived that the United States market was similar to Canada, only larger, and that it was just a southern extension of the Canadian market. As stores were opened they were added to existing Canadian districts.

Entry mode and rationale

Coles used the greenfield mode of entry which, as in the Mark's Work Wearhouse example, management eventually realized would take too long and cost too much money to reach a size and level of concentration to be successful. In fact, the consultant hired to advise on strategic options informed Coles that it would not be possible to continue pursuing the greenfield strategy and that any of its options, other than shutting down, would require a large investment. Management concluded, in retrospect, that the only way to enter the United States was by acquisition.

The rationale underlying the entry strategy seemed to be to follow the real estate opportunities. When locations became available that looked appropriate, they were taken.

Research prior to entry

No research was done prior to entry.

Transfer of retail concept

The Canadian concept was transferred with little modification to the United States. It was implemented in the same "cookie-cutter" style as in Canada. Certain elements of the product mix were inappropriate for the United States, in general, and regional differences within the country were often missed.

Geographic operating area

Coles was extremely dispersed and lacked concentration, operating 58 stores in 24 states.

Store locations

Acquiring good store locations was a major problem. Walden's and Dalton's expansion made it almost impossible for an unknown entity like Coles to secure primary locations. Coles found rents to be comparable or lower than in Canada. However, this may have been a function of the company's secondary locations.

Canadian management

Knowledge and qualifications   Canadian management knew little about the American market and were not connected well enough to the operations in the United States to know the quality of the staff being hired. As the number of stores in the United States increased, they were added to existing Canadian districts and undoubtedly contributed to the existing control problems.

Commitment   Coles ran its business in the United States for 20 years which represents a certain level of commitment. However, there did not seem to be the managerial and financial commitment necessary to expand the company to the size required to compete against Walden's and Dalton's.

Decision-making   For the majority of the time that Coles operated in the United States, decision-making was centralized in Canada with the following exceptions: the hiring of store staff; purchasing in the last couple of years of operations; during the brief tenure of the person hired as Vice-President for the U.S. stores; and possibly after district managers for the United States were eventually hired.

American management

The American managers hired by Coles did not appear to have the expertise needed. There are indications in the case that American store managers did not understand the remainder business which was a significant component of Coles product mix. The person hired as Vice-President for the United States operation apparently compounded the company's problems rather than resolving them.

Suppliers

Coles had its supplier relationships in place and was considered a major bookseller by publishers. However, Coles was unable to take advantage effectively of the substantial advertising allowances offered by publishers because the stores were so dispersed.

Systems

Inventory control systems were inadequate in the United States. Also communication with headquarters and with suppliers was poor.

Competition

The competition was severe. It was probably the major barrier to success for Coles. Dalton's and Walden's dominated the American market with over 1600 stores between them. They also had large parent companies with significant resources. They were also more aggressive. For example, Dalton's started in 1966 and by 1985 had almost 800 stores. During this same approximate time period, Coles opened 58 stores in the United States and 50 stores in Canada.

Over the years as the competition grew, the market divided into companies following a full selection, regular price strategy and those pursuing a discount strategy. The latter became direct competition for Coles at the low end of the market which was where Coles was positioned. However, their prices were lower, their promotional expenditures higher, their stores and selection bigger than Coles. The company either was not able to move with the market or had not seen the split taking place and missed it. Coles found itself in the middle and could not compete.

SHOPPERS DRUG MART

Entry into the United States

Shoppers entry into the United States, similar to the three cases already described, was reactive. A Canadian developer, who was friendly with the president of Shoppers Drug Mart, was building a shopping centre in Florida and required a pharmacy for the location. Shoppers had always wanted to go into the United States and this was seen as a good opportunity. The Florida market was perceived to be a good one due to the number of senior citizens in the area and the fact that there was a large "snowbird" population who already knew Shoppers.

The board of directors elected to open one pilot store, a research and development project. For two years that one store was successful. David Bloom commented, "It was a tremendous pilot test, with minimal risk and great potential." Shoppers added a second store about 80 miles away and then started to open stores, one after another, so that by 1977 it had 37 stores on the east and west coasts.

In 1984 David Bloom, Chairman and CEO, made the decision to leave Florida. The first seven years had been profitable, after which the company started to lose money. Changes were made and the company was breaking even when it was sold. According to Bloom, "We were number five in the market and you can't be number five and survive. You need to be number one, two or three in market share. I'm talking top-of-the-mind awareness. Otherwise, you don't have the advertising and marketing dollars to compete successfully."

In 1984, Shoppers transferred 30 stores to Peoples Drug Stores, recently purchased by Shoppers parent company, Imasco. It sold the seven others to an outside company. Peoples was in 14 states and its market share varied from 10 to 50 percent. Peoples was a breakeven company. However, in 1986 the drug store business took a nose dive because deep discounters moved into the market. Peoples barely broke even in 1986 and lost money in 1987 ($22.5 million) and 1988 ($8.3 million). Imasco formed a retail group and made David Bloom president of the group. This meant that he was overseeing the activities of Peoples Drug Stores in the United States and Shoppers Drug Mart in Canada.

David Bloom re-positioned the American stores, controlled expenses and brought Peoples to profitability in 1989. That same year, the company divested 325 stores in areas it felt were of limited potential. In its remaining major market areas, except one, Peoples became the market leader. In 1990, Imasco sold the remaining 490 Peoples stores to an American drug store chain because it did not have the scale necessary to generate the returns that Imasco required.

Attitude toward entry

Entry into the United States was seen as an experiment. There was only one large competitor and three smaller chains, so it was felt there was an opening for a traditional drug store to enter the market.

Entry mode and rationale

Shoppers used a greenfield entry. It experienced the same problems as Mark's and Coles, as well as the same result. David Bloom, in reflecting on his experience, concluded that the best way to enter the

47

United States was by acquisition of a large chain. Some of his other insights include:

- Growth in the United States requires tremendous capital and unless you are big, you tend to be offered secondary locations. Of course, the cost of an acquisition has to be within reason, to make it a viable option.

- Greenfield sites are good learning devices, but they require an unwavering commitment of resources. Also, it is not wise to use a small pilot test and generalize the results. Shoppers did very well with up to three to four stores because the competition didn't pay much attention. However, as it got bigger, they did pay attention and started using competitive tactics. Site selection became a real problem because the competition started bidding against Shoppers. When Shoppers won, it cost the company a fortune.

- Market share is important and the competition will defend it. Since market share is critical to successful competition, greenfield is not a good choice. How do you build 50 to 100 stores at once? The only time market share is not key to obtaining power with suppliers is when you have a truly unique product, and how many of those are there? You need market share and market dominance in the United States.

Research prior to entry

Shoppers performed qualitative and quantitative consumer research before starting up, including focus groups and mall intercepts. Over time management learned about the degree of price sensitivity in the Florida market, as this comment suggests: "In Florida, if it rains, senior citizens become scientific shoppers. They cherry pick all your specials. So in order to manage gross margins you need a broader mix."

The laws were also different in the United States. Drug stores could advertise prescription prices in the local paper, so senior citizens knew the price of drugs to the penny. This was a concern because seniors citizens had more time on their hands. Shopping was entertainment and they looked for the best price.

Shoppers also did a competitive analysis, according to David

Bloom: "We looked at them under a microscope to determine their strengths and weaknesses. For example, we looked at the number one competitor, Eckerd's, and found they were strong in photo-finishing and had very convenient locations. They had a value image, but not a sharp price image. Their stores were dowdy, old and unimaginative. However, they had 340 stores in great locations so this was one aspect we couldn't overcome competitively."

Shoppers also obtained information from various sources such as the national association for chain drug stores, other associations and industry sources, physical examination of many of the competitors' stores, and its own experience with its initial stores.

Transfer of retail concept

The Canadian concept was transferred with little modification to the United States. It was a franchise organization in Canada and this concept was transferred to the United States. However, in the United States pharmacists were not trained in franchising because franchised drug stores were unusual. Bloom commented, "We should not have used a franchise operation."

Shoppers product mix was narrow compared to other American stores. Stores had a pharmacy with general merchandise, similar to Canada. However, they also carried some other products that were necessary to adapt to its new environment such as fishing rods and sandbox pails. It did not carry electronic items, such as appliances, because they turned over very slowly.

Consumers liked Shoppers' image, service, ambience, the width of the aisles, the lighting and fixtures and the friendliness of the staff. As a result, Shoppers did very well with its first two stores because the locations were great. David Bloom stated, "With good locations you will do good business as long as you are price competitive. Our only problem was that our product mix didn't have high gross margins. We discovered the reason American drug store chains carry so much general merchandise...they are able to satisfy their gross margin requirements because sundries have high margin."

Bloom felt that every area of merchandising, advertising and marketing worked and that the only problem was the lack of a distribution centre which made its product costs unfavourable. Shoppers was too small and needed 75 stores to make this economical and feasible. Shoppers could not find a suitable acquisition to increase its size.

Store locations

Acquiring good store locations was a major problem. David Bloom summarized the problem: "We were unable to get good locations which is critical to success in retail. Also, our locations were spread all over the place."

The stores were in secondary sites because the other chains got the best locations. Developers wanted the best names they could get in their malls. Shoppers had to pay higher rents to encourage landlords to rent to them instead of their major competition. Half of the stores were on the east coast and half on the west coast with no market dominance in any particular region.

Canadian management

Shoppers sent one Canadian to Florida and the rest of the staff were Americans. It did not send one of its best executives. Bloom reflected, "You need a solid management team running the operation who understand the competition and know how to compete with them. You need to send a high profile executive."

American management

Shoppers used American management but it didn't have the very best people. In order to entice people to leave other companies, it found that it had to pay a lot of money and, therefore, it could not get the high performers. American executives did not seem to have the same loyalty to a company as in Canada. Also according to Bloom, "They will cross the street very easily and are very mobile. They are also more risk oriented and are more opportunistic."

American pharmacists were usually managers of the dispensary and were not involved in other aspects of management. Therefore, they were totally inexperienced in operating non-pharmacy operations and a total business. Shoppers also had an "honesty" problem with some franchise managers. Bloom commented, "Since they were not used to the total management concept, they looked at the stores as their own and frequently took money belonging to Shoppers. We are talking over two percent."

Suppliers

In Canada, the company did not have a distribution system because each store did its own purchasing. Shoppers networked with suppliers and had a market share that commanded a certain style of service, delivery and distribution. In the United States, without a distribution centre, products cost three to four percent more than the competition, but prices still had to match the competition.

Competition

The other four chains had a head start on Shoppers and were more dominant in the market. They used a lot of hard sell flyers. The competition was severe according to Bloom, "In the United States, especially Florida, if there are four corners on a street, there will be four pharmacies on those corners. The competition in Florida is fierce."

There was also a big mail order prescription business in the United States that did not exist in Canada.

COMPARATIVE SUMMARY

Table 1 is a summary and comparison of the four situations described in this chapter. In analyzing these cases with 20/20 hindsight, it is easy for the readers and the authors to make judgements about the situations, such as "why didn't they see that?", and to offer recommendations like "the company should have done X instead of Y." Making such statements is easier after the fact, once the necessary information is available and little opportunity exists to test the alternative recommendation. However, these problems were not obvious to the executives at the time the decisions were made and, even if they did see them, they believed that the problems could be overcome. What does prove useful for those interested in doing business in the United States is identifying the most critical factors key to the success of the Canadian business. Also useful is providing an answer to the questions "Are there certain critical recommendations for entering and operating in the United States?" and "How many of them need to be followed to ensure success? Is there one mistake that is a killer, or is failure a result of many factors?"

Reflecting on just the four cases in this chapter yields a set of numerous do's and don'ts. Some of the more obvious ones relating to the *management* of the company include:

- Don't use a greenfield site. Do use the acquisition mode of entry.

- Don't be cavalier in entering the United States. Do ensure that the decision is part of a carefully thought-out strategy.

- Don't try to enter the United States unless you have the financial and managerial resources to allocate to the entry. Do make sure you are committed to the venture.

- Don't try to enter the United States if your own house in Canada is not in order. Do ensure that you are already operating efficiently and have the systems in place to support the expansion.

- Don't go in blind. Do market research.

- Don't try to run the American company from Canada. Decentralize decision-making.

- Don't assign executives who are expendable or who need the experience as part of their career progression to manage the entry. Do assign highly qualified and experienced executives to be responsible for the venture.

Following the above recommendations would provide a good start in avoiding problems similar to the ones experienced by the companies discussed in this chapter. Yet, to Monday morning quarterbacks and casual observers, these recommendations probably look patently obvious. If this is true, it suggests that the question, maybe even the mystery, remains — why have so many knowledgeable and experienced executives missed the obvious and met the same end? Maybe the obvious is not so obvious, except when viewing it from the outside, and in retrospect. It will become clear in the next chapter that these recommendations alone are not enough to ensure success in the United States.

There are critical *market* factors that impact on performance such as consumers' tastes and buying habits, store locations, sources of supply, and the competition. The retail concept which should link the company to its customers also has to be right. We have seen some of these at work in the cases in this chapter. Recommendations on these market factors drawn from the first four cases include:

- Don't transfer a retail concept to the United States just because it works in Canada. Do modify the concept and your product mix to fit the market.

- Don't overestimate your ability to secure primary locations.

- Don't think that sourcing products will be easy. Do make sure you have your supplier relationships established. Remember you have to be big enough to be "somebody" to them.

- Don't underestimate your competition. Do be prepared to combat aggressive, experienced and sophisticated competitors.

All of these do's and don'ts about management and market factors still do not tell the whole story. Read on! There is more to learn.

Table 1 Comparative Summary

	Mark's Work Wearhouse	Chateau Stores	Coles	Shoppers Drug Mart
Dates of operation in the U.S.	1981-1987	1983-1992	1965-1987	1972-1984
Reason for entry	expand	expand	expand	expand
Approach	reactive	reactive	reactive	reactive
Attitude toward entry	why not?	others doing it	same but larger	asked in
Entry mode	greenfield	greenfield	greenfield	greenfield
Rationale	test and protect concept	natural extension	natural extension	experiment
Research prior to entry				
consumer	some	none	none	moderate
competition	no			yes
demographic	yes			yes
real estate	yes			
	yes			
Transfer of retail concept	little modification	minor changes	little modification	without modification
Product mix	like Canada	like Canada	like Canada	like Canada, some changes

Geographic operating area	dispersed	dispersed	very dispersed	dispersed
Store locations	secondary, expensive	poor choices, expensive	secondary, similar expense	mostly secondary, expensive
Management Canadian	did not understand U.S. market	did not understand U.S. market, could not turn U.S. around	did not understand U.S. market	did not understand U.S. market initially
American	questionable	questionable	questionable	questionable
Commitment to U.S.	no	no	early commitment, lacking later	
Decision-making	centralized	decentralized, then centralized	centralized	
Suppliers	problems		no problems	little leverage, high costs
Systems	under-developed	under-developed	under-developed	
Competition	severe	severe	severe	severe
Other	simultaneously expanding in Canada	simultaneously expanding in Canada	some simultaneous expansion in Canada	some simultaneous expansion in Canada

CHAPTER 2

BUYING SUCCESS: A BETTER IDEA?

An interesting question that the reader might ask is what would happen if executives of a company entering the United States followed the advice that was offered at the end of the previous chapter. The advice to those executives regarding internal management considerations, restated briefly, would be as follows: use the acquisition mode of entry; carefully consider your strategy; make sure you have the financial and managerial resources to put into the venture and that you are operating efficiently before you enter the United States; conduct research; decentralize decision-making; and assign strong, experienced managers to the entry. The two companies whose experiences are documented in this chapter, Dylex Ltd. and Canadian Tire Corporation, covered all, or nearly all, the points.

Canadian Tire Corporation (CTC), one of Canada's largest and best retailers, apparently did all the things on that list of advice above, yet the results were similar to those of other retailers. In February 1986, Canadian Tire Corporation sold the assets of White's Stores Inc. This marked the end of four years of operation in the United States during which time the company lost approximately $250 million.

Although, after reading the case, one might question Canadian Tire's long term commitment to the United States operation, it was clearly committed at the start. And what about the research, could it have been better or more comprehensive? Possibly, but could not a company with the size, resources and experience of Canadian Tire create the image it wanted? What made the difference? There were numerous difficulties associated with the company it purchased. However, the case also indicates that market factors — the retail concept, product mix, store locations, the American consumer and the competition — contributed significantly to the results.

Dylex Ltd. is Canada's largest specialty apparel retailer. In 1991 it had annual sales of over $1.84 billion. Dylex used a variety of modes to enter the United States including greenfield sites and acquisitions. The first greenfield entry (Club International) ended in the same way as the cases described in the previous chapter and the information available about this venture confirms parts of the earlier analyses. Two of its other three greenfield entries are currently small operations and they may operate quite well without attracting any competitive retaliation. A third greenfield entry (Club Monaco) is relatively new and is still being tested. Only time will tell whether the company can avoid the problems experienced by Mark's Work Wearhouse, Coles Bookstores, Shoppers Drug Mart and Dylex's own Club International.

Dylex's acquisitions constitute a larger and more complex part of the company's past history. These experiences contribute new dimensions to the "lessons learned" about entering the United States by acquisition and confirm many of the issues related to market differences. In 1987 Brooks filed for bankruptcy followed by Foxmoor in early 1990. In total, this represented an empire of over 1500 stores in the United States and a loss of more than $200 million. On the positive side, the Wet Seal NBO and Club Monaco chains were continuing to operate in the United States.

The cases in this chapter explore all the issues — internal management considerations and external market factors. The authors' conclusion is that a company has to get all the pieces of the puzzle right, not just some of them.

CANADIAN TIRE CORPORATION

Background: 1922–1981

In 1922, John W. Billes purchased Hamilton Garage and Rubber Company which was later renamed Canadian Tire Corporation. In 1928 the company published the first Canadian Tire catalogue and in 1934 it introduced its first dealer operated store. Using associated dealers to operate stores provided CTC with the capital and management resources necessary to begin a major expansion program. Although required to invest money in their stores, and to purchase products from the corporation, dealers were allowed to run the stores as their own businesses.

Canadian Tire became a public corporation in September 1944, but with John Billes and his brother, Alfred, retaining voting control. That same year, CTC diversified its product lines beyond automobile parts and accessories to include sporting goods, tools and household products. Stores became one-stop shopping outlets. The concept was very successful and sales increased 15 percent annually throughout the 1950s.

In 1956, John W. Billes died and left his shares in trust for 23 charities. Alfred J. Billes assumed the role of company president and the company continued to expand. In 1958, the first service station was introduced on an experimental basis. It was a success. By 1981, 84 gas stations contributed an estimated $189 million in sales and CTC was operating 348 stores across the country. Between 1966 and 1988 CTC acquired 100 percent of Midland Acceptance Limited and renamed it Canadian Tire Acceptance Limited. By 1981, Canadian Tire Acceptance Limited had 1,750,000 retail credit cardholders and 170,000 commercial accounts.

When Alfred J. Billes retired in 1966, Dean Muncaster was promoted to president. As the first non-Billes family member to act as president of CTC, Mr. Muncaster was accountable to four groups: Alfred Billes and his family; the heirs of John Billes headed by his son Richard; the remaining shareholders; and the dealer network. The Billes family collectively controlled 60.8 percent of Canadian Tire's voting shares (representing only 8.5 percent of all outstanding shares) and was active in the corporation during this period through management of several stores and memberships on the board of directors.

During 1976–1978, CTC faced slower sales growth. To improve performance, management introduced more competitive prices; developed an innovative TV advertising program with the central theme that "there is a lot more to Canadian Tire than tires"; delivered advertising flyers featuring CTC's "Budget Booster" and "Mileage Maker" promotional offerings to individual homes; conducted market research to identify and promote the most wanted items at popular price points; automated warehouses to lower distribution costs and keep selling prices at the stores as low as possible; and installed computers and electronic checkouts at the larger dealer stores which improved inventory turnover.

The changes were successful: dealer inventory turns increased 39 percent from 3.3 times in 1978 to 4.6 times in 1981. Sales per square foot were $178 in 1981 compared with discount department stores such as K Mart, Zellers and Woolco which had sales of approximately $125 per square foot. Canadian Tire enjoyed "profits during the 1980–81 period that (were) the envy of the retail hard goods industry in North America." Under Dean Muncaster, Canadian Tire built a reputation for being a company with incredible growth and success. Sales rose from $100 million in 1966 to $1.3 billion in 1981.

Company Structure

Canadian Tire had two major components: the Canadian Tire Corporation and a network of associated dealers. This structure was intended to achieve the benefits of both a corporate manager and the entrepreneurial spirit of privately owned businesses.

The corporation

Canadian Tire Corporation was the principal supplier and distributor of merchandise to its dealer network. CTC was also responsible for national advertising and merchandising, dealer recruitment, and a variety of administrative services. There were four principal operating units as of 1987: the merchandising division, the real estate division, the petroleum marketing division, and Canadian Tire Acceptance Limited consisting of financial services and manufacturing.

The merchandising division

The merchandising division was the largest operating division. It developed national marketing programs and supplied and distributed products to associated dealers. This division developed and maintained a national marketing program that projected a clear image of Canadian Tire. The following comment, made by Walter Hachborn, general manager of Home Hardware Stores Ltd., CTC's major Canadian competition, speaks to the division's success: "Canadian Tire had succeeded because of excellent marketing and superior merchandising combined with the fact that they were the first to fill a void in the Canadian retailing market." A minimum of two consumer surveys was conducted each year to determine the success of current promotional campaigns. This research was key to maintaining CTC's competitive strength.

Historically, Canadian Tire's marketing programs emphasized automotive products. In 1981 research revealed that consumers did not strongly associate Canadian Tire with products other than auto parts. As a result, advertising was refocussed to stress Canadian Tire as a place for "more than just tires." By 1985 this image was firmly placed in the minds of the Canadian consumer.

During the late 1970s, management believed that CTC was reaching the saturation point of the Canadian market for store expansion. To achieve sales growth, sales per store had to improve and two major changes were made. The division adopted a "back-to-basics" marketing strategy that "focussed on (the company's) basic strengths in the automotive, home and leisure areas." The resulting promotions emphasized the quality and value of Canadian Tire's products sold under the Motomaster and Mastercraft brand names. For example, the company launched a "built tough; backed tough" television campaign. Additionally, marketing was changed from a national to a regional focus. Programs were tailored to regional areas and included a flexible, regional pricing strategy to improve the competitive position of products.

Catalogues were one of CTC's strongest marketing tools. It published an Annual Value Guide that listed the entire CTC product line, and Fall and Winter supplements to the catalogue. Approximately seven million catalogues were distributed annually across Canada. Other forms of promotion included radio and television advertising, weekly flyers, full page newspaper ads published several times a week, and Canadian Tire "money", a form of discount coupon given to consumers after each purchase, designed to entice customers back to the store.

To supply dealers, the division purchased approximately 32,000 products from over 4,000 Canadian and international suppliers. CTC did not manufacture any of the new products sold within stores. Products included automotive parts and accessories, hardware and household items, and leisure-time products. All of these products were available for sale to associated dealers and approximately 6,000 were mandatory.

The merchandising division actively worked with vendors to develop proprietary products. In 1987, the division offered more than 12,000 Motomaster products and 5,000 Mastercraft home and hand tool products exclusively to Canadian Tire dealers. Other company brand names included PermaFill, Armor Coat, Playmaker, Supercycle, Nugold, Easy Flow and Pulsar.

Products were supplied through the company's distribution system. The system's key components were three highly automated warehouses (one in Edmonton and two in Toronto) which utilized computerized cataloguing of parts. The inventory levels of the warehouses, as well as those of individual retail operators, were monitored by computers. Reorder points of the retail and wholesale levels were automatically triggered on a nightly basis. This ensured a maximum delivery time of two days to retail outlets.

The distribution system was critical. It assisted in the management of costs and therefore helped to produce a profit for the corporation. Inventory turnover and carrying charges were constantly monitored. Also, a key part of Canadian Tire's image was having products available at all times for consumers. The distribution system was responsible for getting the right merchandise, in the right store, at the right time. The division was continually updating the system. For example, 1986 marked the introduction of a "just-in-time" merchandise delivery system designed to reduce inventory investment for both the corporation and dealers. The division also actively researched computer software and hardware for methods to improve the company's information systems.

Other corporate divisions

CTC owned 87 percent of the stores operated under the Canadian Tire trade name, making real estate the corporation's largest asset. Store rental income represented the corporation's second largest source of income. All real estate activity was managed within the company's real estate division and included: 1) identifying prime retail location opportunities and acquiring them; 2) expediting site and construction approvals; and 3) coordinating store construction.

The financial services division was responsible for credit sales, the auto club and insurance. It provided credit to customers and arranged financing for investments such as store computers and diagnostic equipment for auto service centers. The division closely monitored customer service charges, dealer discounts, expense levels and its collection activities. During 1987, credit sales accounted for over $1 billion of CTC's sales.

The petroleum marketing division developed all marketing programs used to promote service station activity. In 1987, the corporation had 132 gas bars in six provinces, 53 Pit Stop lubrication service centers with 59 service bays, and also had propane, bulk oil and diesel for sale.

The manufacturing division was Canada's largest remanufacturer (refurbisher) of automotive generators, alternators, fuel pumps, carburetors, brake shoes and disc pads.

The dealer network

The dealer-manager network was considered the cornerstone of CTC's success and a key part of the corporate culture. Dealers made most operating decisions (for example, personnel and local advertising) and kept a large percentage of the profits generated by their individual stores. They did not pay franchise fees, but were required to invest a minimum of $50,000 in their stores. All merchandise was purchased from CTC and had to be sold at prices not exceeding those set by the company.

CTC was responsible for selecting prospective dealers, a process it took very seriously. Prospective dealers were subjected to numerous examinations and interviews prior to being selected as a trainee. The company could afford to be choosy; it had over 1,000 applications per year for 20 to 25 dealer positions. Once selected, trainees spent three months in in-class training programs followed by six months of in-store training before being posted to a store. Corporate support was always available and dealer support group meetings were numerous. This selection process was successful; CTC had virtually no dealer failures.

Key Success Factors

In the 1985 Annual Report, Dean Muncaster outlined the corporation's key success factors.

1. the *dealer network* which placed entrepreneurs "right at store level."

2. a dedication to *power marketing,* a complex concept encompassing category dominance, intensive advertising and promotion, and price leadership. Category dominance referred to the fact that Canadian Tire stores carried "a larger assortment of its principal products than any competitor in its trading area and sells them at competitive prices." Power marketing was also identified by Burns Fry as one of the company's key strengths.

3. the use of state-of-the-art computer and distribution systems *(innovation and technology)*. Innovation and technology were themes that arose frequently in connection with Canadian Tire and both were evident since its inception. These themes continued through the 1980s with the company constantly investigating new computer systems, new inventory systems, new products and new marketing.

4. a commitment to investing in *modern, well-located retail stores.*

5. *"employee profit sharing and stock ownership* is the last, but far from the least, important key to Canadian Tire's success."

Entry into the United States

In 1977, CTC began developing a master plan for future growth that called for continued Canadian expansion throughout the late 1970s and early 1980s, mainly in British Columbia. Projections indicated that the maximum Canadian penetration of 400 stores would be reached in 1985 (it was reached in 1986). Growth would have to come from improved product mix, new efficiencies in purchasing and distribution, and from carefully controlling expenses.

Mr. Muncaster and his management team began considering options available for continued growth and expansion. Line managers were brought into the decision making process and a consultant was retained to assist in identifying and examining these options.

Several possibilities were considered: 1) investment in the oil and gas sector in Canada. The government had created incentives to invest in this sector but CTC's lack of expertise ruled out this option; 2) vertical integration into manufacturing CTC products. Again, CTC had no expertise in this area. Substantial capital investment would be required and CTC already had a great deal of power in distribution channels due to its size and position in the retail industry; and 3) real estate development. The company had some experience but interest rates were high and unstable at the time, and the risk involved was judged to be too high. The decision was made to attempt to develop a business similar to CTC in the United States. Mr. Muncaster stated: "This is what we thought we would do best. We would have a significant transfer of ability in terms of what we have learnt in the past."

Entry Strategies Considered

Both acquisitions and greenfield sites were considered. Mr. Muncaster stated that "there was some economic evaluation but it didn't take much to realize that to achieve a certain amount of economic mass, we needed to acquire an existing firm." He also commented that grass roots operations had much longer time lines than acquisitions.

Once the entry mode was decided, criteria were established for potential acquisition candidates:

1. Stores had to be close in size to an average CTC store.

2. The company had to have auto service departments associated with it.

3. The company had to have at least 25 established stores.

Six American companies meeting the criteria were identified and inquiries were made to see which could be bought. At the same time, Household International Limited wanted to sell White Stores Inc., one of the six companies being considered, and approached Canadian Tire. CTC management and board members visited White's corporate head office, warehouses and several store locations to assess the opportunity, which resulted in the decision to purchase White Stores. White Stores Inc. was located in the sunbelt area of the United States which had been experiencing phenomenal growth for several years. Long term demographic studies were favorable.

Competitive analysis indicated Texas and the sunbelt markets contained only six major, direct competitors: Sears Roebuck, Montgomery Ward, K Mart, Builders Square, Home Depot and Handyman. None of these carried the same product mix as Canadian Tire, and management believed it had identified a void in the market. The analysis did, however, indicate that Sears, Montgomery Ward and K Mart had significant power in the market. For example, Sears was heavily involved in auto parts and service, and its stores often had 16 or more auto bays as opposed to White's five or six.

Reflecting on this competitive analysis, Mr. Muncaster stated, "We underestimated the impact of nondirect competition such as Wal-Mart and discount department stores."

CTC's Purchase of White Stores Inc.

On November 17, 1981, CTC announced its intention to purchase the merchandising assets of White Stores Inc. The acquisition was completed on February 24, 1982, at a cost of $40.24 million.

White Stores Inc. operated 81 home and auto supply stores in six states (mainly Texas), and supplied 420 dealer-owned stores in 12 states. Sales exceeded $150 million in 1981 and were basically split evenly between corporate stores and wholesale shipments. The company had been losing money for several years.

Half of White's corporate stores were located on company-owned real estate while the remainder were on leased premises. The stores averaged 25,000 square feet, including 15,500 square feet of retail space and six to eight automotive service bays. The stores' product mix included auto service products, lawn and garden equipment, sporting goods, hardware, furniture and major appliances.

The dealer-owned stores averaged 6,000 square feet in size. In 1981, dealer franchise agreements ranged from six months to six years and did not require dealers to purchase their products exclusively from White's.

Annual cash rebates were provided based on dealer purchases from the company. White's merchandise was distributed from four company-owned warehouses which CTC management judged could handle two to three times the volume without additional capital expenditures.

A Burns Fry report prepared in April 1982 estimated that corporate stores had sales per square foot of $40 in 1981, while dealer stores had sales of $47 per square foot. It was estimated that CTC had $178 in sales per square foot of gross retail space during the same period. The fact that the White's chain was old, run down and outdated was considered by some retail analysts to explain the significant difference in sales. Also, as Dean Muncaster commented, "When an operation is losing money it loses its best people." White Stores did not have a strong management base at the time it was bought by CTC.

White's American Market

A retail market analyst from Houston described the market characteristics of the United States and, in particular, the sunbelt states, as follows:

1. In any United States market, three markets were at work: a national one, a regional one, and one based on local climate.

2. Retailing in the United States, and more so in the sunbelt, was highly competitive and highly dynamic (that is, the rate of change was greater in the United States than in Canada).

3. The sunbelt market was witnessing an ever-increasing number of retail entrants who were scrambling to get into very specific market niches.

4. Corporate image and advertising had to be aimed at two very different groups: the English and the Spanish-speaking populations.

5. Promotional campaigns should take into account a high degree of illiteracy and a variety of racial issues.

6. The revenues flowing from oil after 1973 had created a "gold rush" in the area where even poorly run businesses could make money and new people were arriving every day (making the overall population's average age 26).

7. Every neighbourhood in this area varied due to its ethnic composition.

8. Shopping malls predominated since most consumers preferred one-stop shopping.

9. Sunbelt consumers were sophisticated. However they would visit a variety of shops (usually specialty stores) within one mall to meet their needs.

10. Compared to Canada, stores in the United States tended to be larger, especially department stores, for example, where 25,000 square feet would be considered a small area.

11. The American consumer enjoyed a wide range of shopping choices. For example, it would have been typical to see 40 brands of an automotive product available on one shelf.

12. Older downtown areas were considered marginal and these "strip centres" tended to cater to neighbourhood traffic.

13. Hardware and sporting goods stores in Texas were a rarity as every major store sold this kind of merchandise.

14. Some observers considered the Houston area as the toughest market in the United States.

15. Consumers needed to identify with a firm's message (that is, a reason for its existence) in order for it to survive.

Retail analysts identified two potential problems for CTC: 1) White's retail locations were not in prime retail/commercial areas. Instead they were in local neighbourhoods, some populated by non-English speaking Hispanics; and 2) unlike CTC's current operations, stores were company-owned and operated.

On the other hand, some retail analysts were also quoted as saying that White's represented a good fit because the chain's average store size and product line was similar to a typical Canadian Tire store. Additionally White's, like CTC, carried only a few brand names.

The Turnaround Strategy

John Kron, Executive Vice-President of CTC, was appointed President of White Stores Inc. He had been in charge of the marketing, management information systems, and operations in Canada and was considered an ideal choice because, as Dean Muncaster commented, "He was the most broadly based person in Canada and was anxious to do something different." Three additional executives, experienced in advertising, store operations and distribution, were transferred to the United States along with several other junior management personnel.

White's was run as a separate, distinct company. Mr. Kron and his management team had full responsibility for White's. Integration was achieved by Dean Muncaster being involved in all major strategic and capital acquisition decisions. However, he stated that he maintained a distant role to ensure those closest to the market were making the decisions. Control was maintained both through Dean Muncaster's regular contact with John Kron and by having major strategic moves and capital requests approved by the Canadian board of directors in the normal manner.

Prior to the purchase, it had been decided to transfer to the United States what the company knew best — the Canadian Tire retail formula. Mr. Kron stated that "White's will not re-invent the wheel in Texas." To improve the company's sales and profit CTC planned to refurbish and re-stock White's stores to closely resemble a Canadian Tire store in terms of exterior and interior decor and merchandise mix.

As input to the turnaround strategy, CTC management researched the value of White's name, performed consumer research, and set up meetings with existing White's management and dealers. Immediately after the purchase, focus group studies were conducted to determine the image of the White's name (no such research was performed prior to the purchase). White's had been losing money for a number of years and CTC wanted to be sure the company's name did not carry a negative image. The research indicated that consumers did not think about White's often, but when prompted, the common reaction was "oh yes, I remember going to White's many years ago, it was a nice store." Management determined there was sufficient value in the name to retain it. Very little consumer research was completed because, as John Kron stated, "There were not really any questions you could ask. You could ask — do you buy tires or home products and they would say yes. ... It is hard to get an objective view of what would happen 'if' through consumer research."

However, management did study the historical buying patterns of the area using published information. These market studies indicated that Texas had similar buying patterns to rural areas in Western Canada, although the Texas market was more competitive.

To determine which of White's products were selling, meetings were held with head office employees and management who remained after the purchase and with dealer groups. Mr. Kron stated that although the CTC formula was being transferred to the United States, White's people were used to "examine the product line, item by item, and fine tune the formula to fit United States markets." He also stated that White's management, personnel and dealers fully supported the changes being considered. Everyone knew something had to be done about White's performance and there was no resistance to changes made.

The following strategy was designed to turn White's around:

1. All 81 stores would be refurbished and re-merchandised by the spring of 1984, at an estimated cost of $100 million. Up to 22 stores would be closed at any one time for up to two months for the renovation.

2. CTC dealers would be brought in to run some of the stores with a goal of 81 dealer-run stores by the end of 1983.

3. The merchandise mix (currently at 23,000 items) would be phased in gradually. Major appliances and furniture would be phased out to provide more display space. White's was to become the dominant Texas retailer for automotive products, hardware, lawn and garden equipment, and sports equipment (these product lines had been very successful for CTC).

4. White's would spend more money on advertising than the average United States retailer in order to develop a strong, clear consumer image. The dominant form of advertising would be flyers.

5. The name would be retained to take advantage of existing customer loyalty.

6. Loss leaders would be used to gain market share and increase store traffic.

7. To help dealers finance inventories, credit would be given freely, although at prevailing interest rates. If a dealer could not afford a

shipment of goods, the price to the dealer would be lowered and the difference put on a note payable to White's.

8. No additional capital would be required to upgrade warehousing facilities since the four warehouses were at 30–35 percent capacity.

9. The independent dealer network would be reduced to 300 stores by cutting off the outlying dealers. In addition, merchandising and operating strategies would be improved throughout the network. The network was profitable but was less standardized than CTC was comfortable with.

The top priority was to refurbish the 81 company-owned outlets and convert them to dealer operated locations. White's would then reflect CTC's philosophy and corporate objectives. CTC management was quoted as saying, "Management is confident that the Canadian Tire-type merchandising presentation will be successful in the United States."

CTC realized that turning White's financial performance around was not a short term project. However, Dean Muncaster stated that White's was "expected to be in the black in its third or fourth year of operation." Future plans called for expansion beginning in 1985, initially in Texas which had room for an estimated 50 stores. The expansion would create a United States operation that would match, and then surpass, the size of CTC's Canadian operation.

Implementing the Strategy

During the first two years management focussed attention on the store conversion process, the development of infrastructure, and advertising to increase the visibility of the White's name and promote its new image in order to create a substantial and loyal customer base. Six percent of sales was spent on advertising as compared to the industry average of three percent. Advertising was primarily through flyers, and in 1983, a 180-page catalogue was produced for distribution. Since distributing products to the independent dealer network was a marginally profitable activity, planned changes to the network were delayed until the conversion process was complete.

The conversion program was extensive. Each store was closed for a minimum of six weeks while it was refurbished and refixtured. In addition, as furniture and major appliances were phased out, the depth and scope of hardware and automotive products were increased. During the first half of 1982, over 11,000 items were added to White's product line, raising the stockkeeping unit base to over 24,000 items. The entire product presentation was plan-o-grammed and reflected to a large degree the "modular" merchandise concept employed by Canadian Tire.

To ensure that White's had dealers who understood the CTC concept, 22 dealers trained in Canada were moved to the United States to take over newly converted stores. Some Americans were recruited, but this proved difficult due to White's record of poor performance. Mr. Kron commented that American recruits did not receive the extensive training that Canadian dealers received because "there just wasn't time."

In an attempt to replicate another key success factor, state-of-the-art computer systems, White's information processing was technically upgraded with the installation of a new computer and software systems transferred from Canada. Converted stores were supplied with on-line, point-of-sale case register equipment providing the company with a computerized inventory system.

Since, at the time of purchase, White Stores had an image of being run down and unappealing, it was vital that customer traffic be generated in order to introduce the "new" White's Stores. After each store was re-opened, 50 to 60 percent of its merchandise was put on promotion and specialty loss leaders were developed and promoted through flyer advertising. The original plan was to reduce the percentage of promotional items as the stores matured. However, the competitive market situation in the United States forced a higher mix of promotional items than in Canada. To remain competitive, White's maintained the high level of promotional items.

Performance During 1982 and 1983

The conversion process was expensive (estimated at $165 million) and severely affected profit. White's had a net loss in 1982 of $9.8 million and in 1983 it was $29.2 million. When asked to comment on White's performance versus original forecasts, Mr. Kron made the following comments:

- [Our forecasts] didn't consider a worldwide economic slowdown, depressed oil prices, a drought in western Texas and the devaluation of the Mexican peso — events that have stymied sales growth in several trading areas serviced by White's stores.
- We were too optimistic when we started the project. We thought it would take two and a half years to make the operation profitable, but now it will take us three and a half years.
- We underestimated customer loyalty [to other stores] and the difficulty of changing their shopping habits. There is no doubt that the retail competition here [in the United States] is extremely good.
- United States consumers are extremely sophisticated purchasers, cherry picking auto parts and hardware stores for specials.

Mr. Muncaster stated:

- After having been down here for a period, we discovered the differences [in consumer behavior] were greater than we first expected. It was much more difficult to move them away from established buying patterns.
- Also we quite clearly positioned ourselves in the wrong place in the energy cycle in terms of what was going to happen to Texas, Oklahoma, etc. due to the oil price shock. This was compounded by the fact that everyone in the merchandising/distribution business had known for the past decade that the place where everyone was moving, where the growth would occur, was the sunbelt states. Everyone was there, we were the new boy on the block trying to, in effect, reconstruct something that had been allowed to fall into pretty bad shape, and we got caught in the wringer.

White's market research revealed that as many as 17 flyers were placed in a typical United States weekend newspaper for consumers to read. This intense competitive environment made it difficult for White's to capture consumer attention.

1984–1985

By 1984, the conversion process was near completion and the associated expenses were largely written off. Dean Muncaster was optimistic about

CTC's ability to turn White's into a profitable base for United States expansion.

During the year, White's continued converting company-owned stores into dealer operations (13 in total). Management concentrated on developing a more cost-efficient purchasing and distribution system and on assessing the strength of stores within the White's chain. No new stores were opened and several unprofitable ones were closed. Despite these efforts, White's lost $55 million in 1984. This figure included the $14 million expense of closing the Georgia warehouse and several retail stores.

At this time, CTC was receiving a great deal of publicity over its losses. The press was asking for explanations of White's poor performance. Retail analysts were quoted as stating:

- The company stumbled largely because it underestimated its competition in the Texas market.

- The stores look quite bright and attractive, but the locations are not the best. I wish they would open up some stores in growing areas.

- For many United States analysts, the image of White Stores conjures up pictures of a chain that's past its glory days, and reversing this opinion may take more than a face-lift and the estimated $165 million injected into the project so far.

CTC discovered that good locations were far more important in the United States than in Canada. Mr. Muncaster commented, "In Canada, we could have less than prime A locations and draw traffic to our stores. In the United States due to the increased competition this was not possible; you need prime locations."

Despite the problems, Mr. Muncaster and Mr. Kron were committed to turning around the United States operation. As one employee stated, "We have to [make a go in the United States] — it's our future." However, at the same time, both were feeling pressure within the organization to improve White's performance. Dealers not involved in the United States were concerned because stock they received through the profit sharing plan was being affected negatively by the White's results. The new Board of Directors also was not pleased with the losses. Mr. Kron indicated there was a shift in corporate support at this time.

In 1985, it was decided that a strong, experienced marketing manager was needed to improve White's performance. The two managers in charge of marketing were working hard but did not have the experience necessary to handle the difficult job of improving White's image. John Crowley, Vice-President of Marketing in Canada, was sent to the United States as Executive Vice-President of Merchandising. Mr. Crowley was an American by birth with 36 years of retail experience, largely in the United States.

It had been obvious for some time that the only products earning money were automotive products and service. After research revealed that no competitor dominated this product area, a two-pronged strategy was developed. First, a new merchandising and marketing campaign was designed to reposition White's from a one-stop shopping place to a store focussed on auto parts and service. Mr. Crowley stated, "We had to go 180 degrees in reverse of what we were able to do in Canada, away from a broader presentation of lines to a projection of great expertise in the automotive service area." Store signs were changed to read "White's Autocenter Plus" to reflect the new emphasis on auto parts, accessories and maintenance.

In addition, the company moved away from flyer advertising and spent 40 percent of its 1985 advertising budget on electronic media advertising. A TV campaign was developed to highlight the broad selection of auto parts (auto parts represented at least 50 percent of the product mix at each store) and showed customer satisfaction at auto centers.

Second, the uncompetitive hardware and housewares product lines were dropped and all other do-it-yourself home improvement products were de-emphasized. This was due, in part, to a change in the competitive environment. K Mart Corporation, the second largest retailer in the United States, had just announced its intention to expand its nine-store Texas chain of Builders Square do-it-yourself stores. Dean Muncaster stated, "We have found the United States hardware market difficult to enter. They (the competition) have a good lock on the business."

In June 1985, CTC's executive committee of the Board of Directors commissioned Arthur Anderson and Company to perform an extensive management consulting project on White's (estimated to cost $1 million). This project was completed in August and the resulting report recommended downsizing the United States operation. The research indicated three things: 1) White Stores was over-extended in relationship to its internal operation. The company had too many stores, many of which were in poor locations; 2) by attempting to supply dealer operated stores in eastern United States, the company had over-extended itself geographically; and 3) White Store's excess warehouse capacity was increased even further when furniture and appliances were dropped from the product line. These products required more space than other product categories. In order to downsize White's, the report recommended closing unprofitable stores, relocating several stores to larger suburban areas and changing White's management structure.

During the first quarter of 1985, performance improved; sales were up ten percent over the previous year. In April, Dean Muncaster stated, "The early signs of the repositioning seem to be positive, but it's too early to be at all definitive"; however, he did admit that "some preliminary work has been done on a possible retreat from the United States market."

In May 1985, A.J. Billes (co-founder of CTC), then 85 years old, rejoined the Board of Directors full-time. Numerous rumours suggested that relations between Dean Muncaster and the Billes family were strained.

In May, after White's financial results showed losses parallelling those of 1984, despite repositioning attempts, Dean Muncaster was quoted out of context in a Canadian paper stating that CTC would probably liquidate its United States operation. This quote was picked up by United States newspapers and resulted in White's losing bank credit, much of its supplier credit and some employees. On June 15, 1985, Mr. Muncaster was asked to leave CTC just prior to the company's annual meeting.

John Kron was let go as president of White's in August, at which time White's showed a loss of $78.3 million, including a $50 million write down.

Alfred (Fred) Billes agreed to manage the United States operation for a period of two to three months until a new president could be hired. Mr. Billes was sent because the Canadian organization required all of its senior management staff. A replacement for Dean Muncaster had not been located. The changes suggested by Arthur Anderson continued to be implemented. Billes believed that the operation was twice the size it should have been and announced plans to close 18 dealer-operated stores and 21 company-owned stores by December.

It was announced at a trade show in October that all franchise contracts expiring on December 31st would not be renewed. This action resulted in a major lawsuit against Whites, CTC, and the executives of both companies by the 22 affected dealers. Half of the 22 dealers were Canadians, transferred to the United States by CTC. The lawsuit was settled out of court in 1986 for an estimated $5 million.

Hiring a New President

In February–March of 1985, both Dean Muncaster and John Kron had realized that the American operation required a new president and initiated a search through a major American professional recruiting firm. Their relations were strained with certain members of the Board of Directors and as Dean Muncaster stated, "It was just a matter of time before it would be time for both of us to leave (the company)." A Board committee was then formed to work with the American recruiting firm to find an experienced American retailer who could assume the presidency of White's. Everyone involved believed that an American was necessary because it was vital that the president of White's understand the American retail market.

In October 1985, Dean Groussman, an American with a strong retailing background, was hired and Alfred Billes returned to Canada shortly thereafter. Mr. Groussman was hired to find out what could be done to stop the hemorrhaging of losses and implement it as soon as possible. By this time, White Stores was losing approximately $2 million per week and this figure had been increasing rapidly. For example, when Arthur Anderson was conducting its report, losses were estimated at $1 million per week.

Immediately upon entering White Stores, Mr. Groussman began a two-week in-depth investigation of the operation which was possible largely due to the extensive background research conducted by Arthur Anderson. Mr. Groussman based his analysis on his own retail experience, his knowledge of the Texas economy, and his knowledge of White Stores acquired over the previous ten years. An independent review of the Arthur Anderson material was performed as management felt the situation had changed since the recommendations were formed. Losses per week had doubled and the operation was in serious danger of caving in.

Groussman concluded that no aspect of White Stores, as it stood, was profitable or capable of becoming so. Downsizing the operation alone would not create profits for many years and the write-off associated with store closures would only increase the company's losses. Mr. Groussman agreed with Mr. Crowley's and Mr. Kron's earlier conclusion that an automotive emphasis was required. Automotive products were the best part of the present product line in terms of sales/profits and the company had been gaining market share in this area. Management felt automotive products were the only hope for White Stores' future; however, the stores were too large to convert into exclusive auto specialty stores.

It was concluded that White Stores had to be downsized even more extensively than recommended by Arthur Anderson. The associated writedown expenses would result in a significant loss for 1986. Future plans included opening new, smaller stores, in prime locations, specializing in automotive products.

Management presented the conclusions, along with a request for additional funding, to the CTC Board of Directors. They approved the request.

The Sale of White Stores Inc.

One week after the Board approved the proposal, Western Auto Supply Company of Morristown, N.J. approached White Stores with an offer to purchase the company. This offer was presented to the CTC Board along with Mr. Groussman's recommendation that they not accept the offer. He did not feel the offered price was high enough to consider. The Board agreed and turned down the offer.

One week later, Western increased the offer. White Stores entered into a negotiation process with Western. A price was negotiated that made it more advantageous for CTC to sell White Stores than to continue its operation.

On December 21, 1985, CTC announced publicly that a letter of intent had been signed with Western Auto Supply Company. The letter of intent outlined an agreement for Western to purchase White's for US $55 million in cash and notes. Concurrent with the Western–CTC negotiations, Western was being purchased by Wesray Capital Corporation. It was important that this purchase be completed prior to the acquisition of White Stores. All parties involved worked hard to ensure that both purchases were completed before December 31. After this date, the United States tax laws were changing and White Stores' tax losses could not be sold to Western. The tax losses were of great interest to Western and a key item being purchased.

The purchase by Wesray of Western Auto was not completed until December 20th. Western and Wesray then worked quickly to get approval from their 23 lenders for the required financing to purchase Whites. Since it was close to Christmas many of the lenders could not be located and financing was not secured prior to December 31st.

Western still wanted parts of White Stores but without the $250 million tax loss, a totally new contract had to be negotiated. In the meantime, White Stores had started preparing for the sale by reducing its inventory, which had not been part of the original letter of intent, and by having dealers source from other suppliers. The process was beyond the point of no return and, therefore, White Stores could not reconsider selling.

By January 1986, the deal had been renegotiated. Western was no longer purchasing the company as a whole, but its assets. At first, it was determined that White Stores would retain 13 stores which would be used to experiment with the specialty auto store concept. Plans were put in motion to remodel the stores and source products. However, CTC was still without a replacement for Mr. Muncaster and asked Mr. Groussman to join the Canadian organization. He accepted and all of the United States stores were sold to Western.

In February 1986, 40 White Stores, three warehouses and certain accounts receivable were sold to Western for US $24,534,000 and all remaining inventory, office equipment and other assets were sold. CTC retained the name White Stores Inc. in order to maintain the option of using the United States tax losses, incurred during 1981 to 1985 ($250 million), in any future United States ventures.

Some Lessons that Management Learned

The following comments are from senior management involved with the project. CTC took a group of unsuccessful stores and they rethought the process, cleaned up the stores, refurbished and refixtured them, made them nice facilities with a new assortment of merchandise. They concentrated on basically the same categories as Canadian Tire. They took an unsuccessful strategy that customers didn't really want and changed it into a strategy that customers didn't know anything about. The stores had five different product categories unlike anything anyone else had in the United States. The customer had never seen an assortment like this under one roof. Customers were very comfortable with their earlier shopping habits and their early decisions of whom to buy from.

The product assortment transferred to the United States was common in Canada but did not fit with American consumer buying behaviour. In the United States, where all White's stores were located, there generally was at least one, if not more than one, retailer who did a better job on every category that they carried in the stores — better assortments, at better locations with the same low prices. So there was nothing compelling the customer to go to White's. White's had not fit ... there was no fit.

Mr. Kron stated, "I think we should have spent a year perfecting the operations first. What we were doing was bringing people into a store that we couldn't operate properly or efficiently. From an operational point of view that was the biggest strategic error. We should have got good qualified people first. We were trying to get too much out of too few people. In order to capitalize on a heavy promotional program, you have to fulfil the promises. Once you get the customer in the store it has to be a pleasant shopping experience and you take them through the store and get the halo effect. We weren't doing that. There was that degree of inexperience on the part of staff so you couldn't present the whole merchandising program. In addition, there was a disproportionate effort on promotional items. This was one of our biggest errors."

It was agreed that too much effort was put on promotional items and not enough time was spent considering the rest of the product mix. One senior manager commented, "Your promotional items must relate to what is in your store. If your customers find a pleasing assortment of products to select from after they are there, they will stay and shop. A lot of White's promotions did not reflect the rest of the store. For example, if you advertise garbage cans and customers come in and don't find a good selection of housewares or found that Wal-Mart had a bigger and better selection, there was no reason for customers to stay and shop. They [White's] weren't able to close the sale because their assortment was not that strong, except later in auto products."

Mr. Kron identified the following additional factors as being key to White's poor performance:

1. White's didn't have enough stores in suburban areas to take advantage of the heavy promotional campaign. "In order to hit the consumer with adequate frequency, you have to over-advertise and we were wasting an awful lot of money because we didn't have enough store locations."

2. There was a shift in corporate support when it became obvious that White's would not make money in the projected time frame. "You need total corporate commitment to make it in the United States — it can't be withdrawn when things go badly."

Mr. Muncaster's assessment of what went wrong is conveyed in his list of things he would do differently if he were to enter the United States again:

1. Look for a successful company with a good management base and be prepared to pay the necessary price. "If you don't have the right people in a business then your opportunities to run a successful business are much less." Mr. Muncaster considered it very difficult to infuse the necessary talent who understood the market. He also stated that it was very hard to change a company's image and turn around its performance — "it's much easier to purchase a successful company."

2. Acquire a company with a narrower product line and smaller stores.

3. He would still have sent Mr. Kron to the United States to run the operation but he would hire a first-rate American retail person, who knew the market, to be Kron's next-in-command. Mr. Muncaster stated he thought it was important to have someone he knew and trusted overseeing the United States operation.

4. He would have conducted more and different research. Specifically, he would thoroughly test consumer response to the store's concept. He would not have gone in assuming the concept would work.

5. Instead of having the United States operation reviewed yearly, the initial proposal would clearly lay out the long term commitment and time line required to succeed in the United States.

At the time of this case, Canadian Tire had a committee in place charged with looking for good acquisition candidates in both Canada and the United States. Management would not disclose the industries being considered but stated that any United States candidate would have to fulfil the following criteria:

1. The company must be financially successful at the time of purchase.

2. It had to be in a growth industry.

3. It had to have strong management in place that could be retained after the purchase.

Reflecting on the Experience

Reason for entry and approach

Management believed that the company was reaching the maximum penetration level possible in Canada. To continue growing and expanding, management decided to enter the United States.

Dates of operation in the United States

1982–1986.

Attitude toward entry

CTC management was *proactive* as they began to investigate various possibilities for expansion. This investigation was part of the strategic planning process that involved the senior management team, line managers and a consultant. In the end they chose to stay with what they knew best and did very well — the retail business. They may have become more *reactive,* however, in their ultimate decision about the company to acquire in the United States.

Entry mode and rationale

CTC management chose to enter the United States with an acquisition. Acquisitions and greenfield sites were both considered but management realized that a certain economic mass was necessary to be successful which would only be available by acquiring an existing firm.

Research prior to entry

Management established criteria for the potential acquisition and identified six companies that met the criteria. As enquiries were being made as to which companies could be bought, CTC was approached by the owner of one of the companies on the list, White Stores, that wanted to sell. Management and board members visited White's head office, warehouses and some stores prior to the decision. Demographic studies and competitive analyses were conducted. Competitive analyses indicated that there was a void in the market; no one carried the same mix of products as CTC. However, management underestimated the indirect competition such as Wal-Mart and discount department stores. The stores were old, run down and outdated. However, research into the value of the company name and consumer research came after the purchase as part of the planning of the turn around strategy.

Transfer of retail concept

Prior to the purchase, the decision was made to transfer the CTC retail formula, and it was transferred with only minor modifications to product lines.

Geographic operating area

There were 81 company-owned stores in six states and 420

dealer-owned stores in 12 states. There was no market dominance.

Store locations

The stores were in secondary locations, not prime retail/commercial locations. There were not enough stores in growth markets such as suburban locations.

Canadian management

Knowledge and qualifications   Apparently, four thoughtful and experienced executives were selected and transferred to the United States along with additional junior managers. Between them they had experience in almost all the critical functions of the company but no experience in the United States. Twenty-two Canadian dealers, trained in Canada by CTC, were sent to the United States to take over newly refurbished stores. Eventually, another senior marketing person was sent to join the team. It is interesting to note that this person was an American by birth and had 36 years of retail experience, much of it in the United States. It was this executive who initially suggested that White's had to move away from its broad product and focus on auto parts, accessories and maintenance.

Commitment   CTC was initially committed as evidenced by the sending of senior executives and the investment made in trying to turn White's around. That commitment started to wane when losses kept occurring and a schism developed between Dean Muncaster and the Board.

Decision-making   Decision-making was decentralized but links were maintained at the strategy and policy level.

American management

White Stores did not have strong management when CTC acquired it. The company had been losing management during its years of continuing financial losses. It also was difficult to attract qualified Americans to train as dealers because of White's reputation. Eventually, Dean Groussman, an American with a strong retailing background, was hired as president. When White Stores was sold, Groussman joined the CTC in Canada as Dean Muncaster's replacement.

Suppliers

There are no indications that this was a problem.

Systems

Computers, point of purchase equipment and computerized inventory control systems were utilized. Canadian Tire certainly had the necessary expertise in this area to transfer to the United States.

Competition

The situation was highly competitive. There were six major competitors, including some with auto care centers, and numerous indirect competitors who had been underestimated. The number of competitors continued to increase.

DYLEX LIMITED

Overview

During the 1980s, Dylex Ltd., Canada's largest specialty apparel retailer with 1991 annual sales in excess of $1.8 billion, had experienced both dramatic successes and failures in the United States. Beginning with the purchase of apparel manufacturer Tobias Kotzin in 1980, Dylex continued its United States expansion acquiring the NBO stores, Brooks Fashion Stores and the Wet Seal chain in 1984, and the Foxmoor chain in 1985. It opened Club International in 1985 and Harry Rosen and Club Monaco U.S. in 1989.

In 1987, Brooks filed for protection from creditors under Chapter 11 of the U.S. bankruptcy code. The majority of Foxmoor specialty stores was sold to Edison Brothers and the balance of the chain was liquidated under court protection in early 1990. This represented an empire of over 1,500 stores and a loss of more than $200 million. Club International was sold to Merry Go Round in 1991.

On the positive side, Dylex's Wet Seal and NBO chains were flourishing in the United States and Club Monaco was being tested and refined before embarking on any expansion plans. Wet Seal's apparent success was instrumental in shaping Dylex's current approach to the United States. The Wet Seal experience will be described in Chapter 8 in a discussion of two Canadian retailers that seem to have learned how to do business in the United States as a result of previous experiences there.

Company Beginnings

Dylex Diversified Limited began operation in 1967 with the Posluns family and James F. Kay acquiring Tip Top Tailors and merging it with their own business interests. The new company comprised the Tip Top chain (20 stores), the Fairweather chain (13 stores), the Posluns' clothing manufacturing businesses and a group of manufacturing companies in plastics, housewares and lighting. The partners saw an opportunity in the growing Canadian retail market to create a group of specialty apparel retailing chains and they embarked on an aggressive expansion and renovation program.

The name, Dylex, short for "Damn your lousy excuses!", reflected Posluns' brusque management style. At the same time, he also took a laissez-faire attitude to management, promoting a high level of entrepreneurship within a large corporation. "If you made it work, I didn't care what you did."

In August 1968, after one year of operation, Dylex had sales of $38 million and operating profits of $796,000. The retail operations comprised about two-thirds of the company's business, with manufacturing providing the other third. During this first year, 17 new retail stores were opened, largely in major regional shopping centres, including the launch of a new family specialty chain, Family Fair.

In its second year, Dylex acquired three retailers — Harry Rosen Men's Wear, Fashion Council and Valu-Fair — as well as dress manufacturer Nu-Mode. Fashion Council merged with the Fairweather chain to provide new management and growth momentum to the latter group.

In 1969 Dylex acquired a 50 percent interest in the Town and Country stores. The manufacturing interests were also continuing to expand through the purchase of National Knitting Mills, and in early 1970, the acquisition of Manchester Children's Wear. The Fairweather chain opened the first Big Steel boutique within the Fairweather stores. However, by the following year Big Steel had become independent.

Dylex's total sales passed $90 million in 1970, with $54 million generated by its retailing operations and the remainder from apparel and home products manufacturing. Dylex retail chains continued to expand across Canada in the many new regional shopping centres then under development. In 1971 there were 117 stores, excluding Town and Country, with total retail sales of more than $66 million. Productivity had reached $86 per square foot compared with $63 per square foot in 1969. Two more acquisitions took place in 1972 when Dylex purchased a 51 percent interest in Thrifty's and a 50 percent interest in Shoe Shoppe.

Five years after founding, Dylex had grown to 158 stores, with plans to open more than 48 new outlets the following year. Management decided in early 1973 to concentrate on being a specialty fashion retailer and apparel manufacturer. The company grew nationally with 78 new stores and a 50 percent increase in selling space. It also acquired a one-third interest in the Forsyth Manufacturing Company. Expansion continued in 1975 when Dylex acquired a 50.1 percent interest in Suzy Shier. In order to service the Tip Top, Harry Rosen, Fairweather and Braemar divisions, a 160,000 square foot central distribution facility was opened in Etobicoke. The centre, with computer controlled conveyors, was the first of its kind in Canada.

After ten years, Dylex had more than 400 stores and combined sales of $262 million. Braemar, originally merchandised as part of the Fairweather division, was set up as a separate chain. The following year Dylex acquired a 50 percent interest in Bi-Way stores, which operated 30 outlets in southern Ontario.

The first decision to sell part of Dylex was made in 1980, as the Family Fair division had not been achieving the company's profit targets. Yet expansion continued with the opening of the first BH Emporium outlets in Toronto. By the end of 1980, Dylex's combined sales totalled $670 million and the number of stores had increased to 779.

In 1982, a 250,000 square foot distribution centre was opened in Mississauga to supplement the existing distribution centre in Etobicoke. During 1982 and 1983, Dylex bought the remaining interest in Thrifty's and Bi-Way, making them both wholly-owned divisions. In 1984, the Harry Rosen chain began its women's division with the opening of six outlets in addition to its 13 men's wear stores.

Dylex's combined sales passed the billion dollar mark in 1984. That year Bi-Way started entering other provinces beginning with Nova Scotia, and an expansion plan for the 50 percent owned Drug World was developed. In May 1988, the 50 percent owned Shoe Shoppe Limited was sold to Rizzo & Rizzo Shoes.

Dylex continued to expand in Canada by acquiring 50 percent of The Monaco Group in February 1989. The company also purchased the balance of the Town and Country division which it closed down in 1991. Braemar, which had been an associate company, became a subsidiary in which Dylex retained a 75 percent ownership, and expanded through the operation of another chain of stores, Braemar Petites.

Canadian Corporate Structure

Dylex began as a unique and largely decentralized group of entrepreneurial companies. A corporate group of central services provided the operating divisions with specialized functions at competitive market prices. These included retail accounting, real estate, store construction, warehousing and distribution.

Wilfred Posluns played a strong supporting role for the Dylex subsidiaries. He did not exercise hands-on management, but built and motivated his managers through the provision of advice and knowledge, and acted as a sounding board to help them run their operations efficiently. They were free to pursue their own strategy as long as they made money. However, if results were not achieved, the division head was replaced.

This loose corporate structure remained in effect until 1989, when management was reorganized to adapt to the requirements of the changing marketplace and the company's lagging fortunes. In June 1990, Lionel Robins became Dylex's new president. He presided over a nine-member executive committee of vice-presidents and heads of divisions and was given the task of exerting some control over the chains within the Dylex group. More emphasis was placed on strategic planning and overall direction. Companies in the group now had to develop, justify and meet a strategic plan and report to an executive committee. A formal strategic planning process was implemented in 1991 whereby each company developed its own strategic plan which supported annual and monthly budgets. Variance reports and action plans were generated monthly, with a second tier being completed quarterly.

In the early 1980s, a contentious issue surfaced between Posluns and Kay regarding Kay's assertions that an agreement existed relating to the way he and the Posluns family were to vote their common shares and to buy–sell arrangements pertaining to these shares. Five years later the relationship between Kay and Posluns finally disintegrated and Kay launched a suit against the Posluns family asking for the court to rule the partnership agreement valid. The board then ousted Kay and made Posluns chairman. The court battle would take years to resolve and would likely result in the exercise of a buy–sell clause with one party (i.e. the best offer) buying out the other.

Entry into the United States

Chief Financial Officer, David Posluns, noted that Dylex "had captured approximately ten percent of all apparel retail sales in Canada in the 1980s. It was thought to be more difficult to grow to 12 or 14 percent of the incremental market share in Canada than to enter the vast United States market." During the mid 1980s, Posluns and Kay continued to work together though their relationship was strained. It was under these conditions that Dylex began its expansion into the United States by buying Brooks and Foxmoor in partnership with AEA, a private New York investment group specializing in acquisitions and leveraged buyouts.

Dylex took its first step into the United States earlier in 1980 by acquiring a 70 percent interest in Tobias Kotzin, a Los Angeles based manufacturer of clothing for young men. Realizing the approaching limits to growth in the Canadian retail market, Dylex began its expansion into fashion retailing in the United States in June 1984 with the acquisition of 50 percent of NBO stores which owned 14 men's wear stores in the New

York metropolitan area. That same month, Suzy Shier acquired a 78 percent interest in Wet Seal, an 18-store women's wear chain in southern California. Two years later this interest was increased to 86.8 percent. Also in June 1984, Dylex acquired an interest in Brooks Fashion stores which operated more than 750 women's wear outlets in 48 states. The acquisition was made through a newly formed company, BR Investors, in which Dylex held 39 percent. AEA Investors Inc. held 39 percent and senior members of the Brooks management team held 22 percent. In the following year, BR Investors purchased the Foxmoor chain, a retailer of junior women's apparel with 614 stores throughout the United States and Tip Top men's wear opened five stores in the greater Chicago area under the name Club International. 1985 saw Dylex's combined sales, including its recently acquired United States interests, totalling $2.3 billion with net earnings of $47 million.

Dylex experienced its first decline in earnings in seven years in 1986, mainly as a result of losses incurred by BR Investors Inc. in the United States. Dylex's share of the BRI loss was $22 million or 46 cents per share. Overall net earnings (before a $1.1 million extraordinary gain) were $25 million or 51 cents per share.

Expansion of existing Canadian divisions into the United States started in the late summer of 1989. Harry Rosen opened a store in Buffalo, New York, and Club Monaco opened six stores in California through a licensing agreement with the Monaco Group.

Greenfield Entries

Club International

In the first quarter of 1985, Tip Top, Dylex's medium priced men's wear division in Canada, opened five stores in the greater Chicago area under the name Club International. Management had been exploring the United States with the view to opening stores on a test basis. General Manager Don Evans was quoted in the 1984 annual report as saying at the time that "an extensive preparation process preceded Tip Top's decision to enter that particular metropolitan area [Chicago]. We wanted to minimize the risk factor in making a move. The climate conditions are similar to those in Canada, so our buying patterns have not been significantly altered."

The plan was to monitor the success of the chain and, if it showed good potential, to establish an American organization. Sales productivity lagged and the stores were not profitable during the second year. Run by Canadian management as an extension of the Canadian operation, the stores and merchandising were similar to the Tip Top stores in Canada.

Productivity improved over the next few years but the chain was not profitable. By the end of 1989 it had expanded to 10 stores, all in the Chicago market. As David Posluns stated, "Canadian management was not focussed enough on these stores; it was one of 10 or 12 chains. Therefore, they moved to American management." The company appointed an American as President in May 1990 and Tip Top was still searching for the right merchandising formula to attract the American consumer. However, in the recession of 1991, the decision was made to sell the Club International stores.

Harry Rosen

This upscale men's wear retailer, of which Dylex owned a 51 percent stake, opened a store in the Buffalo market. The move was intended to take advantage of the large customer following, as indicated by market research, that the company had in Buffalo. It was a question, as Posluns noted, of taking advantage of a logical opportunity as Harry Rosen had good name recognition in that market. There were no plans to expand further since moving into another market would require a large investment to create market awareness. Sales declined during the recession and there were a number of bankruptcies in the mall in which the store was located. The store was situated next to Bonwit Teller which closed, further weakening Rosen's end of the centre and compounding the recession induced problems.

Club Monaco

The Monaco Group began in the late 1970s as a separate company in Toronto. By 1985, it had two divisions, Club Monaco and Alfred Sung, and was a public company. Dylex bought out the public shareholders in

1988. Dylex purchased approximately 50 percent of the shares; insiders retained a portion; and the balance was owned by a venture capital group that had been funding Monaco. The Sung and Monaco divisions split. Dylex took a majority interest in the retail side. It owned approximately 60 percent of Club Monaco and 100 percent of Club Monaco in the United States which was started as a trial to test the viability of the concept.

Late in 1988, David Posluns became involved in Club Monaco in the United States. At the time he had been running the Foxmoor real estate division in New York and, due to his experience in mergers and acquisitions, he was asked for his opinion on the acquisition of Club Monaco by Dylex. Believing that Club Monaco had potential to be successful in the United States, he left Foxmoor to head up Club Monaco and to test the concept in the California market. California was chosen as the test market since it had 25 million people, many of whom had moved there, and were continuing to do so, from all parts of the United States.

Posluns' knowledge of the real estate market enabled him to acquire quickly six locations, providing an immediate base of operations sufficient for a test. A cross section of different markets was chosen to test the concept such as the sophisticated downtown Beverly Center in Beverly Hills, several suburban locations, and a more remote area. Locations were in northern California, which was believed to be representative of the northeast mentality, and in southern California where the mix of attitudes was thought to be more representative of the United States generally.

The stores were opened in fall 1989, and by mid 1991 they had met with some success. Although results varied by store, downtown locations tended to outperform suburban stores. The company was attempting to capitalize on the successes and make them work in all six stores. Since most of the merchandise was imported, change was a slow process, as commitments had to be made far in advance. Posluns related that "by the time you recognize you've even had to adjust something, you are a year into it, and you have already committed two seasons out for the fabric, etc. So to make changes takes a long time." The Canadian product assortment was used as a base for the United States stores with the intention of adjusting it for the new market. During the previous two years, management had moved to include merchandise from local sources as well. They also hired a merchant from California who was helping to guide Club Monaco Canada to meet Club Monaco United States' needs. Brand names were important for the American consumer.

Physically, the stores were similar to those in Canada, incorporating the simple, clean look, in an average space of approximately 3,000 square feet. Initially, the company did some advertising; however, it did not intend to continue the program until the concept and mix was right. In addition, since the stores were spread throughout California, it was difficult to advertise economically. The United States office, located in Santa Monica, was headed by David Posluns and consisted of a number of buyers and various other administrative functions.

Posluns' role as Chairman was to oversee growth and to give direction to the company. In addition, he was responsible for real estate, finance, and communications between Club Monaco Canada and Club Monaco in the United States to ensure they worked effectively together. He lived in California for 18 months after the stores were opened and then moved back to Canada. Since that time, he has travelled frequently to California to oversee the operations.

There was little functional interaction between Club Monaco and Wet Seal (another Dylex owned company in California). However, they did capitalize on what they could from an administrative stand point, such as joint medical and insurance coverage. Posluns noted that when Club Monaco started out, it took advantage of having a local affiliate there, for example using Wet Seal's warehouse facilities. This was later discontinued.

There were no immediate plans for expansion until management reached what they considered to be the right mix. Testing with a small store base was obviously less costly, and the company wanted to be sure of their direction before expanding. Management felt that there was great potential as Club Monaco's niche was devoid of direct competitors.

Acquisitions

Brooks

The Brooks acquisition was a joint venture with Brooks' original owners and AEA Investors Inc., a private New York investment group whose partners included some large United States financial institutions and retired senior executives of leading United States corporations. The investment banker who represented the owners had introduced Dylex to AEA. Together they formed a new company, BR Investors, to acquire Brooks and its wholly owned subsidiary, T. Edwards, through a leveraged buyout at a price of approximately US $350 million. AEA investment practice had usually been to retain its holdings for five years or less. In the event that AEA decided to sell or reduce its holdings, Dylex had the option to increase its position and acquire voting control of BR Investors. Dylex's interest in Brooks was reported as investment income.

Dylex President, Wilfred Posluns, stated that the reason they used the acquisition mode to enter the United States was "because we didn't want to impose our Canadian retailing formula on a large and unfamiliar market." Dylex Chairman James Kay noted that they needed "people who have succeeded and grown in that environment." Although the operations were run autonomously from Dylex, ideas were exchanged about store design, computer systems and merchandising techniques.

Brooks defined its market as women ranging in age from 16 to 35 who wanted current styles at reasonable prices. Its affiliated T. Edwards chain targeted a higher income customer who had "graduated" from Brooks in age and lifestyle. Brooks was profitable at the time of purchase; however, it began to lose money within a short period of time after it was acquired. Sales declined by nine percent on a same store basis in 1985, and expansion was postponed until sales and margins could be stabilized.

To turn the situation around, Dylex and AEA Investors Inc. acquired the interest of the minority shareholders of BR Investors increasing their ownership to 48.5 percent each from 39 percent. The voting equity in BR Investors was shared equally by Dylex and AEA. The original owners and managers left the business. Both Wilfred Posluns and Irving Teitlebaum from Suzy Shier/Wet Seal visited Brooks on a frequent basis.

New management was appointed to BR Investors in 1986 and this group held approximately three percent equity in the form of non-voting shares. Barry Aved from The Limited was appointed President and CEO of Brooks. Wilfred Posluns became Chairman and Chief Executive Officer of BR Investors in the first quarter of 1986 in addition to continuing as President and Chief Executive Officer of Dylex. Dylex invested an additional US $75 million in a newly authorized class of BR Investors preferred shares. Half of this additional investment was provided by AEA's purchase of Dylex Class "C" preferred shares, US $25 million was financed by borrowing and US $12.5 million was provided from cash. Dylex was carrying a debt load of $150 million for Brooks.

During 1987 Brooks reported heavy losses, and on October 31, 1987 Dylex wrote down its investment in Brooks by C$118 million. The total loss attributable to Brooks (including operating losses) was C$153 million. On December 7, 1987 Brooks Fashion Stores Inc. filed for protection under Chapter 11 of the United States bankruptcy code. Operating losses and high interest charges from approximately $300 million of debt had severely drained Brooks' cash flow. Under Chapter 11, Brooks was given protection from trade creditors and interest payments were suspended while the company prepared a court supervised reorganization.

According to David Posluns, Brooks failed largely for two reasons. First, the founding family were "cashed out so generously that they lost a lot of their incentive to work hard." Secondly, the "leverage was so high that there was no room to make mistakes. When the original management and owners failed to produce results, it grew into a huge problem and was difficult to manage."

In retrospect, according to David Posluns, "They should have left it as an investment, lost the original $50 million, and called it a day. However, because the Canadian banks were major debt holders, Dylex felt obliged to try and save it, sinking in more time and money; but, after it lost its momentum, it was impossible to turn it around." In fact, the banks had been very supportive and were so confident that Dylex would succeed that the company, buoyed by this strong support, committed more deeply than they might otherwise have done. In the end, Dylex lost its money and its relationship with the bank.

Foxmoor

In 1985, a year after the purchase of Brooks, Foxmoor became available. Brooks' management, still consisting of the Saul family and original management, wanted to buy Foxmoor and amalgamate it with the Brooks chain. At first, Dylex was hesitant to do so. However, a compromise was reached whereby they would acquire the company, but it would be run as a separate entity under the guidance of Brooks, but not be totally managed by Brooks.

Both chains were similar in terms of their markets, catering to the junior customer. Brooks was slightly larger with 750 stores, compared to Foxmoor's 614, and both were national. The Foxmoor stores were smaller in square footage and the merchandise was priced slightly lower than that of Brooks. As stated by David Posluns, "If Brooks had operated well, it would have been feasible to put the two together." Though there was a fair bit of overlap in their locations, this did not matter because the market was growing quickly. The idea was the more frontage in the mall the better. The strategy of gaining maximum frontage was the same for both the Canadian and the United States market.

Brooks itself had been growing through the acquisition of the Nobby Shops with stores in the mid west and on the west coast. They were, therefore, often operating two or three Brooks stores in a mall under different names with a different front. Brooks' management also directed the affiliated T. Edwards chain of 73 stores that carried young women's apparel at slightly higher prices. Brooks' president stated at the time that "with the addition of Foxmoor, there will be approximately 1,400 stores with as many as four of our outlets in some shopping centres."

Together the two chains ranked within the top ten specialty ladies apparel retailers in the United States in terms of number of stores. The outlets were spread throughout the United States with the heaviest concentration in the north east, Florida and California. By Canadian standards, such growth would amount to a major gain in market share. But, as Dylex Vice-President Chris Schwartz commented, "It's still only a drop in the bucket for the United States." With the addition of Foxmoor, David Posluns felt that Brooks "took their eye off the ball."

Foxmoor was unprofitable when it was purchased. In order to reverse the chain's sagging sales and profitability, BR Investors installed a new president, Philip Brouse from the Jean Nicole Stores, and relocated some of the original Foxmoor management. Certain administrative functions were left in Massachusetts, where the company was originally based, while others, particularly the merchandising division, was brought to New York and located across the street from the Brooks building. Brooks and Foxmoor had separate presidents, but they had certain common departments such as traffic, imports and real estate, as Dylex did in Canada. Brooks' management were involved in all the strategic, financial and real estate concerns, although the Canadian company was not heavily involved. The senior Dylex management visited once a week for a day to oversee the operations.

In 1985, total sales increased by 30 percent and Dylex's share of net earnings was US $1.6 million. However, this profit, along with that of the other United States divisions, was eliminated by interest and acquisition costs.

Foxmoor's sales increased by 20 percent store for store in 1986, reaching approximately $170 per square foot, and the company made a profit. Management renovated 43 stores, sales for which increased by 30 percent.

During 1987, sales were up slightly but earnings deteriorated for several reasons. A severely competitive retail environment in the fourth quarter caused the company to reduce prices drastically in order to move inventory. The company had bought heavily to support an optimistic sales plan, but when planned sales did not materialize, large inventories had to be carried. Management sought to reduce inventories and increase turnover by lowering imports to 16 percent from 24 percent of purchases, and replacing them with domestic goods that required shorter lead times. Assortments were broadened with less depth carried in each style.

In November 1987, Dylex invested $45 million in Foxmoor which eliminated the bank debt. Management aggressively continued to turn the company around. Capital expenditures in 1987 were approximately $10.5 million, dedicated largely to renovating 45 stores, opening eight stores and relocating five. Plans for the following year included 31 renovations and the addition of five new stores. At the end of 1987, Dylex reached an agreement in principle with AEA to acquire all the remaining shares of Foxmoor.

In 1988, Foxmoor's results did not improve and its loss was approximately equivalent to the preceding year. Charged with returning Foxmoor to profitability, two new co-presidents were appointed, Glenn Palmer from Macy's New York to head up the merchandising team and Ed Thomas, the CFO of Foxmoor, to be responsible for store administration and operations.

During the fall of 1988, Dylex increased its investment in Foxmoor to 100 percent and decreased its investment in Brooks to 5.5 percent as a result of the Brooks' Chapter 11 settlement with the banks and AEA. Despite all their efforts, heavy losses continued into 1989, and the decision was finally reached to begin exploring ways to reduce the size of, or sell, Foxmoor. During the first six months of 1989, Foxmoor lost C$12.8 million. In October 1989, Dylex agreed to the sale of 229 of its 601 Foxmoor stores to the Edison Bros. chain of St. Louis, and in December it announced a writedown of C$42 million for the estimated disposal costs of the Foxmoor chain. Earnings for 1989, *excluding* Foxmoor operations, were $17 million or 36 cents per share, compared to $39 million or 83 cents per share in the previous year. The Foxmoor writedown in the third quarter resulted in an overall loss of $61 million or $1.28 per share compared to a net profit in 1988 of $30 million or 63 cents per share. Finally, in January 1990, Foxmoor sought and was granted protection under Chapter 11 of the United States bankruptcy code to complete its own liquidation.

What originated as Brooks' plan to purchase Foxmoor in order to expand its retail concept ended with Dylex running Foxmoor as part of the restructuring, and ultimately, with the failure of Foxmoor. Posluns felt that, on the part of Brooks, the Foxmoor deal had been largely a real estate transaction of buying leases and had required a great deal of cash since it had not been profitable when it was purchased.

The acquired company was also strategically vulnerable. According to Posluns, a shift in mall retailing had been a contributing factor in Foxmoor's failure. Foxmoor had excelled in providing inexpensive junior sportswear apparel. Chains such as The Limited were better marketers for the moderate to upper moderate market, while discount, off price, strip centre based retailers captured the lower end of the market more cost efficiently. This meant that low price mall operators, such as Foxmoor, were squeezed out of the market.

NBO

Dylex acquired a 50 percent interest in the NBO stores in June 1984, the same month that it purchased the interest in Brooks through BR Investors. With this purchase it entered the off-price men's wear business with 14 stores in the New York City area. The clothing was current, stylish merchandise that was sold at less than regular price. This was made possible by trading on the large production capacity of United States manufacturers and acquiring items from stock over-runs.

Since its inception, the chain had changed from being "bare bones stores with the minimum of fixtures and sales help" to providing the customer with a pleasant shopping environment with all the amenities, in addition to low prices. Two stores were opened in the Washington area in 1984, and plans were to open four to eight stores per year, concentrating on specifically targeted regional areas. NBO management continued to run the company after the purchase. Interaction between Dylex and NBO was largely in areas of strategic and financial planning.

Sales during 1985 were $67 million and the company contributed to earnings. Sales and earnings were planned to increase by ten percent in 1986. By 1987, the company had grown to 26 stores in the Washington and New York markets, and profit margins "were excellent with sales increases of 20 percent" during the year. In April 1988, an agreement in principle was reached to acquire the remaining shares of NBO for US $29 million.

The end of 1989 saw an increase in the number of stores to 36, still concentrated in the two markets. Intense competitive pressures in the New York discount market resulted in somewhat lower margins in 1989. However, with sales over $100 million, the company achieved a return on sales of approximately seven percent.

Wet Seal

In the same month Dylex acquired the NBO stores in mid 1984, its Suzy Shier division purchased a 78 percent interest in Wet Seal, an 18-store women's wear chain located in southern California. Including the Brooks acquisition, Dylex had purchased three American chains within one month. Wet Seal appeared to be headed for success and was profitable. This chain demonstrated a marked change in Dylex's approach to the United States which is the culmination of learning from a number of years of doing business there. Some of the differences in strategy and operations from other Dylex entries into the United States are included in the analysis and summary at the end of this chapter for the purpose of comparison at this point. The complete account of the Wet Seal experience can be found in Chapter 8.

At the time of writing, if the balance of the stock held in Wet Seal was sold, the annualized return on total investment would be in excess of 70 percent per annum (over the seven years 1985–1991) which translates into approximately a $55 million return.

Management's Perception of the United States Market

Effect of regions

Posluns found that the different regions definitely had their own constitution, makeup, and their own economically driven forces. Each had it's own image and required a somewhat different marketing approach. Though the large national chains had been very successful, they did not really change their marketing approach from one end of the country to the other. Niche marketers felt that there was room to capitalize on that fact. This was seen as the reason why Wet Seal was successful, because it was delivering what the regional market wanted.

The American consumer

In general, the American consumer was seen as far more price sensitive, discriminating and knowledgeable. Americans find prices in Canada appalling. Posluns noted that one of the problems is the lack of choice in products in Canada. In the United States, for example, they sell in bulk more often which means that they can offer a lower price per unit. There are fewer options available in Canada.

Club Monaco had recently opened several "boutiques" within department stores in Tokyo, Japan. Posluns likened the Canadian and Tokyo consumers to each other, noting that they were more structured and utilitarian. The American consumers, on the other hand, tended to be more individualistic and fashion-oriented. Product mix, therefore, had to be adjusted more for the United States market than for the Japanese market!

United States competition

There was far more competition in the United States than in Canada, which in turn, had made the retailers more competitive. Each region was so large that it could support its own retailers. However, many of the regionals had grown up and had invaded each other's markets providing competition to both the national and regional companies. The local/regional competition tended to be specifically focussed on narrow segments of the market. For example, if a retailer decided to develop a beach/surf-related theme in California, they would find the competition so intense that they could never capture that market. Thus, while the national chains are a formidable barrier, the local chains have a strong impact often in a more specialized way.

One of the chief differences between American and Canadian retail competition, that consumers have many more choices in the United States, was perceived to be due to the larger number of department stores in the United States. As these stores have traditionally anchored shopping malls, there tended to be a greater proliferation of malls within a trading area in the United States. At one freeway exit, for example, it was not unusual to find several malls anchored by department stores such as Sears, Penny's, May, Nordstrom, Neiman Marcus, Dillards or Montgomery Ward. In Canada there are only four conventional department store chains to act as anchors, and since they do not want to locate too near their existing stores, it has resulted in fewer malls. In Posluns view, the department stores were definitely more competitive and had much greater impact in the United States When they held sales, for example, there was a significant drop in business for other stores in the mall.

Since the competition was so intense in the United States, there was more emphasis on competitive pricing and it became a bigger issue. Posluns felt that consumers were more aware of prices. "If merchandise comes out of the box too high to begin with, the market will teach you a lesson very quickly. If competitive to begin with, then you have to continue to match the competition."

He suggested that the average industry markup might be 60 percent in the United States and 65 percent in Canada. Due to the large scale of operations in the United States, companies could often buy at a lower cost than they could in Canada. Margins in Canada had recently come under tremendous pressure due to such factors as free trade and would likely continue to fall.

Markdowns were more aggressive in the United States and there was "more of a discipline to freshness." The philosophy is more aggressive... if something does not work then they get rid of it. Markdowns have been substantial during the past few years within the department stores.

The discount competition in the United States was found to have an enormous impact. For example, a basic oxford cloth shirt at Club Monaco Canada was a very strong item. Relative to the general marketplace in the United States the shirt was higher quality; however, it was not nearly as successful there. This was attributed specifically to the discounters where a similar, lesser quality shirt was available for $15 less. Thus, not only was there competition for the more colourful part of the assortment in the basic areas from the Gap, for example, but for the real basics, the discounters were serious competition. Consequently, one of the merchandising strategy changes was to move away from that element of the mix toward the more fashionable part of the assortment.

The opportunity to comparison shop was great and people took advantage of it. Posluns felt that the weather played a large part in mall structure and location. Where the weather was not a factor, people tended to go from one mall to the next and comparison shop. Since Canada's weather is inclement for more of the year than a lot of places in the United States, there are not as many outdoor malls. In the United States there is always a strip mall across from a major mall, feeding off the traffic from its larger neighbour.

Advertising

In some respects, advertising was easier in Canada, largely due to population and media concentration. Posluns commented that, "If you can hit Toronto that is going to be almost 40 percent of the whole country and you can't do that in any single city in the United States, so you have to have a different kind of campaign."

Local chains tended to do more radio advertising, but a national chain such as the Gap was seldom found to advertise on the radio. Transit shelters and magazines were more common media for many of the nationals. In their perception, radio was used much more frequently in Canada. Since there was so much more competition in the United States it was more difficult to obtain good market coverage. As an example, there were 20 radio stations in Los Angeles, five of which might cover a specific target market. In order to obtain good coverage, one would have to buy a considerable amount of air time. The differences between the stations were marginal, and advertising with one station would only cover a tiny segment of the potential market.

On the other hand, since the market is so regulated in Canada, there are fewer radio stations. One or possibly two stations can generally cover the target market.

Since Club Monaco arrived in the United States, one of the leading national apparel retailers had launched a major advertising campaign throughout North America. Posluns noted that they had not advertised their change in market focus before that time, and that it was very strong competitive positioning. They shifted more in line with where Club Monaco was headed, becoming more sophisticated.

United States developers and real estate

Since there were more department stores to anchor malls in the United States, there was more opportunity for malls to set up close to one another and compete. In order to secure locations in Canada, there was little choice between major malls and street locations, thus giving the landlords more control over the market.

From Posluns' experience with Club Monaco, being a new and different concept in the United States, he had received calls and letters weekly from developers during the two years they had been open. He noted, however, that due to the current economic climate the landlords in Canada today were much more flexible than they had been in the past. Some were offering off balance sheet lending in the form of build-outs and developer support for inventory, though not to the same extent that their counterparts do in the United States. There have also been changes in the secondary and tertiary malls in the United States as a result of the recession, with developers offering more incentives to retailers than they did before.

Posluns noted that most specialty stores lease their premises since they are largely located in high traffic malls. A few notable exceptions exist, such as the Charming Shoppes, which own some malls in the United States and lease to other retailers. Dylex leased all their locations in both Canada and the United States.

Rents were found to be lower in the United States than in Canada; however, as a counter-balancing force, the margins were also lower. Since there was more competition between malls and leasing agents, the rents were lower.

Days of operation

In Posluns' view, the Canadian government forced retailers to close many days during the year. In the United States, however, there are numerous holidays during which schools may be closed, but businesses and retailers are not. Americans get a surge in mall activity, for example, on Washington's Birthday, Memorial Day and Columbus Day.

According to the United States Consulate there are no national holidays when stores must close, other than Christmas. It is left up to the individual owners to decide on which days they want to open, and they are free to negotiate with their employees on this basis, subject to certain state regulations.

The situation in Canada is different. While the federal government does not require stores to close, many of the provinces force retailers to close on statutory holidays, i.e., Nova Scotia, New Brunswick, Quebec, Ontario and Manitoba all close for at least six statutory holidays and on Sundays (except Ontario, which now allows Sunday shopping). The western provinces, including Saskatchewan, Alberta, British Columbia and the Yukon Territory, are ruled by municipal by-laws. In Saskatchewan, most of the municipal by-laws restrict Sunday shopping; however, this was not being enforced. In Alberta, retailers must pay employees time and a half for holidays. In British Columbia stores can all be open with only one small municipality barring Sunday shopping.

In Posluns' view, government regulation, particularly in Ontario, will result in the failure of many Canadian retailers in this decade.

Lessons that Management Learned

Dylex has been through a seven-year learning process with respect to its United States operations, having failed in three attempts, succeeded in two, and presently testing and refining two before further expansion is contemplated.

Failures

David Posluns cited the most important reasons for Dylex's failures in the U.S. as the following:

Brooks
1. The original owners/managers were cashed out so generously they lost their incentive to work in the same way as they had in the past.

2. Leverage was so high that there was no room to make mistakes.

3. It should have remained as an investment and Dylex should not have spent millions more in an effort to turn it around.

Foxmoor
1. It was unprofitable when it was purchased.

2. It was largely a transaction of buying leases but it required a great deal of cash to make it profitable.

3. It was strategically void.

Successes

In Posluns' view, the most important reasons for Dylex's successes are the following:

Wet Seal (described in detail in Chapter 8)
1. Excellent management consisting of a Canadian CEO and an American Vice-President.

2. A strong regional niche approach.

3. Outstanding buying.

4. Sufficient local market importance to obtain merchandise first.

5. Commitment to the junior market when others had abandoned this segment.

6. Commitment to summer merchandise all year round as opposed to "chasing the seasons" as the national chains do.

NBO

1. Strong management.

2. A solid, distinctive concept.

Tests

Club Monaco Indications are positive. However, further refinements will be implemented before expansion is considered.

Reflecting on the Experience

Greenfield sites

Looking at the greenfield entries, one sees some of the same problems that appeared in the four cases in Chapter 1. Although management indicated that Club International engaged in extensive preparation prior to entering the Chicago market, it was not sufficient. The company, like Coles, was run as an extension of the Canadian operation by Canadian management who were not focussed on the stores. There are indications also that the merchandising formula was not right. By the time the company hired an American president it was too late as the recession of 1991 took its toll.

The Club Monaco situation appears to be a combination of good management decisions, but also produces a feeling of déjà vu. We have seen that results in a test situation may not reflect reality when expansion occurs. The good news seems to be in the facts that David Posluns has direct experience in the United States and that the merchandise mix was being adjusted with the help of a merchant from California.

On the other hand, greenfield sites to test retail concepts may work and the feedback from the stores appears to be valuable, but the question remains can the company expand from this base to become a significant chain? Because of its small size and geographical dispersion the company was experiencing difficulty in advertising effectively. The decisions about the expansion mode, and locations, will be critical ones.

Acquisitions

The acquisitions will be summarized separately because of the different experiences each presents. It should be recalled first, however, that the reason for entering the United States was growth and that management's attitude was that it would be easier to grow in the United States than to pick up an incremental share of the Canadian market.

Brooks   This acquisition adds a new element to understanding the difficulties that Canadian retailers have encountered in their forays into the United States. In this particular situation it was the leveraged buy-out (LBO) that was so common in the 1980s. Like many other LBOs, management discovered that even though the firm was generating an operating profit, the profit was not enough to cover the interest payments on the debt. In this situation it was not even necessary to add the impact of a recession to drive the company into Chapter 11.

The case also raises the issue of a change in the original owners' motivation after they "cashed out generously." The idea of keeping qualified original owners as managers who know the market is a good one so long as they continue to work hard and to take responsibility for the business as they did when they owned it. If any of the arrangements associated with the sale change their motivation, then the advantage is lost.

Foxmoor   The acquisition of this company compounded the problems already being experienced with the Brooks operation. Unlike Brooks, this company was not profitable when it was purchased. Canadian Tire could not turn around an unprofitable company with a lot of dedicated management attention, but in this case Brooks' management "took its eye off the ball," and senior Dylex managers only visited once a week for a day. Foxmoor, just like every other company described in this book, encountered severe competition that it seemed unable to overcome. Similar to the Coles situation, when this market split between the stores such as The Limited who were concentrating on the moderate to upper moderate price market, and discounters in the lower end of the market, Foxmoor was caught in the middle and squeezed out.

Wet Seal With Wet Seal, Dylex purchased a company already operating in the United States that had developed a niche and that was important to its suppliers. A competent team combining the talents of an American merchant and a Canadian operating executive was assembled and seemed to be leading the company well.

COMPARATIVE SUMMARY

The experiences of the companies described in Chapter 2 illustrate a number of important points and allow us to refine the "lessons learned" from the earlier comparative summary that analyzed the greenfield entries.

- Don't assume that an acquisition will guarantee a successful entry into the United States. A poorly managed company that is unprofitable may not be salvageable, at least at a cost that the new owners are willing to incur. Companies that are losing money and management talent are probably doing so for very good reasons which may not be easily changed.

- Don't assume that entry into the United States will be inexpensive. Canadian retailers often have bought poor performing companies because they were cheaper and management thought they could turn the companies around. There probably is a price to be paid beyond which a satisfactory return is not possible. Although the authors believe that this price may be higher than managements originally expect to pay, it may be less than they actually end up paying. The cost of bad acquisitions has probably been as great as, or even exceeded, the cost of buying a top company. Make sure you are prepared to pay the price of entry as you will probably do so either in the beginning or in the end.

- Leveraged buy-outs (LBOs) can be dangerous. Although this may be a general lesson from the 1980s, the cases in this chapter show why. In an intensely competitive environment where there is significant pressure on margins it may not be possible to earn enough to cover interest expense.

- Size alone and importance to suppliers will not ensure success. These two factors were significant barriers to success for greenfield companies and they are good reasons to go the acquisition route. However, also ensure that the retail concept is right and that the management is strong.

- Don't let your eyes and appetite overwhelm your ability to digest the meal. Rapid expansion puts tremendous strains on management and qualified human resources may not be available in the company to support the expansion with the degree of expertise that is required. The "B" team does not run acquired companies any better than it does greenfield entries.

- Don't assume that strengths at home will transfer to the United States. It was seen in this chapter that a Canadian retail concept does not work any better when it is imposed on an acquired company than it did in the greenfield mode if it is not right for the market.

- It is best to assume that a product mix needs to be different in the United States and that the American consumers are different than Canadian consumers. This seems to be an almost universal lesson that Canadian retailers have learned.

- Although realizing that the United States is different is a necessary first step in successful entry, it alone is not sufficient unless the American operations are managed as well as the parent company. Canadian executives need to confront the reality that they may not understand the American market place and that American management probably is a necessity. Decentralization and autonomy which, in theory, will provide management in the United States with the ability to respond to market differences and demands only works in proportion to the degree of experience and skill of the management team.

- Don't assume that all American executives and middle managers are highly qualified simply because they are American and have some experience in the marketplace.

- Don't underestimate the competition. Another universal lesson from the cases so far is the intensity of the competition in the United States. Continual pressure is put on margins and the market is dynamic with new competitors entering and the segments shifting.

- Entering the United States market is a continual learning experience.

Table 1 Comparative Summary

	Canadian Tire Corporation	Dylex: Brooks Stores	Dylex: Foxmoor	Dylex: NBO	Dylex: Wet Seal
Dates of operation in the U.S.	1982-1986	1984-1987	1985-1990	1984 to the present	
Reason for entry	approaching limits to growth	approaching the limits to growth in Canada			
Entry mode	acquisition	joint venture/acquisitions Brooks was LBO		acquisition	acquisition
Profitable when acquired?	no	yes	no	yes	marginally
Rationale for acquisition	greenfield too expensive	U.S. is different	gain maximum store frontage	niche expansion opportunity	opportunity, fair price
Approach	proactive	proactive	compromise		proactive
Attitude toward acquisition	it can be turned around	management will keep it profitable	hesitant		base for test, experiment
Research prior to acquisition?	yes	unknown	unknown	unknown	little

alternative companies					
company analysis	yes				
consumer	yes; not before purchase				
competition	yes, but missed some				
demographic locations	yes; some				
Transfer of retail concept	without modification	don't impose retail formula on large, unfamiliar market		American retained, distinctive	distinctive regional niche
Product mix	like Canada	American	American	American	local
Geographic operating area	81 company stores in 6 states, 420 dealer stores in 12 states	823 stores in 48 states	614 stores across the country	small chain, 36 stores in 2 markets	growing, 90 stores in 5 sunny states
Store locations	secondary				good
Management Canadian	did not understand U.S. market	did not understand U.S. market, left American management in charge, visited occasionally		strong	strong

	Canadian Tire Corporation	Dylex: Brooks Stores	Dylex: Foxmoor	Dylex: NBO	Dylex: Wet Seal
American (with acquisition)	questionable	questionable	questionable	strong	strong Americans hired
Commitment to U.S.	committed at start, lagged as losses mounted, renewed commitment with new entry in car care market	Dylex appears to have a strong commitment to establishing itself in the United States			
Decision-making	decentralized	decentralized	decentralized	decentralized	autonomous
Suppliers	no indication of problems	no indication of problems		no problems	important to suppliers
Systems	yes	fair	poor-fair		
Competition	severe	severe	severe	severe	severe
Other		rapid expansion in both countries, Foxmoor strategically vulnerable, caught when market split		profitable	good name, shaping policy for U.S., profitable

CHAPTER 3

ALL THAT GLITTERS...

PEOPLES JEWELLERS LIMITED

In December 1986, Peoples Jewellers acquired Zale Corporation of Dallas, Texas and became the largest jewellery retailer in the world.

Background

In 1919, Frank Gerstein opened the first Peoples jewellery store in downtown Toronto. His idea was to sell jewellery on credit to the masses, an unheard of practice in Canada at the time. He built his business by selling jewellery at "50 cents down and 50 cents a week." The shocked aristocratic jewellery establishment rejected the idea and said it would never work. However, Peoples survived the depression and by 1957 it was a national company with 18 stores and a mail order business. Frank's son, Bertrand Gerstein, had the foresight to understand the effect shopping malls would have on Canadian retailing. He guided Peoples' aggressive expansion program into most major shopping centre locations in Canada. By 1972, Peoples had 98 stores. In 1972, Bertrand's son, Irving, assumed the presidency. The 1970s was a "boom" period for jewellery retailing and Peoples grew to be the second largest jewellery retailer in Canada with 300 stores.

The growth ended in the late 1970s when the Canadian market became saturated with malls. To maintain sales growth, Peoples was repositioned with a more fashion-oriented, consumer-responsive marketing strategy. Irving developed a new motto, "Our customer is our boss"; stores were renovated; and merchandising programs were developed to identify Peoples as an innovative fashion leader in jewellery. Peoples also became aggressive in closing stores that were not meeting sales and profit goals. The strategic re-orientation was considered very successful.

Peoples Operations

Peoples Jewellers consisted of two divisions, Peoples and Mappins, which operated under three trade names: Peoples, Mappins and Mackenzies. In total, the divisions held 19.2 percent of the Canadian jewellery market. Henry Birks and Sons controlled approximately 21 percent of the market. In 1987, Peoples had sales of $195.4 million and Canadian earnings before taxes of $12.9 million. In 1987, the company operated 291 retail stores across Canada, most of which were leased with terms ranging from four to 25 years, and employed 2,400 people.

Peoples division

The Peoples division was positioned to attract a target audience in their twenties to late thirties, "youthful, positive shoppers who know what they want and expect a wide selection of trendy, upbeat items combining quality and value." Irving Gerstein considered retail locations to be the single most important point of communication with customers. Therefore, Peoples stores were designed to entice customers to enter. Each store looked "exciting, dramatic, glittering — with show-type lighting, handsome new display cases, and merchandise segmented and strongly identified by clear acrylic hanging overhead signs for more convenient shopping." In addition, the stores had large point-of-purchase displays and fashion jewellery displays that customers could "touch, feel and try." The objective was to make the stores appear more accessible.

A report produced by Burns Fry in December of 1987 estimated that 65 percent of the company's total sales, $130 million, were attributable to the Peoples division. The report also estimated that, on average, stores had sales of $660,00, a gross profit margin of 52 percent, and sales per square foot of $215.

Mappin division

This division targeted customers predominately in their late thirties through forties, and older. Its customers were described as "upscale, sophisticated shoppers who give high priority to quality and tradition."

Mappin stores were designed to evoke an image of style, craftsmanship and quality. Fashion displays and promotions emphasized up-scale, high-fashion jewellery. However, only 15 to 20 stores under the Mappin trade name were in districts that could support a strictly high-end jewellery store. The remainder of the stores were designed to be an alternative to Peoples stores, within a single mall. These Mappins still featured upscale items, but also catered to customers with middle incomes.

The Burns Fry report estimated that sales from this division were approximately $70 million, or close to 35 percent of Peoples total sales in Canada in 1987. The report also estimated that Mappins stores achieved sales per store of about $740,000, with a 49 percent gross profit margin, sales per square foot of about $460, and gross profit per square foot of $225.

After the Mackenzie chain was acquired, the trade name was retained to allow Peoples a third trade name within a given mall. The stores carried lower priced merchandise than Peoples or Mappins, because the stores' target consumer was in the lower income segment of the population.

Peoples management structure

Irving Gerstein did not involve himself a great deal in the day-to-day operations of the company, but rather concentrated on setting its strategic direction. His management style relied on process. He stated, "If you manage the process, then decisions aren't hard. If you have gone through the right process, decisions fall out."

To keep himself informed of what was going on in the organization, Gerstein used two strategies: 1) he worked closely with the Senior Vice-President of Finance and the Vice-President of Merchandising and

Operations. Each of these individuals, in turn, kept informed of activities within their functional areas; and 2) he managed by walking around and talking to people. It was not uncommon for him to be found walking through the head office, stopping to talk to everyone from managers through to secretaries. He also made a habit of visiting stores as often as possible throughout the country.

Communications were mainly informal in the head office. Irving met regularly with his management team but not on a scheduled basis. The two vice-presidents felt that they had substantial input into major company decisions and that Irving valued and encouraged their ideas and participation.

Entry into the United States

During the 1960s and 1970s, Canadian retailers experienced rapid growth as a by-product of the shopping centre trend. Irving stated that "retailers were able to ride the wave and become prosperous," but by the end of the 1970s the trend, and retail growth, were over. Rather than opening 20 to 30 stores each year, as had formerly been the case, Peoples was closing more stores than it was opening. In order to revive its previous growth trend, the company turned its attention to the United States market. Irving felt that if a company could sell to a market 3,000 miles west, there was no reason it couldn't sell to a market 90 miles south. At the time the decision was made, no specific analysis was completed on the United States market.

In 1978, the company examined United States jewellery chains to find one that was compatible with Peoples and that required minimal changes. After investigating several possibilities with no success, Irving met an American jewellery consultant who introduced him to the White chain, headquartered in Salt Lake City with 14 stores in Utah, Montana and San Francisco. The subsequent investigation of the White chain consisted of an analysis of its financial status, including projections of future earnings, as well as an examination of its operations for compatibility with Peoples. In 1978, Peoples purchased 80 percent of the company. The jewellery consultant purchased the remaining 20 percent and became President. Over the next two years, the chain expanded to 50 stores.

However, the acquisition was not profitable for Peoples. Although the stores were operating at a profit, it was not enough to cover the carrying costs of the investment. In May 1982 the operation was sold to a United States corporation at a loss of $8.1 million. The American management was quoted as saying that Peoples failed to understand the key market differences between Canada and the United States, and tried to institute Canadian procedures that did not work south of the border. When asked why the operation ran into trouble, Irving Gerstein and the Senior Vice-President of Finance outlined the following reasons:

1. Stores must be placed in new malls which have very high rents compared to older, more established malls. It is difficult to get good locations in malls when you are not a leading jeweller in the area. Mall developers offer prime locations to established, well-known jewellers first. This creates bidding competition and dramatically increases rents. In addition, less than ideal locations severely hinder sales performance.

2. Building a new chain required large cash inputs. The cash flow from the United States operation, plus additional funds, were required to finance the expansion. In addition, the company ran into United States capitalization rules which required Peoples to invest more cash than they had planned.

3. "A Gerstein was not president." Both men stressed this as a key factor in the problems of the United States operation. "You are not totally in control of your destiny."

This first experience gave Peoples a general exposure to the United States jewellery market. It discovered that credit played a much more important and integral role in the United States than it did in Canada. The experience also convinced Irving that it was almost impossible to enter the United States regionally, if growth is your objective. He advised, "Go big or don't go at all." Canadian companies, no matter how large they were in Canada, did not have the clout necessary to negotiate favourable deals with suppliers, builders or distributors when they entered the United States on a small scale. These factors created increased costs compared to the larger American competition which made competing successfully extremely difficult.

The Zale Corporation

In 1924, Morris B. Zale opened a store in Wichita Falls, Texas. Like Frank Gerstein, he believed in "jewellery affordable for the masses." In 1957 Zale began an expansion program focussed on the rapid shopping centre growth. Zales grew from 80 to 1,500 stores over the next 25 years.

To maintain growth Zales discontinued advertising its outlets as "diamond stores" and developed a marketing campaign based on the fashion-oriented slogan "leading with style." In 1986, to move further in this direction, the company announced a plan to increase its selection of fashion jewellery by 50 percent. It also announced a $74 million inventory writedown. However, during 1986, Zales senior management directed most of their energy to warding off the purchase attempts by Peoples Jewellers.

Prior to being acquired, the Zale Corporation consisted of a manufacturing division which was the world's largest jewellery manufacturer; five international offices; a credit division with the most sophisticated jewellery credit system in the world; and three retail operating divisions: Zale Jewellers, Guild Division and Diamond Park Division. Despite the fact that Zales was the largest jewellery retailer in the world, it still had only 6.5 percent of the total United States jewellery market as of 1988. The market was extremely fragmented with the four largest jewellers holding only 8.3 percent of the total market. Zales next largest competitor, Gordon Jewellers, was less than half the size of Zales in terms of total sales.

Collectively, Zale's three retail divisions had sales of $938.6 million and earnings before interest, taxes and unusual items of $39.0 million in 1987. The Zale division consisted of over 700 stores operating under the name "Zales." The stores were aimed at "middle America," especially the younger and lower income customers, with merchandise primarily in the medium-price range of $75 to $450. The stores averaged 1,200 square feet. The Guild Division, Zale's traditional division, was aimed at upper income, older customers. Merchandise was typically higher priced, ranging from $240 to $1,000, and stores averaged 2,100 square feet. Established in 1955, the division was a loose mix of established chains. By 1985 the division had more than 300 stores operating under a variety of different trade names. At that time, the decision was made to progressively consolidate the division under 10 to 12 names whose marketability was assured. The Bailey Banks & Biddle chain, founded in Philadelphia in 1832, was chosen as division leader. The Diamond Park Division consisted of 267 "stores" which operated in spaces leased within department stores such as Filene's, Dillard's, and Marshall Fields. Diamond Park sold primarily lower to medium priced items in the $50 to $250 price range. Each "store" was tailored to its host store. In the previous four years, the division had almost doubled its store base and its merchandising had improved. As a result, outside analysts and Zale management considered it to have tremendous growth potential.

The Acquisition of Zale Corporation

The acquisition of Zale Corporation occurred in two stages. In 1981 Peoples purchased 15 percent of the company's stock as an investment. In 1985 the company initiated procedures necessary to obtain control of Zales.

The initial investment

In late 1980, Irving Gerstein briefly examined the United States jewellery market and concluded that Peoples should invest in Zales. He did so without much analysis and without examining a Zales financial statement. He knew Zales was the largest jeweller in the United States and was highly respected. When asked about the decision, Irving made the following comment, "I just did it. I didn't even look at a financial statement for Zales." He felt his informal knowledge, acquired by virtue of operating in the jewellery business, was more than enough information to justify the purchase.

The initial purchase of stock created concern for the Zale board of directors. In December 1980, when Peoples had successfully purchased five percent of Zale stock, the Zale board sued Peoples, alleging that it was fronting for another organization with the intention of taking over the company. The lawsuit was resolved when Peoples agreed to sign a standstill agreement stating that it would not purchase more than 21 percent of Zale over the next 21 years. Any attempt to purchase more than 21 percent would have to be done with the approval of the board of directors. Peoples could not approach the shareholders directly. The agreement also gave Zale the option to purchase 17 percent of Peoples stock prior to March 1982. However, the Zale Corporation took no interest in Peoples and decided not to exercise the option. This lack of interest may have been critical. Irving felt that had Zale owned 17 percent of Peoples, the company would not have gone ahead with the takeover of Zale.

Within the restrictions, Peoples continued to purchase Zale stock. The initial goal was to purchase close to 20 percent of the stock in order to account for the investment using the equity method of accounting. By September of 1981, the company had purchased 17 percent of Zales stock at a cost of $64.3 million and was allowed three seats on the board of directors. This was sufficient to create significant influence and Peoples stopped purchasing stock. Zale eventually sold additional stock diluting Peoples investment to 15 percent.

Irving was adamant that Peoples had no intention of obtaining control of the Zale Corporation at that time. The idea seemed ridiculous due to the difference in size. Zale was over ten times the size of Peoples and he was sure that Peoples would have been unable to obtain the financing because it did not have the necessary collateral. The intention was to be a passive investor, who could participate in the growth of the Zale Corporation without the usual headaches associated with operating in the United States.

Leading to the takeover

The three seats on the board of directors and Irving's membership on the company's audit committee gave Peoples a unique opportunity to learn about Zale, its competitive environment, its operations and its key management. However, Peoples was not involved with the executive committee and, therefore, had no say in strategic decisions. "In many ways it was this exposure to the issues, without the ability to make decisions at the board level, which ultimately led to Peoples' determined pursuit of Zale Corporation in 1986."

Irving indicated that once he was inside of the company he became very concerned over its ability to achieve growth in the future. He saw that, although the company was the industry leader in the United States, it was plagued with problems. *The Globe and Mail* quoted him in 1986,

"If Zale were performing in the United States in the manner I thought it would, we would be very pleased to be sitting back here watching its substantial growth over the years. But we are now sitting here in 1986 saying we are concerned about the ability of the company to create value for its shareholders."

According to Peoples management, areas of concern were:

1. Zale's organizational structure. The company was large and complicated which meant an excessive non-selling staff, an abundance of red tape, and management and decision making that was far removed from the customer.

2. Zale's marketing approach. Zale's extensively used expensive national TV advertising that Peoples did not consider an effective use of funds. In addition, stores were not being used as effective merchandising tools.

3. Zale's vertical integration. Zale's was the world's largest jewellery manufacturer. The manufacturing orientation was impeding its ability to deliver the right products to customers at the right price.

4. The board's decision to sell the European/United Kingdom division. The operation had only been in effect for three to four years and was just starting to reach its potential.

5. Price discounting. In February 1986, Zale's announced a $74 million inventory writedown to create reserves to cover negative gross margins that resulted from price discounting to clear obsolete inventory.

6. The investment's expected performance. Peoples was losing money on its 15 percent share in Zale because dividend payments were not covering the interest carrying charges. The equity value of the investment (after interest) was decreasing every year. Zale stock was not performing well and Peoples' bank became concerned with the company's ability to carry the investment.

In 1985, as a result of these concerns, Irving and his management team considered Peoples' options with regard to its investment in Zale: sell the stock or purchase control of the company. They decided their best option was to pursue purchasing Zale. Irving felt that Zale's performance could be improved significantly if the company became more focussed, costs were cut and the organizational structure was simplified.

Once the initial financial analysis was completed, the company approached Drexel Burnham Lambert Inc. to arrange financing for the acquisition. Over the next few months, Peoples' management and Drexel developed a complete financial analysis.

The purchase process

During 1986, Peoples made a total of four offers. The first three were merger offers, to be financed with public debt, made directly to the board of directors of Zale in accordance with the requirements of the standstill agreement. All three offers were rejected. Resistance came mainly from the Zale and related Lipshy families who controlled 34 percent of the stock and dominated the board. After rejection of the third offer, Drexel wanted more equity to secure the transaction and Irving felt it was becoming necessary to limit the risk of Peoples' shareholders. As a result, Peoples teamed with Swarovski International Holding AG, a Swiss company.

After the third offer, it also became apparent that Zale shareholders were putting pressure on the Zale board to accept any further offers. In addition, the United States government announced that it would be changing the tax laws regarding capital gains, starting in 1987. Taking advantage of this position, the Peoples/Swarovski joint venture made a final offer on October 29, 1986. It was the first offer of straight cash to acquire the shares by tender and was for substantially more than the trading value of the shares on the New York Stock Exchange. After further discussions with Zale, revolving around severance agreements, the offer was accepted November 23, 1986, provided the deal was closed by December 31 to allow shareholders to take advantage of the 1986 lower tax rates on capital gains.

Public reactions to the purchase were mixed. Several analysts were quoted in the media as considering the purchase to be a mistake on the part of Peoples. Conversely, other analysts thought the purchase was a wise move. Management's reaction was that the risk was not high due to the nature of the financing arrangement: Zale itself was used to finance the purchase. Irving was quoted as saying, "It is important to understand that Peoples' risk in having fifty percent of Zale is limited to its original investment in 1982."

After the purchase

The joint venture agreement between Peoples Jewellers and Swarovski International Holdings allowed Peoples full management control of Zale Corporation. Swarovski remained a silent partner. It was Peoples' task to determine how to turn Zale into a growing, increasingly profitable investment.

On December 29, 1986, Irving Gerstein took full management control of the company upon the resignation of the company's chairman and the two vice chairmen of the Board. He called a meeting of the company's senior management to outline the "new" direction for Zale. During this meeting he indicated that he intended to move aggressively in order to turn Zale into a more profitable organization. His vision for the company was based on four principles:

1. Zale is a retail jeweller; retailers make their profits across two feet of counter space.

2. Zale will have a simple organizational structure.

3. Zale will minimize the distance between the customer and the chief executive officer.

4. The customer is the boss; everything we do is to serve the customer.

These four principles described the culture that Irving wanted to create and formed the framework for all changes made to Zale Corporation. In his communications to Zale employees, he stressed that the future of Zale rested on the above-mentioned principles. He believed that the key to success in retailing was achieving customer satisfaction. The principles became so prevalent and well known that coffee cups were created with the principles written on them in gold. As a symbolic move, Irving announced that the executive dining room would be closed immediately. Executives would no longer be separated from the remainder of Zale's staff.

The Vice-President of the Store Operations indicated that Irving was very interested in "how things really worked in the company, how people thought and felt about things, and especially what their attitudes were." Irving interviewed key executives of Zale to become more familiar with the company and its management talent; to identify problems, opportunities and areas for improvement; and to aid in selecting a management team with which he could work.

One executive stated that Irving Gerstein's personal style encouraged the exchange of ideas. "Ideas that were suppressed in the old system came out of the woodwork." Armed with this information, Irving began making changes to the company.

Changes to the Zale Corporation

The changes made between January and April 1987 included:

1. Reorganizing the structure along functional lines.
2. Refocussing the company's business on jewellery retailing by disposing of manufacturing operations.
3. Reducing the number of non-sales personnel by over 1,100.
4. Repositioning the company's marketing strategy away from promotional discounting and emphasizing value, fashion and exclusivity.
5. Broadening the range of products offered and improving advertising programs.

Reorganization

The first change was to simplify Zale's organizational structure. At the time of the acquisition, Zale had a divisional structure with each division having a chairman, president and vice-presidents. The head office acted as a holding company. The general strategic direction of the divisions was left to divisional management. Each division acted autonomously and very little communication occurred between divisions.

This structure did not suit Irving's personal philosophy about how to run a business, nor did it suit his management style. The new, functional structure consolidated the divisions, removed redundancies and allowed senior management to be reduced significantly. All of the management interviewed felt that the new structure made Zale more efficient and consumer-responsive.

In selecting people to head each functional area it became apparent that personal philosophies and personal chemistry would prevent the existing team from operating smoothly. Some executives believed in price-off promotional strategies to increase customer flow and had a difficult time believing in Irving's "vision." After several discussions it was agreed by those involved that they should leave the company.

Peoples' Senior Vice-President of Merchandising, Marketing and Operations, Nick White, was transferred to the Zale operation as Senior Vice-President of Merchandising. This person was an American with industry experience in the United States who had joined White's in Salt Lake City when it was owned by Peoples. He transferred to Canada in 1981 and worked there six years before transferring to Zales. In addition, two of Zales' executives were promoted into the positions of Senior Vice-President of Store Operation and Senior Vice-President of Finance.

Within six weeks of the takeover, Irving had his management team in place who, along with Irving as president and CEO and his assistant, were responsible for running the Zale Corporation. Irving often referred to this team as "the office of the president."

Closing manufacturing operations

The biggest change was the closing of manufacturing operations in January, 1987. The decision was relatively easy since Irving's vision for Zale stated that it should be exclusively a retailer; also, Zale senior management had been recommending this move for several years, so there was no resistance to the idea. In the past, Zale had only given lip service to being market driven; "the company was really manufacturing driven," stated one executive.

Early in January, Irving held a management meeting to discuss closing the manufacturing operation. He learned of an earlier internal study that concluded it would take two years to wind down the operation and relocate the distribution process. The operation consisted of 95,000 square feet of office space and employed 500 people in activities such as diamond purchasing, product development, distribution, and staff departments such as accounting, finance and data processing.

Ignoring the internal study, Irving decided to close the operation immediately. During the next 120 hours, $75 million of inventory, all the data processing equipment and the furniture and fixtures were shipped to Dallas headquarters. Within five days of closing the manufacturing operation, Zale was shipping goods from Dallas, its new distribution centre.

Expense reduction

Zale's expenses had to be reduced significantly and its profits increased. During this stage Irving relied heavily on input from Zale management. He was quoted in the Zale company magazine as saying, "I am relying heavily on the expertise and visions of the senior officers who make up our new organizational structure to map out the final details and strategies as we move ahead."

Members of the newly formed management team developed a budget they felt was realistic. However, they had a guideline: the budget would have to cover the interest expense of the acquisition. The budget matched closely with the one previously developed by Peoples and Drexel. Zale would go after an aggressive EBIT (earnings before interest and taxes) of $100 million, 25 percent above the company's interest expense. Improved performance would come from expense reduction, a different marketing approach to improve sales, and tying bonuses to performance measures.

All members of the management team were encouraged to participate in an exchange of ideas. In fact, Irving gave the management full credit for coming up with the ideas that were implemented. He stated that, "They [the management team] came up with the ideas to reduce expenses. They determined how to reduce the staff by 1,600. I let them do what they wanted. They knew what to do. They just needed someone to create the atmosphere for them to do it."

1. Expense Reduction. Non-selling staff was reduced by 1,600 or 35 percent. This removed duplication and redundancies and improved the efficiency of the organization. Five hundred employees were from the closed manufacturing operation.

Expenses were reduced by approximately $80 million as a result of wage savings, the elimination of manufacturing, and a reduction in the advertising budget of $35 million. The new management's position was that they did not have the advertising power to draw additional customers into a mall. Customers came to a specific mall for many reasons other than Zale jewellery stores. Therefore, it was Zale's job to ensure that customers already in the mall made it into a Zale store. This position led to increased use of point-of-purchase advertising, mall advertising and direct mail advertising. National advertising was determined to be unnecessary.

2. Marketing Approach. Zale stopped using price discounting as a means to increase customer flow. Irving believed in quality products at a good price at all times, and felt that discounting sent a message that the price was too high in the first place. The company chose to no longer differentiate itself on the basis of price but rather value, style, fashion and uniqueness.

The management team also changed the merchandise mix of individual stores. Since previous management had identified department stores as their main competition, they had stocked their stores similar to a department store — broad lines with little depth. To change this strategy to one of a specialty store, narrow lines with depth, the best sellers were identified and slow movers were eliminated from store inventory.

The new marketing strategy also focussed on diamonds. Zale had a 60-year relationship built with customers by way of diamonds. Several years earlier, in an attempt to appear more fashionable, Zale de-emphasized diamonds by moving them to the back of the stores. The new Zale management felt that the company could not be profitable unless it perpetuated its position in the profitable diamond market. Therefore, diamonds were moved to the first third of the store, the most productive section in a retail store.

Another key element to the marketing and merchandising strategy was promotion. It was felt that the stores could be used more effectively for promotion purposes, an important issue since advertising expenses were cut so dramatically. One executive stated, "We wanted to service our customer more productively. We wanted a store that is a perfect communicator of our offer to not only preempt the competition by being different, but we give the customer a reason to shop by virtue of how the store is displayed, merchandised, and by our service.... We redisplayed the showcases. We took that best selling item and put it in a special display. We put a sign with a picture of the item and its price on top of the showcase, then we put another sign on the ceiling above the showcase."

This change provided a clear message to the customer and a very focussed direction for salespeople within the organization. Salespeople knew what to emphasize in terms of product and also that service was considered key to increased sales.

Promotional advertising was centred upon credit. According to one executive, "Zale had one of the finest credit organizations in the United States. This meant that Zale could make offers to customers in terms of the extension of credit or the communication of credit offers, via direct mail that was preemptive in the marketplace except for an organization like J.C. Penny's or Sears. We took our best selling product, our unique product and we tied it into a very strong credit message. We said, 'We can offer you great jewellery at the lowest terms.' We offered instant credit of $2,000 in twenty minutes. This communicated great value plus unique design to the customer."

3. Bonus Structure. Once the EBIT figure of $100 million was agreed upon by all the senior management within the organization, Irving announced that bonuses paid to all key managers would be tied to achieving the figure. One executive commented, "When the executives' incentives were set around the EBIT figure, it focussed everyone on a crystal clear, hard objective." In addition, store managers had their bonuses tied to the sales plan (60 percent), shortage figures (20 percent), and the expense plan (20 percent).

The management of change process

During the four month period, and for a time afterwards, the organization was in shock. People were leaving and the company's culture was changing.

Irving and the management team took the following approach to the change process: (1) make the changes quickly to minimize the upheaval time; (2) keep employees informed as much as was feasible; (3) get as many people involved in making the changes as possible; (4) let actions speak. Don't hide anything, but don't spend a lot of time talking about doing something — do it; (5) make objectives and changes as clear as possible; and (6) treat people fairly that are dismissed from the company. The way you treat people who are leaving reflects how you will treat people who are staying.

One of the key reasons given for the success of changes was that the company recently had been purchased. When an organization is taken over by a new company, change is expected and tolerated. An executive commented, "There was a great willingness on the part of people to change or at least reserve judgment on change." By May, employees seemed to be pleased with the changes in the organizational structure and in the company's merchandising strategy. However, there was a great deal of uncertainty and scepticism. Management assured the remaining employees that their jobs were secure.

Once the fall marketing program was implemented and the company's performance started to improve, the scepticism began to disappear. The successful Christmas season (the company out-performed the retail industry) gave the whole company something of which to be proud. Morale was high as everyone seemed to be internalizing the success. Overall, the changes made to the organization were seen as a big success by all those interviewed.

The Relationship Between Zale and Peoples

The fact that Irving Gerstein became president of Zale and his Canadian Senior Vice-President of Finance and Administration became his assistant made it obvious that Peoples would be active in the management of Zale. The two men continued to spend on average two days a week in Texas even long after the purchase. Once a month they would meet with Zale's senior management in a formal meeting that provided a mechanism to discuss key issues. Other than this meeting, the remainder of the communication between them was on an informal, ad hoc basis. Meetings were set up when necessary. Irving was not a big believer in formal meetings and committees. He stated, "When you are running a company with an $85 million interest bill, you don't sit around having committee meetings."

Other than through Irving, or his assistant, there was no formal contact between the two companies. Peoples was managed separately and its senior management had minimal contact with Zale senior management. Therefore, the relationship between Peoples and Zale was very much affected by Irving Gerstein's management style.

Irving Gerstein's Management Style

Irving Gerstein was usually described as energetic, proactive and very good with people. He was known to be a quick study who sized up situations easily. He believed in being flexible and described himself as having a "do it" mentality. The following story, told by his assistant, gives an indication of his proactive, "do it" style:

When the manufacturing division was sold, Zale was left with $145 million in manufacturing inventory. Included in the inventory was $80 million dollars worth of loose diamonds. A diamond expert was asked to determine the best way to dispose of these diamonds. His analysis concluded it would take two years to sell them and Zale would recoup two-thirds of their value. Irving had the diamonds distributed into ten boxes with each box valued at $8 million dollars. He called the top five American jewellery suppliers and told them the boxes were for sale at $8 million dollars apiece. If they purchased a box they were guaranteed Zale's business. Suppliers, eager for Zale's business, quickly purchased the boxes and Zale recouped the full value of the diamonds.

The following comments from the senior management of Peoples and Zale provide a description of his management style:

- Irving's management style is one of giving very clear and firm direction but giving great latitude in terms of accountability for you to carry it out. He is very clear as to what he wants done, but how he wants to do it, he usually leaves a great deal up to the people who work for him.

- Irving is clearly the boss. He wants and encourages participation, he spends lots of time getting out thoughts on things.

- Irving never tells you what to do, instead he gives you an idea and asks you to think about it. He makes you own what you are doing.

- He is very good at working crowds. He makes people feel that he is genuinely interested in them. He charms and thrills people.

- He manages by walking around and talking to people.

- He tends to create an atmosphere in which decisions become obvious by the weight of the facts on the table.

- Irving is not a tinkerer, not a meddler. He does not second guess people, he supports you but likes to be kept informed.

Each of the senior vice-presidents felt that they were responsible, as a team, for handling the day-to-day operation of Zale. "Irving manages the process, we manage the business." Irving agreed with this comment. As mentioned earlier, he was a great believer in process: "If you have gone through the right process, decisions fall out."

Irving's management style appeared to be the result of two things. First, he insisted on being kept informed of all changes in plans, and any surprises, in each functional area. This way he could monitor the company's progress and be involved in important decisions while allowing his management team to make day-to-day decisions. His assistant felt that one of his own key roles was to help create and foster a culture where Irving was kept informed of what was going on. This was very different from the individualistic culture under previous Zale management. Second was his personal confidence. He was confident enough to listen to others' ideas and to change his mind when presented with additional information. As one of his management team commented, "Irving's confidence allows him to be flexible and adaptable. He is looking for the right way, not his way.... He has strong opinions but he is not afraid to change them." However, when Irving felt he was right, he knew how to steer people in his direction.

Irving also allowed senior management a tremendous amount of input into the strategic direction of the company.

Was Zale Managed Differently than Peoples?

Irving was very clear that he managed the two companies separately and differently. "You can't manage a company the size of Zale in the same way as Peoples." However, he stated that his basic management style was the same; the philosophy of how to manage people was the same.

A management team member stated, "Irving is more hands-on in Canada... not in daily operations because Irving is not involved in day-to-day operations and he never has been, it's not his style. He spends more time following up on certain types of detail in Peoples that he would not deal with in Zale. He clearly has the ability to personally affect by virtue of his own leadership style, his own charisma, the mood, the motivation of Peoples because he knows most of the people here. I consider this a real advantage."

In an organization the size of Zale that was not possible. In Zale, Irving relied more heavily on his senior management team which comprised highly skilled, good managers who knew Zale and how it works. The same executive commented, "The level of professionalism between the two businesses [Peoples and Zale] is exceptionally different. Generally their [Zale management] skills, their experience sets are much broader not only in terms of variety but also in terms of depth of knowledge than you will find here [in Peoples].... The opportunity is there to manage the business from the point of view that says, we have in Zale a professional management group. They have high levels of management skills in whatever area they are dealing with, as well as skills to manage people and to implement things."

The difference in the level of professionalism was considered to be largely a function of organizational size. A large organization like Zale had the money, challenge and drawing power to recruit professional management talent. In addition, the pure size of the United States retailing industry allowed people within the industry to obtain a broad level of experience.

The fact that Zale was an American company was another reason it had to be managed differently. Irving stated the following soon after the purchase, "I have made it very, very clear. There will be no consolidation of Peoples in Canada with Zale. They will be two separate stand-alone operations. We are not taking Canadian management down there.... I feel strongly that Canada is not the United States and the United States is not Canada. I come with no baggage, and they have an extremely talented professional management team. My role will be to create a framework for them to make Zale Jewellers the most exciting environment for a customer to be in."

When asked to identify differences between Canada and the United States, in terms of operating a business, the following observations were given by senior management. Each indicated that the differences between Americans and Canadians were subtle.

- Americans are more individualistic, operate more independently than Canadians. Consensus management is more important in the Canadian system.

- Canadians are more formal in their business and personal dealings. There is more of the European restraint between people at the business level.

- Canada has a more homogeneous, accepted value system in politics and economics. The United States is far more diverse. The value systems between regions can be very different. There is more homogeneity when you move from the north to the south (i.e. Vancouver to Seattle) than when you move east to west (i.e. Los Angeles to New York).

The competitive environment was identified as being different in the two countries by all but Irving Gerstein. Irving stated that since the North American jewellery sector was highly fragmented, both countries had strong competitive environments. Others felt the United States business environment was much more competitive, due to the increased number of players and the marketing experience of larger competitors as indicated by the following comments:

- The United States is far more competitive in every area than in Canada. The desire for independence is more obvious among United States management.

- A product differentiation offer alone wasn't enough to make success. We needed a broader, extended approach to marketing (than in Canada) that would uniquely differentiate ourselves from the competition. In the United States no product is unique (unlike Canada). If it is not already there, the competition will copy it immediately.... The issue is taking the product that is being sold and figuring out how to do it better than your competition in terms of how you market.

- The level of specialization in retailing is unbelievable in the United States. Segments and products are broken down and companies specialize. The United States population is large enough to warrant this. This makes entry into the market difficult. You need focus and clarity of offer, which is difficult if you have a broad product mix.

Management Explains Performance in 1989

Irving Gerstein, and all the members of his American management team, were very clear that the first year and a half of operation had been a huge success. Performance goals were met and surpassed by over 15 percent. Company morale was higher than it had ever been. When asked why the acquisition was a success, Irving Gerstein and Charles Gill gave the following reasons:

1. Peoples had bought a leading company in the United States — it was off track but still a leader. It had good store locations and customer recognition. Zale had a dominant position in the market so the company had the clout necessary for growth. The leading position in the market also allowed Zale to make changes that the rest of the industry would follow. Zale was able to be proactive, not reactive.

2. Irving was able to sit on the board for several years prior to the take over. This gave him a good feel for the company which permitted the rapid turnaround. He had a good feel for where the company should be going.

3. The management talent existed in the company. This was key. No one had to be hired outside the company; therefore, the people managing the company knew Zale and how it worked. The management in place was extremely talented and competent.

4. Irving and his assistant were running the company. No CEO was brought in. They both had enthusiasm for performance and were able to create it in Zale.

5.They had a very clear focus on what they wanted for performance. This was communicated to management and management bonuses were tied to this EBIT figure. This focussed the whole company and gave it a clear, hard objective.

Peoples Jewellers Update: Three Years Later

Until March of 1989, the results at Zale had been consistent with expectations. At about the same time, Irving Gerstein and Charles Gill became aware that Gordon Jewelry Corp., Zale's major competitor with 625 stores in the United States, was available. Charles Gill stated that although they were not looking to make such an acquisition, there were two major reasons why they finally decided to purchase Gordon's. First, the Zales store assortments had been transformed into more high-end jewellry and giftware merchandise. This left the large lower income consumer segment open, and Gordon filled this gap, fitting into the company's program to serve the total market. Second, Gordon represented an opportunity to add 625 stores without increasing the company's overhead base. Gill pointed out that Zale had difficulty with the financing of Gordon: "The marketplace had changed radically. To raise $100 million before had not been too hard. To raise money for Gordon, it was necessary to go to three continents." Peoples spent $313 million to acquire the Houston-based jeweller.

The operating results in 1990 were fine for both the Zale and Gordon divisions. In fact, Gordon outperformed its targets and Zale was not far off. Gill added, "Today, Gordon continues to be the most profitable division, especially in the current recession when people tend to trade down."

The United States operation was under some financial constraints during the early part of 1990, but it was not until August of that same year that the real problems began. Gill commented, "In August of 1990, the impact of the Gulf War eroded consumer confidence and reduced traffic in the malls. This coupled with the economic slowdown decreased sales in the United States into 1992."

In May 1991, Irving Gerstein moved to Texas to deal with Zale on a full-time basis. Charles Gill continued in Canada as President of Peoples Jewellers. At this point, Dennis Bookshester, who had been hired in December 1990, resigned. Bookshester had extensive department store experience and had been hired to run Zale, while Gerstein planned to concentrate on global opportunities available to Zale.

By March 1991, the difficulties led Peoples management to meet with their banks to discuss Zale's financial position, but they still hoped that things would improve. However, consumer confidence continued to erode and, as Charles Gill noted, "If you have a normally structured company you can withstand this, but if it is highly leveraged, it becomes very difficult to withstand."

It also became difficult for Zale to sell its United States stores because of their poor performance.

As the Christmas season approached, the picture was not improving.

The recognition that Zale was not going to meet certain obligations moved its management toward a dialogue with its creditors. One of the company's creditors, a Dallas securities dealer called Barre & Co., thought it was more appropriate to pursue such discussions within Chapter 11 of the United States Bankruptcy Code, and filed a petition on January 1, 1992. This made it impossible for Zale to continue without the protection of Chapter 11. Charles Gill commented, "Fundamentally, some of our receivables financing was pulled because of the fact that someone had filed under Chapter 11. So, we ended up consenting to Chapter 11 later in January."

As Gill also noted, "Under Chapter 11, the first thing you do is arrange for financing." Fortunately, Zales management had developed a business plan once it began having difficulty. The strength of this plan assisted the company in raising $510 million that allowed them to continue to operate. They then began to implement the plan, closing over 400 stores, changing the organization back to a divisional structure, and making a number of changes to operations. As of May 1992, Zale was meeting its business plan.

When asked about the future, Gill pointed out the difficulty in speculation. He concluded, "It is fair to say that we will end up owning a significantly smaller percentage of Zale. The thing that needs to be understood is that we have a very solid business in Canada that has allowed us to do the things we have done, and that will continue. I don't think the problems that Zale has had were operational. With Zale we ended up being whipsawed by the twin effects of a recession and a leveraged financial structure. And, the recession coupled with the war that the United States has gone through has brought it to one of the most severe times that people have seen in a long, long time."

Finally, Irving Gerstein stated, "Our goal is to return Zale to profitability in the 1990s. While we might prefer different circumstances, we feel we can still achieve [that goal] under Chapter 11 protection."

Reflecting on the Experience

In the Peoples Jewellers case it appears that almost all the important issues were covered:

- Management already had experience in the United States and understood that it was a different market.
- Peoples acquired the market leader which was profitable.
- Although no formal research was done, more practical and valuable information was gathered by management working in Zales as part of the board of directors and from years of experience in the United States jewellery market.
- The company's strategy was changed to reposition it and to make the company more responsive to customers. At the same time expenses were reduced. During the approximate period 1989–1991, $125 million was taken out of Zale's and Gordon's expenses.
- Zales had good store locations and tremendous leverage with developers and suppliers.
- Peoples and Zales had strong, experienced management.
- It had the systems necessary to manage and control the company. An auto-replenishment of inventory system was implemented throughout the entire Zale organization permitting the reduction of inventory levels. It also developed a computer-assisted transaction system which was a sophisticated point-of-sale system.
- Zales was profitable for a number of years after it was acquired.
- And then it was forced into Chapter 11. What happened?

Perhaps the most obvious problems were the high level of debt and the major expansion just in time for the recession of 1991. These factors, working together, probably negated all the things that management did do correctly. However, Peoples was not the only retailer that apparently had hit upon a winning formula for entering and succeeding in the United States that ran into difficulty in the first two years of this decade. The next case about the Grafton Group describes a different strategy (from the one Peoples chose in purchasing Zales) that apparently was also succeeding, but ended in disappointment as well.

THE GRAFTON GROUP

Background

In 1961, Lowville Limited, a holding company, purchased Grafton Limited, a retailer with 11 stores in southwestern Ontario. In December 1969, the company merged with Jack Fraser Limited, a chain of menswear stores. In March 1970, the company's name was changed to Grafton Group Limited and over the next seven years it expanded rapidly through a series of Canadian acquisitions. Near the end of the 1970s, the company began to find that acquisition opportunities in Canada were limited. Since management was interested in continuing to expand, they began opening new retail chains and looked to the United States for acquisition candidates.

In 1989, Grafton consisted of five subsidiaries (including Seifert's Inc. in the United States); four specialized in retailing and one manufactured and sold wholesale bedroom and bathroom decorative products. Grafton's organization in Canada is presented in Table 1. The number of stores in each company is shown in parentheses.

Grafton Group acted as an overall strategic management company for the subsidiaries. Day-to-day operations were the responsibility of subsidiary presidents. In addition to strategic direction, the parent company provided centralized services to the subsidiaries in areas where economies of scale provided competitive advantages. For example, many of the information systems were centralized, as were real estate and buying. Coordination and control was achieved through an annual budgeting process that was presented to the parent company and the Board for approval. Subsidiaries also reported performance results regularly to Grafton Group's management.

Grafton Group: three years later

By mid 1992 the Grafton Group's collection of companies had virtually unravelled. In 1991, the Grafton Group reported major losses

Table 1 Grafton Group Ltd. (Canada)
1989

Grafton-Fraser Inc. (100% owned)	Elks Inc. (65% owned)	Maher Inc. (100% owned)	Toby Industries (100% owned)
Jack Fraser (170)	Elks Menswear	Maher Stores (116)	Home furnishings
George Richards (25)	Dapper Dan	Julia Division (45)	
Grafton & Co.(20)		Copp Division (51)	
The Loft (116)		Footpath Division (8)	
Sideffects (43)			
Apparel Clearance Centres (21)			
Nabour Stores (41)			
Licensed Men's and Boy's Wear Departments in Woolco (120)			

(number of stores in parentheses)

partially due to reduced consumer spending as a result of the recession, the GST, unemployment and increases in cross-border shopping. Elks filed for bankruptcy in January of 1991, and several other stores were closed including the Nabours, Apparel Clearance Centre, Loft, Sideffects and Dapper Dan divisions. Further exacerbating their problems, on July 29, 1991, the company announced that it had been advised that the F.W. Woolworth Co. Limited would not be renewing the license agreement between it and Grafton–Fraser Inc., which was to expire January 2, 1992.

The Grafton–Fraser subsidiary received protection under the Companies Creditors Arrangements Act (CCAA) on December 23, 1991, and attempted to restructure. In January 1992, subsidiary Maher sought protection from creditors under the CCAA. In April 1992, Maher had declared bankruptcy and a month later it was sold to Bata Shoe. In addition, in May of 1992, creditors of Grafton–Fraser Inc. approved the sale of 90 percent of the company to Toronto developer Cadillac

Fairview Corp. Ltd. and Grafton–Fraser's Executive Vice-President Glenn Stonehouse. The Grafton Group had undergone a major reorganization which left it with 10 percent of Grafton–Fraser and 45 percent of Seifert's in the United States.

With respect to its American subsidiary, 1990 was the first time in Seifert's history that the company reported a loss. The company cited the fact that major retailers in the United States were using price cutting tactics during the year to secure cash flow and Seifert's was forced to follow in an attempt to maintain market share. In addition, escalating location and wage costs were reported. In February 1992, the Grafton Group lost control of Seifert's, as part of a debt reduction agreement with the parent company's secured creditors in Canada.

It appears that Seifert's problems were not operating or management oriented. Rather, a combination of parent company debt and a deep recession created problems that led to the decreased equity in the United States chain.

Entry into the United States

Like most Canadian retailers, Grafton Group benefited from the rapid growth in shopping centres during the 1960s and 1970s. This expansion plus several acquisitions resulted in an average company growth rate from 1969 to 1979 of 23 percent in sales and 58 percent in net income. Grafton's phenomenal retail performance led to the following comment by a well-known investment analyst, "It [Grafton Group] is one of the best managed retailers in the country."

Near the end of the 1970s the shopping centre trend and major Canadian retailing growth were coming to an end, and Grafton was facing limited growth opportunities. The company's management began considering the United States market for expansion. However, Grafton's management were cautious and seemed to understand the United States was a different market with a different set of suppliers. They also believed that Canadians, and Canadian formulas, might not function there as well as they did at home.

Grafton's management was confident that a United States acquisition was the best method for international expansion because they thought it would be too difficult to start up a greenfield company. They also believed that they would need people that understood the market which the company did not have, or hire them, which would be risky.

Grafton hired an investment advisor to help locate a suitable acquisition candidate. The company had successfully used this approach several times when making Canadian acquisitions. At the time of the decision to acquire a United States retailer, no specific analysis was completed on the United States market. Management established only one criterion for the potential acquisition, that the company be a retailer of soft goods.

In late 1978, Grafton was presented with an opportunity to purchase a private company named Seifert's Inc. owned by two brothers. Seifert's was a chain of 50 ladies wear stores in the United States midwest. Negotiations took approximately six months to complete in order to work out the purchase arrangements and to perform sufficient analysis on Seifert's to ensure it provided a good opportunity for United States entry.

Grafton completed an extensive review of Seifert's before purchasing it. The analysis included an investigation of the financial situation; merchandising philosophy; the business and its growth potential; all store conditions, locations, markets, images and management talent. Once the analysis was completed, Grafton's management was sure Seifert's represented an excellent opportunity for expansion and growth in the United States. Therefore, in July 1979, Grafton agreed in principle to acquire Seifert's Inc. One concern was ensuring that Seifert's maintained a strong, competent president who understood the American midwest market. Grafton's senior management felt strongly that a Canadian could not take charge because the lack of market knowledge would lead to too many mistakes. As a result, Grafton management negotiated to have James Seifert remain with the company for five years as its president. Mr. Seifert's main condition was that Grafton leave sufficient funds within the company for expansion projects.

Seifert's Inc. at the Time of the Purchase

Seifert's Inc. was founded in 1953, in Cedar Rapids, Iowa when the Seifert brothers recognized that younger consumers (15 to 30) after World War II had become increasingly interested in sportswear and retailers in their area were not selling products to satisfy this interest. They opened stores averaging 4,000–5,000 square feet in smaller Iowa communities of 5,000 to 30,000 people, and stocked mainly sportswear apparel designed for females of all ages from juniors to missy women (mature women who wore sizes 12 to 16). As the company evolved, stores began carrying other apparel but sportswear still represented over 60 percent of the store's product line.

The approach was successful and the chain had been growing steadily since the early 1950s by focussing on entering small and medium sized areas. Just prior to the acquisition, the company opened or acquired 13 stores and several more were opened early in 1979. At the time of the purchase, the chain consisted of 50 stores in seven states with the greatest number (28) by far in Iowa. Burns Fry estimated that Seifert's 1978 sales were US $18 million. The company was profitable.

Parent-Subsidiary Relationship

From the beginning, Grafton's management had no intention of actively managing the United States operation. Mr. Seifert was allowed a great deal of autonomy in running the company. The American retail concept and implementation were not changed. No changes were made to the organization subsequent to the acquisition. As a result, the acquisition seemed like a minor change for the Seifert organization. Control was established and maintained through a budgeting and financial reporting system that was structured around Seifert's data processing equipment. The equipment was quite different from the Canadian organization's, but was considered suitable for both Seifert's and Grafton's requirements. However, the company's reporting systems were upgraded to manage the new reporting and control requirements.

Seifert's Performance

Over the period from 1979 to 1988, Seifert's underwent numerous changes as a result of rapid expansion, increasing competition and tough United States economic conditions. By 1988 Seifert's was almost four times the size as when it was bought by Grafton. It had 195 stores in 24 states and the District of Columbia. The company's organizational structure was designed around three merchandising divisions: Seifert's, Mark

Henri and Seifert's Plus; and four operational divisions: midwest, west, south and east.

Operating divisions were established because Seifert's senior management was aware that different regions in the United States had different cultures, competitive environments and consumers. Divisional vice-presidents were charged with keeping stores responsive to the environment and had responsibility for all operating issues including staffing. Products were sourced from New York, Los Angeles and the Far East. Forty percent of all products purchased were under private label programs and 30 percent of these were manufactured in the Far East for Seifert's. Increasing competition, higher rent expenses and economic conditions had made it vital to closely monitor and control product costs. Overall the U.S. operation was managed as an inverted pyramid, with the customer being the final boss. To ensure customer satisfaction, everyone's performance within Seifert's was tied to the success of the company.

COMPARATIVE SUMMARY

A comparative summary of the Grafton and Peoples experiences is presented in Table 2.

Table 2 Comparative Summary

	Grafton Group	Peoples: White Jewellers	Peoples: Zales
Dates of operation in the U.S.	1979–present	1978–1982	1981 purchased 15% interest; 1986 – 100%; still operating 1992
Reason for entry	approaching limits to growth	retail growth ended in Canada	grow
Entry mode	acquisition	joint venture acquisition	joint venture acquisition; junk bond financing
Profitable when acquired?	yes	yes	yes
Rationale for acquisition	U.S. different; greenfield too difficult		
Approach	proactive	proactive	proactive
Attitude toward acquisition	keep it running as is and expand	grow from regional base	go big or don't go at all
Research prior to acquisition?	yes	some	informal research
alternative companies	yes	yes	no
company analysis	yes	yes	from the inside
consumer	some	no	from experience

144

competition	yes	no	from experience
demographic	all	no	no
locations		no	no
Transfer of retail concept	kept U.S. concept	transferred Canadian procedures	repositioned existing concept
Product mix	American	American	American
Geographic operating area	195 stores in 24 states plus D.C.	50 stores	1,500 stores across the country
Store locations		difficult to get good ones due to size; expensive	good
Management Canadian	did not understand U.S. market	did not understand U.S. market	understood market from experience and some managers originally from White's transferred back to U.S.
American (with acquisition)	qualified	generally good; some returned to Canada with Peoples	strong, experienced
Commitment to U.S.	yes		yes
Decision-making	autonomous		decentralized but links for strategy and finance
Suppliers	no indications of problems	not important to suppliers	very important; high leverage

	Grafton Group	Peoples: White Jewellers	Peoples: Zales
Systems	yes		reorganized company; sophisticated information and control systems
Competition	severe		strong competition
Other		profitable but could not cover interest payments	transferred principles; strong Canadian and American management team

CHAPTER 4

MORE FOOD FOR THOUGHT

PROVIGO INCORPORATED

Overview

Provigo Inc. had company-wide sales of $6.1 billion in fiscal 1990. Headquartered in Montreal, the company was a broad based distributor in the food (wholesale and retail), health and pharmaceutical, convenience store and specialty retailing sectors including catalogue showrooms and sporting goods chains.

In 1977, Provigo made its first foray into the United States market through the purchase of Loeb Ltd. whose subsidiaries included Market Wholesale, a northern California food wholesaler, and Tidewater, a food wholesaler operating in the Chicago, New York and Chesapeake Bay areas. Eleven years later Provigo bought 11 Petrini and 15 Lucky–Alpha Beta supermarkets in the San Francisco bay area. Shortly thereafter they opened five discount food stores in the same area. In 1989 five of the Lucky–Alpha Beta stores were closed, and early in 1990 four more were closed and one was sold. The remaining five have been converted to the Petrini banner. In addition, the sale of Tidewater Wholesale had been announced. Expansion was planned for the retail sector after the existing stores were fully consolidated.

The 1990 results (year end January 27, 1990) were mixed for the United States operations. Both Market Wholesale and the discount retail operation showed a profit while the Petrini chain lost money. Despite the disappointing performance of the United States division, which posted a $10.7 million loss compared to a profit of $13.8 million in 1989, Provigo appeared determined to succeed in California, and had plans to spend $15 million to renovate the existing Petrini stores and a further $15 million for a frozen food distribution centre. Total Provigo company results deteriorated in 1990 posting a $51.4 million loss compared to a profit of $51.5 million the previous year largely due to restructuring and write-downs taken in the third quarter 1990.

Background

Provigo was formed in 1969 by the merger of three Quebec wholesalers with little or no direct retail presence. Sales of the newly formed company were approximately $200 million and grew to $300 million by 1974. In 1974 the company launched the Provi-Soir chain of convenience food stores in Quebec which subsequently became the market leaders.

Three years later, with the acquisition of Loeb Ltd. and its subsidiaries, sales had risen to $2 billion. Loeb was primarily a food wholesaler to Ontario and Quebec based IGA stores but it had other subsidiaries: Horne and Pitfield (Alberta IGA Food Wholesale), National Drug (a Canadian health and pharmaceutical wholesaler), Market Wholesale (a food wholesaler based in northern California), and Tidewater Wholesale (a food wholesaler operating in Chicago, New York and the Chesapeake Bay area). This acquisition was Provigo's initial exposure to the United States market. As Yvan Bussières, President of Provigo Inc., stated, the main intent of the acquisition was "not so much to secure a position in the United States as to extend its wholesale activities in Canada."

Other acquisitions followed:

- In 1981 came the acquisition of the Dominion Stores supermarkets in Quebec. Consistent with the company strategy, most of these stores have since been franchised. Also that year Sports Experts, a Quebec sporting goods wholesaler selling to the Sports

Experts franchised stores, was also purchased. Provigo's annual sales reached $3.3 billion.

• In 1985 Pierre Lortie joined the company as Chairman and CEO and continued the acquisitions, thereby further diversifying the company base. Sales of Provigo Inc. reached $4.8 billion that year.

1. Collegiate/Arlington, a Canadian sporting goods chain, was purchased.

2. The first Brico store was opened near Montreal. This was a new concept, a-do-it-yourself home improvement, renovation and decoration warehouse store.

3. A 22 percent interest in the catalogue showroom chain, Consumers Distributing, which operated in both Canada and the United States, was acquired. Again, Bussières pointed out that when Provigo purchased this initial interest in Consumers Distributing, it was for the purpose of diversification rather than the acquisition of a United States operation. The United States stores were performing poorly and were dramatically rationalized, closing the west coast stores and paring down the eastern operation for a total of 77 closures within the first year. To cover the cost of retrenchment, Consumers made a provision of $26 million. With Consumers Distributing also came Toy City which operated 20 "toy supermarkets." The following year Provigo increased its ownership to 100 percent. At this point Consumers consisted of 200 catalogue showroom stores and 27 Toy City stores across Canada.

Consumer's east coast United States stores were continuing to lose money and the remaining catalogue showrooms were sold in 1988. Provigo had not been closely involved on a day-to-day basis with Consumers Distributing in the United States.

• In 1986, Provigo continued to acquire companies:

1. Institutional Food Service Companies in Quebec was purchased and Medis Health and Pharmaceutical Services (formerly National Drug) developed into Canada's leading drug and pharmaceutical wholesaler.

2. In the same year Provigo acquired 11 Petrini supermarkets and 15 Lucky–Alpha Beta supermarkets in the San Francisco area. The latter were changed to the Quality Food Store banner, and both were to be supplied by Market Wholesale. A discount food store operation was also launched in the same area with two stores opening during 1988. In Canada, Provigo acquired seven Alberta supermarkets from Safeway, plus seven supermarkets from Steinberg in Quebec.

• In 1989 sales had reached $7.4 billion which represented a growth in sales of 37 times since the first year of operation 27 years earlier.

Sales had almost doubled under Pierre Lortie who resigned in October 1989. He was replaced shortly thereafter by Yvan Bussières who was appointed Senior Vice-President and Chief Operating Officer and, as of April 3, 1990, was made President. Provigo had become increasingly diversified, entering the pharmaceutical and unrelated retail markets. Partially as a result of this direction, income suffered, declining in 1989 to $0.61 per share from $0.80 per share in 1988. In order to reverse this trend, senior management decided to pursue the company's original franchise in the food business and divested its unrelated operations. In 1990 Provigo sold the companies in its money-losing health and pharmaceuticals group. It also sold Consumers Distributing and was in the process of selling Sports Experts. Provigo focussed again on its core food businesses.

Food group

The food group was the sole remaining group in 1990. The Canadian division was made up of both wholesale and retail operations. The latter operated under some 22 different banners both company owned and franchised, the most important of which were Provigo, Axep, Proprio, Jovi, IGA and M/M. In this mature market, Provigo has pursued a segmentation strategy whereby, in addition to the conventional supermarket, it has also entered the discount market and has filled the void between convenience store and conventional supermarket. Key to its success was the vertical integration of their distribution systems whereby the wholesale division had a controlled and captive market in the corporate and franchised retail stores.

The United States division accounted for 13 percent of the sales in 1990. The same market strategy of market segmentation and vertical integration was being pursued in the American market as well. There were plans to expand the United States retail food operations as part of the long-term strategy.

The Convenience Group was included in the Canadian Food Group. It operated only at the retail level selling convenience products through a network of franchised stores, the largest of which was Provi-Soir. In addition the company operated retail gasoline outlets in Ontario, Quebec and Alberta.

Company Strategy

Very simply stated, Provigo's strategy had been focussed on vertically integrated marketing distribution formats selling to its captive customers — franchised or affiliated owner-operated retailers. This combination of centralized low-cost services consisting of merchandise buying and distribution, marketing programs and retail support services provided a powerful force in a highly competitive mass merchandising environment. A comparative analysis of the five major food distribution companies, namely Oshawa, Steinberg, Loblaw, Metro Richelieu and Provigo, showed Provigo's ten year average return on equity at 19.7 percent with Oshawa a distant second at 12.3 percent.

Perception of the United States Market and Reason for Entry

Management realized in the mid 1980s that extrapolating a repeat performance of the previous ten years sales increases would yield huge numbers in the neighbourhood of $40 billion. In order to maintain the organization on an aggressive track, it became obvious that there must be further market penetration. At that time, diversification was regarded as an essential part of the expansion process. The view and rationale for movement into the United States market was set forth by Pierre Lortie in December of 1986. He argued that with Provigo's market share rapidly approaching the upper limits in the Canadian market, and industry growth moving at a slow pace, the United States was the obvious choice for increased market penetration.

In addition, starting in 1987, the Canada Combines Act would make future acquisitions much more complex. If an acquisition threatened the competitiveness of the Canadian marketplace, it could be held up and subjected to legal procedures which could either delay or possibly kill a transaction. Due to Provigo's size and their desire to grow, problems could easily arise.

It was also believed that the trade negotiations with the United States for a free trade agreement, which were underway at the time, would result in a reduction in the tariff and non-tariff barriers between the two countries. This openness would ultimately lead to the possibility of large United States retailers and distributors moving into the Canadian market, thus negatively affecting investment opportunities in Canada and increasing the competitiveness of the market.

Finally, a position in the United States market would also provide exposure to new marketing practices and advanced technologies originating in the United States.

Lortie believed that it was imperative to increase Provigo's United States presence and that the expansion would most likely be through acquisition. He was well aware that the acquisition process was fraught with risks, quoting studies which showed that only 20 percent of acquisitions by American companies in the United States were really successful.

Research Prior to Entry

Use of outside resources

With this view and a long-term strategy to expand in the United States market, several studies were commissioned to evaluate acquisition opportunities. The first was prepared by Management Horizons, a division of Price Waterhouse, headquartered in Columbus, Ohio. This report, completed in 1986, assessed the United States wholesale and retail markets with a view to evaluating optimum opportunities at both the industry and commodity level. It also reviewed the dismal performances of Canadian retailers that had entered the United States via acquisition, and recommended success requirements for United States acquisitions. In summary, the recommended requirements were as follows:

1. Acquisitions must be consistent with corporate strategies and objectives.

2. Failure is minimized with an individual on staff who is experienced in merger, acquisitions and integration.

3. Acquisitions should be viewed with realistic expectations and objectives in terms of the value which the new company will add.

4. Participation by new owners in day-to-day management is required from the beginning.

5. Effective incentives should be designed to retain top management of the acquired company.

6. Prior to making an acquisition decision, market and company research should be undertaken to reduce risks associated with unknown factors.

The findings of the report also indicated that the retail sector was preferable to the wholesale sector. Following this study, a number of others were carried out for different markets. A group headquartered in Boston reported on the California market, identifying Petrini among others, as a good acquisition candidate. Since Provigo had inherited the Market Wholesale operation in California through its purchase of Loeb, it had an interest in expanding in this area. Following the company strategy of controlling its retail outlets either through corporate ownership or franchises, Provigo sought to establish a retail network in this market.

In addition to using a consultant to identify acquisition candidates in California, Provigo also employed a consultant to explore the Boston market. He identified the critical success factors for the intended retail concept in descending order of importance for this market as location, price, quality, variety, cleanliness and weekly specials. The relative importance of these factors would vary depending on retail concept and market. He highlighted four top acquisition candidates and ranked them through a consumer perception study with respect to the critical success factors.

Use of internal resources

During 1988 and 1989 Pierre Jette, Provigo Assistant-Treasurer, provided senior management with detailed studies and information on the United States market, conditions favourable to acquisition, and potential candidates.

Prerequisites for market entry

From the various studies, both internal and external, the presence of certain favourable market conditions was identified to ensure maximum potential success for the acquisition. Markets were examined for their level of competitive fragmentation as measured through market share. For example, if the top players within a region held less than 60–65 percent of the market and no one was disproportionately high, i.e. greater than 20 percent, the market was considered to be fragmented providing a favourable environment for acquisition. The presence of LBO'd competitors was seen to provide an opportunity for entry since high debt would not allow these companies to compete strongly on price. (LBO, or leveraged buyout, refers to a method of acquiring a company whereby the acquirer puts up a small fraction of the purchase price and the rest is financed by banks and investors, secured by the assets of the company purchased.) Economic growth, population growth and the absence of a formidable player in the market were all criteria determining the attractiveness of a market.

The importance of power based on regional, not national, concentration was stressed and the key success factors of regional competitors were identified as better buying power, advertising efficiencies, distribution efficiencies, efficiencies of regional management, self distribution, store format development and regional leverage.

Prerequisites for acquisition candidates

Jette observed that acquisition prices were very high. A survey of sales showed that the price paid for recent acquisitions had varied from 15–35 times earnings producing an average of 20 times. LBOs had driven up prices supported by the availability of junk bond financing and relatively low interest rates. Foreign buyers had also contributed to the high prices. Generally, the larger the firm, the higher the price multiple.

Management examined the development strategies of world class food distributors and the correlation of those strategies with relative return on equity performance. The selection criteria established for acquisition candidates were smaller companies located within a fragmented and economically diversified market with strong management. Ideally the company would be in close proximity to the Canadian operation.

A number of acquisition candidates were identified. Background and financial information was collected and a potential strategy was developed for each. An action plan was initiated based on a comprehensive base of knowledge.

Entry into the United States Market

Before dealing with the California retail acquisition, some discussion of the United States operations inherited through the purchase of Loeb is necessary.

Loeb

With the Loeb acquisition in 1977, Provigo fell heir to two United States wholesale operations — Market Wholesale in California and Tidewater in the Chicago, New York and Chesapeake Bay area. The California company was prospering; however, Tidewater was losing money at the time of purchase.

According to Yvan Bussières, Loeb had had plans to sell the two distribution centres in Chicago and New York. These markets were both highly competitive. He noted that competition was strongest in growth areas in the United States especially on the west coast. In retrospect, the company might have chosen lower growth areas in which to expand their United States business, as the high growth centres were targeted by many American firms which increased the already intense competitive nature of the market.

The Chicago and New York centres were subsequently closed as was the remaining Chesapeake Bay operation. Its principal market was military bases in the east, a declining segment in light of the existing political climate.

California acquisition

The first acquisition, consistent with the long-term growth strategy of intended United States expansion, was in California. As indicated earlier, this market was a priority for retail expansion since Provigo already operated Market Wholesale. The consultant's report showed that chains were increasing, and the independents, who were their main customers, were decreasing, thus making it important to establish their own retail distribution network.

To that end, in 1988 Provigo purchased 11 Petrini supermarkets which already was one of its customers in the San Francisco Bay area. This base was further expanded several months later through the acquisition of two stores from the Palo Alto Co-op and 15 Lucky–Alpha Beta stores. Alpha Beta and Lucky, two large supermarket chains, had recently merged, but due to California competition laws, had been forced by the government to sell off a number of their stores. In addition to these acquisitions, Provigo opened five discount stores in northern California under the Better Buy and Cost Less names and were planning two more openings in 1990.

The 15 Lucky–Alpha Beta stores were changed to Quality Plus shortly after the acquisition which proved to be a major error. The new name did not mean anything to customers and the stores suffered a sales decrease of 25 percent. Provigo subsequently sold five of the Quality Plus stores and converted a further five to Petrini where the trading area demographics fit the upscale concept. The company closed four and sold one of the remaining five.

Over an eight-month period, three different retail concepts had come to Provigo with three different groups of people and cultures. There were plans to expand both Petrinis and the discount chain after the existing stores were consolidated and the necessary management, technological changes and renovations completed.

Description of the United States Operation

Locations

All 29 stores acquired/opened in the 1988–89 period were located in northern California, largely concentrated in the San Francisco Bay area. For an upscale concept such as Petrini, the stores were well positioned, as the market was characterized as young (40 percent of its inhabitants are between 25 and 50 years of age), affluent (first in effective buying income out of the 48 continental states), mobile (nearly two automobiles per household) and with a lifestyle that was considered "upscale" (interest in wines, foreign travel, gourmet cooking, real estate investment, home computers, etc. way above the national average).

The stores were in demographically correct locations for their respective target market. The five stores located in unsatisfactory trading areas were closed or sold.

Physical characteristics and merchandising

The Petrini stores average 25,000 square feet of gross leasable area. Since they were appealing to a more selective and higher income market segment, merchandising and store exteriors were more attractive and sophisticated compared to the discount stores. Quality, full service specialty departments and upscale selection were promoted through store layout, presentation and display. Although by American standards Petrini merchandising was relatively sophisticated, Bussières noted that Canadian food stores are "more lively, colourful and more of a show," particularly in Quebec, partially because "we can obtain more display (allowances) deals here than in the United States."

The discount stores, consistent with their strategy and cost structure, assumed a self-serve warehouse-type environment. They were almost twice the size of Petrini at 45,000–55,000 square feet of gross leasable area. Price was the key differential advantage, and many canned and dry goods were displayed in cases.

Productivity

The productivity of the United States retail stores was less than that of the Canadian operation. In 1990, Petrini was averaging approximately $400/sq.ft. compared to $475/sq.ft. in Canada and much higher for many of the franchised stores. Bussières predicted that when changes in the United States division were completed, which would include some franchising, productivity should be at least equal to that of the Canadian stores. He pointed out that generally food retailers in the United States generate more profit than in Canada.

Rents

The United States locations for both Petrini and the discount stores were largely leased and rents were generally comparable to those in Canada. The company intended to buy wherever possible in the future, as they had been doing for a few years in the Canadian market.

Franchising

Provigo's general strategy had been to franchise corporate stores. Their experience showed that franchising produced an instant sales increase of 15–20 percent. In 1990, four of the discount stores were franchised in the United States. Management intended to test two Petrini stores in 1990 but wanted to "have their house in order first."

Labour

Store level

Bussières stated that the labour market was not so tight in the United States as in Canada. Wages paid to store staff in California were generally on a par with those in Canada. A cashier, for example, after three years service would be paid the equivalent of $10/hour Canadian in both countries. Ontario was approximately 10–12 percent higher, and he also noted that wages at Petrini were somewhat higher, though this was offset by a higher gross margin.

Unlike many other United States markets, the unions in California were very strong and the contracts were tough. Workman's compensation was usually expensive and was completely paid by the employer. While a benefit package in Canada amounted to 30–35 percent of basic salary, in California it was 40–45 percent.

The quality and attitude of sales personnel differed from their counterparts in Canada as Americans had a higher regard for working in the retail supermarket environment.

Management

In Provigo's experience, the quality of management was good in the United States. Top level management was more demanding in terms of compensation, with middle management similar to those in Canada.

Products

Petrini

The Petrini stores began as meat markets in the 1930s. Since then, they had developed into full line grocery stores offering quality and choice, specializing in produce and full service meat, fish and deli products. In addition, they were known for their large assortment of wines, and some stores had take-out food and teleflorist services. They carried a selection of private label products developed through Market Wholesale but these accounted for only ten percent of their total assortment.

The discount stores

The discount stores were almost twice the size of Petrini in square footage and stocked approximately 21,000 stock keeping units including fresh meat and produce, commercial deli, bulk foods, bakery goods, dry groceries, dairy, frozen foods, liquor and general merchandise. Private label goods were purchased from Market Wholesale under the Home Garden label and accounted for approximately ten percent of grocery sales. Although other Market Wholesale customers carried the Home

Garden label, it still provided a competitive advantage to Provigo's own stores.

In addition to the private label program developed through Market Wholesale for the retail market, Provigo, along with other distributors in California, was also promoting the Nutriclean Program. Under this system seven or eight types of produce were tested each week for chemicals and pesticides. Tests were carried out in Washington, where a data bank was kept of clean producers, to which all participating members had access. Bussières noted that Canada had much tougher laws with respect to environmental standards than did the United States; however, these issues were becoming more important in California than in the eastern United States. American consumer groups were well represented, well organized and lobbied far more often than their counterparts in Canada.

The same Nutriclean system was used in Quebec, but Provigo did not advertise this fact. The Canadian public tended to be more critical with respect to environmental issues and Provigo's size and stature in the Quebec market made the company vulnerable to attack by environmentalist groups.

Regional Differences

Although some of the differences between Canada and the United States were similar to those found in California, there were a number of factors which were unique to the California market.

- The ethnic make-up is a case in point. Provigo's stores were located largely within the San Francisco Bay area having a population of approximately 6.7 million of which only 60 percent were white anglos and the balance was made up of other ethnic groups of which a large proportion were Hispanic. The latter was predicted to reach 50 percent by the year 2000. The Asian population was also significant. Provigo sourced Asia for specialties which came labelled in all languages; however, Spanish labelling was not an extensive part of the overall program.

- Unions tended to be stronger than elsewhere in the United States and Bussières commented that more patience was required when dealing with the California unions.

- Tax laws were different in California, and legal and employment regulations were difficult with regard to such issues as staff terminations and franchise agreements.
- Consumer taste differences were very significant. Bussières cited, for example, that a California store would sell four to five times more frozen food than a store in Canada and the green peas sold in Canada would not sell in California as they were too sweet.

Competition

Two major chains, Lucky's and Safeway, shared nearly half the $15.7 billion retail market. The balance of competitors were small family run regional chains and independents, like Petrini.

Safeway, an LBO with almost 25 percent market share, had a strong advertising program, 24 hour service in all stores, wide selection and good presentation. Debt service had been heavy. However, through divestitures and expense reduction, operations had improved and it was again profitable.

Alpha Beta had recently been acquired by American Stores making the combined business the largest national retailer. A number of Alpha Beta stores were converted to the Lucky banner. However, the California attorney general prevented Lucky and Alpha Beta from operating all their stores under the same advertising campaign and banners. As noted earlier, Provigo acquired the stores they were forced to sell. Lucky had traditionally been the low-price leader in the market. However, with the high debt incurred by American Stores ($2.5 billion) it was questionable whether they could continue to occupy this position. They had a strong advertising program and were focussing on expanded selection through "perimeter" departments.

Albertsons, a 30-store chain serviced by its own wholesale operation, was expanding and several new retail players had announced their entry into the market arena; Fred Meyer, Wal-Mart and Price Saver had sites in Sacramento and Central Valley.

Three area companies including Fleming, Certified Grocers and Market Wholesale largely split the wholesale business serving the small regional chains and independents. However, a recent market entrant, New Co-op, was expected to erode this market and capture a 15 percent market share. Fleming was expected to be the major loser in this competition and was retaliating by pursuing the retail business presently held by the other wholesalers.

Management in the United States

The United States operation was managed by six senior executives headed by a Chief Operating Officer in California who reported directly to Bussières, Chairman and CEO of the United States division. Of the six senior executives, one was Canadian and five were American. The Board of Directors, which met quarterly, was made up of Bussières, the CFO for Provigo, the COO of the California operation, Executive Vice-Presidents of Provigo Inc., and one President from the Canadian food operation. It was Bussières' intention to have an all-American team in the United States and to bring outside people onto the board, in particular two from California.

Developing a management team after the Petrini purchase presented a problem. Mr. Petrini, then in his late eighties, had ruled the business without strong senior or middle management. Provigo kept several of the Petrini middle managers, as well as several from Lucky–Alpha Beta, and put a Canadian in charge of the retail operation. Bussières stated that the mixing of the divergent cultures had been difficult.

Initially, Bussières was in California every ten days, but then reduced it to approximately every six weeks. When the organization was finalized, the United States president would meet with senior management in Montreal twice a year. In January, the presidents presented their strategic plan, action plan and budget, and the senior management committee met in May. The California division was operated in a relatively decentralized manner. With the exception of strategic planning and systems where some intervention from head office was necessary, Bussières felt that the other areas should be comparatively independent as were those in Canada.

Technology

There was a high level of technology in Provigo's Canadian operation; however, the United States operation was not technologically sophisticated. Bussières intended to develop the United States operation to be on a par with the one in Canada.

Future Development in the United States

The results of the United States operation were mixed. Market Wholesale and the discount stores were profitable; however, the Petrini chain suffered a large loss in 1990. The Lucky–Alpha Beta purchase proved very costly for Provigo. The stores were unprofitable to start with, violating one of the company's own rules not to buy a turnaround situation in the United States. Secondly, the change in name to Quality Plus proved disastrous, and then, when Provigo made the decision to convert them to the Petrini banner, many of the locations were unsuitable and had to be sold or closed at great expense. These problems and resultant writedowns, coupled with generally difficult retail conditions, resulted in significant losses for the year ending January, 1990.

Provigo faced several challenges over the next few years. Petrini was saddled with heavy overhead costs that had to be brought into line through cost reductions or sales expansion, allowing Provigo to turn a profit quickly enough to satisfy impatient shareholders. Provigo had owned the stores for a relatively short period of time and was forecasting a profit within 18 to 24 months.

Despite the difficulties experienced, management was positive regarding the long-term outlook in the United States and intended to expand both the discount and Petrini chains and to renovate the existing Petrini stores. Expansion to other parts of the United States, particularly in the east, was under consideration.

Free Trade

Insofar as the effect of free trade on Canadian food distribution channels was concerned, Bussières thought that it would be limited at the wholesale level. The major impact would be felt by the manufacturers, many of which were subsidiaries of American companies.

At the retail level, American food companies coming to Quebec would be at a disadvantage due to language. Bussières stated that other Canadian food retailers have shied away from the Quebec market for that same reason. He thinks it would be possible, but not likely, that United States food retailers might come to Canada. Successful entry into the concentrated Canadian market would require a concept other than that of a traditional supermarket. Superstores or hypermarkets are one possibility; however, this concept is not well developed in the United States and the Canadian market is largely covered by Loblaws in this respect. He would expect this type of entry to originate from Europe, particularly France or Germany where the hypermarket is well established. (A hypermarket is loosely defined as a food store containing an approximately equal amount of department store type merchandise, especially drugs and health and beauty aids.)

One way open to United States food retailers is discount food chains or warehouse clubs. Price Club, an American company, had already entered Canada as will be described in Chapter 7.

In general, Canadians stand to lose at the manufacturing level, and potentially gain at the wholesale and retail levels through entry into the United States where cheaper and more numerous sources of supply abound and competition tends to be more fragmented and characterized by the proliferation of smaller family firms.

Provigo Update: Two Years Later

In September of 1990, having incurred significant losses, Provigo hired an independent consultant to define the strategic options with respect to the United States operation. The choice was straightforward: stay in the United States and grow, or withdraw. Provigo chose the former, and by the year ending January 1991, Provigo's American operations generated an operating income of US$3.5 million compared with a loss of US$5.1 million the previous year. The year ending January 1992 was also positive, though due to problems in the Cost Less division it was not as profitable as 1991. Thus, despite severe economic recession in the United States, and particularly in the California market, Provigo had succeeded in turning around the United States division in less than the forecast time of 18 to 24 months.

Management was now happy with the Petrini division which had previously been the major stumbling block to their success. A new vice–president had been appointed and over 60 percent of the stores in the 18 unit chain had been renovated. The product mix was changed to some extent, and services and prepared foods were added, thus improving overall margins.

The discount operation, which had been profitable from the beginning, suffered reduced profits during 1991. Most of the reduction was due to the fact that a licensee of three of the Cost Less discount stores filed for protection under Chapter 11 of the United States bankruptcy code. Provigo took back the stores as corporate stores, refurbished them, and was in the process of rebuilding the business. During the summer of 1991, they appointed a new manager for the discount division and were very pleased with the recovery and progress of the chain. By 1992, they had seven stores and were considering opening two more within the next year.

The wholesale division, Market Wholesale, had always been profitable. It, however, had run into some problems due mainly to increased competitive pressures from competing wholesalers who had lost a number of their retail customers to a new wholesale company called Westpack. This, of course, resulted in lower sales and profits, but by early 1992, business was coming back again. A new vice-president had also recently been appointed in this division and the operation was expected to continue to show a profit.

During May of 1991, one of Market Wholesale's longstanding customers, New Deal Supermarkets, wanted to sell their chain of 13 stores. In order to maintain this customer, Provigo agreed to buy the chain with the view to selling it when it could find an appropriate buyer. This chain of smaller supermarkets was profitable when it was purchased and was still making money in 1992. Provigo was preparing to sell the stores in 1992.

On the management front, in addition to hiring new managers for each of the three divisions, Provigo had also appointed new systems and finance managers. All the management in the United States was now American with the exception of Claude Savard, President and Chief Operating Officer, who was Canadian. The mix appeared to be working well.

Provigo, as most other retailers, was feeling the pinch of the recession in both Canada and the United States. New entrants into the Canadian market, such as the Price Club, were making conditions even more challenging. Overall, sales and net income were up over the previous year and efforts were being focussed on increasing market share and reducing costs in these highly competitive markets.

As far as the future was concerned in the United States, Provigo intended to focus its growth on the Cost Less division first, with some expansion of the wholesale business. Longer term management would focus on expanding Petrini's. In the short term, all operations would be confined to the California market, which had good growth potential. Previous plans to look at opportunities in other parts of the United States had been put on hold for the time being, until market conditions improved.

LOBLAW COMPANIES LIMITED

Overview

Loblaw is the largest food distribution company in Canada and has the largest United States involvement of any Canadian food distributor. Loblaw's United States operation is the National Tea retail chain which focusses on markets in and around New Orleans, Louisiana and St. Louis, Missouri. The company has been operating in the United States for 45 years. Its executives have developed an experience base and perspective on doing business there that other executives may find illuminating. This case focusses on the restructuring and management of its operations in the United States which provide valuable insights for other companies.

In 1989, Richard Currie, the President of Loblaw Companies Limited (Loblaw), was reviewing Loblaw's United States operations. During the 13 years Currie had been president, Loblaw's United States operations had been restructured and downsized from 892 stores in 1975 to 102 stores in early 1989. Also over this period, the United States operations declined from contributing roughly a third of Loblaw's volume to comprising a fifth of the business. More importantly, however, the restructuring process had reversed the unprofitable status of the United States stores in 1976. 1989 was expected to be the most profitable year for the United States stores.

Background

Loblaw's foreign operations were rooted in Garfield Weston's strategy to expand the business outside of Canada. The natural markets for such expansion were the major English speaking countries around the world: the United Kingdom, South Africa, Australia, New Zealand and the United States. In 1933, the United Kingdom was the first foreign country entered by Weston with the acquisition of Mitchell & Muil Ltd. Subsequently, various food related businesses were acquired in Great Britain, South Africa, Australia and New Zealand.

George Weston Ltd. entered the United States in 1947 through the acquisition of a minority stock position in Loblaw Groceterias which operated stores in New York State at that time. Loblaw Groceteria Company was founded in 1919 by two partners, Theodore Pringle Loblaw and J. Milton Cork. In 1955, George Weston Ltd. obtained voting control of the company, and in 1956, Loblaw Companies Limited was incorporated as a subsidiary of George Weston Ltd.

Garfield Weston's strategy for entering markets outside Canada was based on a key criterion: The mode of entry would be through acquisition of number one competitors in their particular regional markets, not through greenfield companies or co-ventures.

The acquisitions were financed internally. The United States companies that Loblaw acquired were "friendly takeovers," and in most cases the management in place at the time of takeover were left in their positions and only replaced over time as required. Management from Loblaw Canada did not play a large part in the United States subsidiaries. As key management were left in place, the acquisitions did not require diversion of significant management resources from the Canadian operations.

In the 1960s, a corporate reorganization placed the overseas holdings under the control of Associated British Foods PLC, while the United States holdings continued to be managed by Loblaw. In 1963, Loblaw gained control of the National Tea chain of retail stores in the United States. By 1984, the holdings in South Africa had been divested.

By 1988, George Weston Ltd. held roughly 77 percent of the publicly traded shares of Loblaw. George Weston Ltd. was a diversified food and resource company with close to 60 percent of its publicly traded shares held by Whittington Investments Ltd. (Canada), a holding company owned by W. Galen Weston. Other holdings of George Weston Ltd. included Weston Foods, Weston Resources and Weston Research Centre.

In Canada, Loblaw was the number one grocery retailer in terms of sales. Return on sales had been steady over the 1979 to 1987 period, but had dipped in 1988, mostly due to a temporary dip in the profitability of Canadian operations. The only other Canadian-owned food retailers that had made a significant entry into the United States market were Provigo Inc. and Steinberg (Smitty's in Phoenix). In the United States, the Loblaw-owned subsidiary, National Tea Company, ranked 37th in terms of sales.

When Currie took over as president in August 1976, the United States operations were an integral part of the business, accounting for one-third of sales. However, at that time Loblaw's United States operations were unprofitable, and a turnaround strategy was required. In 1976, Currie began restructuring in both Canada and the United States by selling off unprofitable operations and reinvesting the cash flow in upgrading the remaining assets.

Restructuring of Wholesale Operations

The restructuring of wholesale operations had several thrusts. The first was linked to Currie's belief that control over procurement was crucial.

Creation of Intersave United States

A 100-percent-owned procurement subsidiary was created, Intersave, with a division operating in both Canada (founded in 1975) and the United States (founded in 1980). Essentially, Intersave took on a wholesaler's role for Loblaw. Intersave looked after procurement and all that it entailed: selection and management of suppliers, development and sourcing of private label brands, and ensuring that favourable discounts were obtained by purchasing at optimal quantity levels. Intersave was not involved in distribution.

Divestiture of Western Grocers Inc. (Denver, Colorado and Albuquerque, New Mexico)

Loblaw owned an 84 percent interest in a Canadian subsidiary, Kelly Douglas. Kelly Douglas in turn owned 100 percent of Western Grocers Inc. which was based in Denver, Colorado and had been acquired from the affiliated National Tea in 1976. In 1977, Western Grocers abandoned the retail market, selling 31 of its 33 stores. In 1982–83, Western Grocers' remaining assets were sold to Super Value Stores of Minneapolis.

Divestiture Of Peter J. Schmitt Company Inc. (Buffalo, New York)

Peter J. Schmitt Company Inc. had begun operations in the 1880s with a grocery store in Buffalo. Further stores were added and in 1925 the company began its food wholesale operations which ultimately became the major business. Loblaw acquired 100 percent control of Schmitt in 1975. Schmitt operated 16 corporate retail stores under the Apple, Bells and Loblaws trade names and serviced 204 franchised outlets. Its operations extended across New York and Pennsylvania and its annual sales were $1.5 billion. In 1988, Loblaw completed the restructuring of its United States operations by selling Schmitt.

In the 1988 annual report, Currie explained the divestiture as part of a capital restructuring: "While the business was solid and made a reasonable profit, it was clear that its asset base was not equal to its major competitors and that major capital expenditures with uncertain returns would have been required in any attempt to secure its future."

Restructuring of Retail Operations

National Tea was founded in Chicago in 1899 when it opened its first National food store. Loblaw's ownership in the chain began in 1956 with a minority 27 percent position and evolved into 100 percent ownership with the buyout of all minority interests by 1981. During the 1950s and 1960s, National Tea embarked on an ambitious expansion, placing itself in many diverse markets. By the start of the 1970s, National Tea had grown to become North America's 11th largest supermarket chain, but the profit performance had deteriorated so sharply that drastic action was required. In 1976, Currie made the decision to radically restructure the National Tea retail chain by paring away its unprofitable locations, so much so that by 1989, National Tea was the 37th largest grocery retailer in the United States

Rationalizing National Tea

In 1975, National Tea had eight divisions (based in Chicago, Milwaukee, Minneapolis, Indianapolis, New Orleans, St. Louis, Denver and Davenport, Iowa) with a total of 892 stores. In 1989 there were only two divisions, one in St. Louis (National Tea) and the other in New Orleans (under the Real Superstore and Canal Villere store names) with a total of 102 stores. The process of restructuring had led National Tea to divest six divisions and to exit the Chicago market where its origins and head office were located. In the two remaining divisions, only the good locations survived. The weak outlets were sold off to competitors or closed down.

St. Louis, Missouri division

The St. Louis area resembled Toronto in size, but was not as affluent. Demographically, it was similar to the Kitchener–Waterloo–Cambridge market (location of the Loblaw-owned Zehrs) in that it had a very high percentage of people of German background. The stores in this division operated under the National Tea trade name.

Over the period 1981 to 1986, Loblaw had been engaged in a vicious price war in the St. Louis market with Schnuck's (a family-run enterprise) and Kroger (one of the largest food retail chains in the United States). This price war finally ended when Kroger decided to leave the St. Louis market in 1986 and Loblaw purchased 26 Kroger outlets for $28 million. Loblaw added these stores, and their $250 million in sales, to their existing base in the St. Louis area. Loblaw closed down 12 of the Kroger outlets and renovated the remaining 14 which were then added to the 44 National Tea outlets.

The Kroger acquisition left Schnuck's and Loblaw as the leading competitors in St. Louis. The remaining competition consisted of a local discounter and a warehouse chain called Shop & Save (owned by Wetterau) and a locally owned upscale chain called Dierberg's. By 1989, National Tea enjoyed sales of over $900 million with an approximate market share of 30 percent. Schnuck's had 65 stores and a dominant share of the market, and Currie commended Schnuck's as a competitor: "A family-run business has distinct advantages over a public company. A family business can operate on cash flow and squeeze its competition on earnings in order to gain market share. The Schnuck family decided to make St. Louis their market. In the end, Kroger flinched, and we didn't."

The acquisition marked a turnaround for Loblaw's St. Louis operations. Currie elaborated on the impact of this acquisition: "In St. Louis, the 26-store Kroger acquisition of December 1986 has now been successfully integrated into the 58-store St. Louis division. There has been a steady improvement in profits in the latter part of 1988 and this is expected to continue."

New Orleans, Louisiana division

The New Orleans market was very different from St. Louis. The Louisiana economy had been decimated as a result of the decline of its key petroleum industry and New Orleans had been economically depressed since the oil decline of 1982.

In the fourth quarter of 1988, Loblaw began the process of rationalizing the New Orleans division, where the National Tea had 69 stores operating under the Real Superstore and Canal Villere trade names. Currie discussed the decision to rationalize: "Many of your company's stores are modest, conventional supermarkets struggling to compete using unionized labour in an over-stored, non-unionized, negative growth market. Recent labour concessions have been helpful, but clearly labour rates are only part of the problem. There is a small core business of conventional stores that has the potential to operate profitably even in such an environment. The four Real Superstores — in Baton Rouge, Lafayette and New Orleans (two) — provide for any growth potential. The extraordinary provision in this year's accounts ($16.7 million net of tax recovery) recognizes that a strategic reduction of our exposure to this market is required. This will involve sale or closure of a significant number of stores (25 stores) and consolidation of some administrative functions in St. Louis, enhancing the competitive position of the remaining New Orleans stores."

After the rationalization was completed, Loblaw had 44 stores remaining in the New Orleans division.

Loblaw's Performance 1976–1989

Operating income from the United States divisions had been positive since 1977, but when measured against sales and assets, profitability in the United States lagged behind Canadian performance.

By 1989, Loblaw operated in five states surrounding Missouri and Louisiana in the central–midwest region of the United States. With the St. Louis price wars over and the wholesale and retail restructuring completed, Currie had a positive outlook on the United States operations: "With the unprofitable portion of the conventional New Orleans business written off, there is a reasonable expectation that 1989 will be National Tea's most profitable operating year in the past decade."

The investment community shared Currie's optimism, as indicated by this Midland Doherty research report citing a major turnaround in Loblaw's United States operations: "In the United States, the turnaround is real, and it is one of the key reasons for our revised earnings estimate for 1990.... The big news is in St. Louis, where the situation has finally turned after several years of price war and double couponing. In fact, the company's National stores are showing very good operating margins, and we anticipate improvement over the forecast period."

Typical operating margins for United States supermarkets ranged from 2.1 percent to 2.6 percent. Currie indicated that well run chains could expect 3.0 to 3.5 percent of pre-tax profits which was the same upper range as in Canada.

Looking to the Future

Currie saw the advent of the Free Trade Agreement (FTA) as a near-term disaster that was necessary to wake up Canadians, but that in the long term promised great benefits. One important issue that had to be resolved for the grocery industry was marketing boards which numbered almost 100 in Canada, and which had led to great cross-border disparities that in many cases seemed to be nothing more than protection of profit levels for selected Canadian farmers. Currie cited the example of chicken where Canadian prices were much higher than American.

Currie saw the FTA as setting up a level playing field. The potential for the FTA to threaten Loblaw's Canadian operations was not something Currie feared, unless an American company set up retail outlets in Canada to be supplied from the United States. Currie did not see this possibility occurring but, in any event, Loblaw could easily distribute from the United States into Canada. Its store strength might also be a barrier to a United States entrant.

A competitive entry from a United States retailer would probably require that entrant to acquire an existing Canadian retailer and there were no available retailers on the market. The huge capital costs and tougher zoning regulations involved in establishing a greenfield entry into Canada acted as a significant barrier to entry.

However, major United States food retailers such as SuperValue and Tops Friendly Supermarket had recently entered the Canadian market. According to Currie, "they think they're more efficient."

Expansion of United States Operations

In 1989, Loblaw did not have plans for expansion in the United States. However, if future expansion were to occur, it would be by acquisition, not greenfield, because it would take too long to build sufficient critical mass through a greenfield strategy.

If Loblaw were considering a United States acquisition, Currie would manage all key aspects of this process. The process for selecting such a hypothetical acquisition candidate was sketched out by Currie. First, the candidate would have to be one of the best run American food retailers, all of which were family-owned businesses: "Many of the great retail businesses in the United States are all family run stores — Wal-Mart, Nordstroms, D'Agostino, Wegmans, Albertsons, Publex, Butt. But right now, the prices are too high."

Beyond the paramount price criterion, Currie's strategic agenda for a hypothetical United States acquisition would focus on the following questions:

1. What is the quality of real estate? Loblaw was not looking for hidden value, but quality of real estate was important purely from the perspective of size, location, parking and competition — "when you have good real estate, you can make it into anything!"

2. What is the size of the chain?

3. What is the density and history of the competition?

4. What are the cost structures?

Of the top five American food retailers that Currie would be interested in, the number one company, Wegmans (Rochester, New York), had the best locations and physical assets. Wegmans had big, profitable stores and had won dominant market share — "that's why we left Rochester."

Another chain that impressed him was Albertsons, the eighth largest grocery retailer in the United States ranked according to sales. Currie felt that both Wegmans and Albertsons succeeded in building the right type of stores rather than blindly pursuing market share.

Regionally, Currie wanted to avoid big United States cities located in the northeast such as New York, Philadelphia and Baltimore, with the exception of Boston. Statewise, Texas didn't appeal to Currie because of its economy, nor did California because of its quixotic laws and high labour costs — Currie preferred the American midwest.

Currie speculated that if Loblaw was taking over management of a new acquisition, he would be inclined to appoint a Canadian manager or an American who had spent meaningful time with the business in Canada. He thought that one reason for lack of success among Canadian retailers running American operations was that they hired Americans as senior management: "You have to put your known people in. Initially you will stagger. In the long term, you will build a great business. With an unknown American, if it falters, you can't fix it; if something goes wrong, you won't solve it. Location and cost structure are the most important criteria. A great merchant can't make a dog location work. Food retailing is not a merchant dominated business — it is real estate dominated. It can take 20 years to get a dog store right."

Centralization vs. Decentralization

Currie had instilled a profit orientation in Loblaw. He firmly believed in allowing his management free rein over their operations, and had decentralized the decision making surrounding local marketing strategy, merchandising display, and personnel/operations. All divisions had the authority to set their own tactics but strategies and commitment of capital had to be agreed to by Currie. Currie met with his United States managers four times a year to review financial, strategic and marketing plans.

Prior to Currie's ascent to the president's role, Loblaw lacked any centralized management of its Canadian and American operations. This factor was an important cause in the decline in performance. Currie felt that the key to any successful retail operation was centralization of the decision-making process in three areas: real estate locations, financial management and co-ordinated procurement.

Real estate locations

Real estate is where the vast majority of capital dollars are spent. Loblaws had not developed close relationships with any development companies and sought out good food store locations outside of shopping centres. "Developers used to give Eaton's or Simpson's the knock down price and make Loblaws pay more, even though we were the real traffic generators."

In Canada and the United States, Loblaw preferred to own its locations. In the previous 13 years, it had signed about 30 leases, while opening many more corporate owned stores. Loblaw had a population density goal of 50,000 people within seven minutes of their locations in urban centres.

Financial management

Control through strict financial management was key in Currie's mind. He had a series of ratios that he used to measure performance. "No one can hide from these measures."

Trading profit (a pre-tax, pre-interest, pre-depreciation measure of profitability) was the key measure, in addition to pre-tax profit divided by total assets. Loblaw targeted a pre-tax profit margin of 2.5 percent in the United States (vs. a United States supermarket industry standard of 2.1 percent to 2.6 percent) and 2.5 percent in Canada.

Since the ultimate value of labour was its ability to create value added, another important ratio to Currie was labour productivity, measured by gross margin (value added) divided by dollars of employee compensation. In 1988, Loblaw had 11,400 employees with their United States operations compared to 28,700 in Canada.

Procurement

The third area important to centralize was procurement. Buying for both Canada and the United States was concentrated through separate Intersave subsidiaries which were wholly owned by Loblaw. Currie recognized the potential for enormous corporate savings through more efficient buying: "Buying accounts for 80 cents of our sales dollar and all of our P&L dollars." Loblaw's had decided to "go it alone" and set up their own buying operations rather than forming a buying group alliance.

All United States buying was done in the United States. The Robinson–Patman Act regulated that suppliers had to offer identical deal terms to all competitors. But the United States market had changed from a purchaser's market when the Act was first drafted to a supplier's market today.

All President's Choice and Green private label products were developed in Canada, but were primarily sourced in the United States and were widely sold in the United States and Canada. Approximately 20 percent of President's Choice label products were sourced from Europe where they were shipped directly to either Canada or the United States.

United States sourcing was encouraged because there was an enormous supplier base. The United States had many factories that were dedicated to manufacturing private label products and had the capability to make products to Loblaw's specifications. One such manufacturer, Red Wing, was located just outside Rochester and featured an enormous factory almost exclusively devoted to private label manufacturing.

The bilingual labelling legislation had obstructed United States manufacturers from coming to Canada, but had not had the opposite effect on Canadian manufacturers. Loblaw occasionally shipped to the

United States its bilingual products, but American consumers did not seem to care. "We ship uniqueness, not cost."

Use of Outside Resources

Loblaw viewed design and research needs on a regional basis. Loblaw used a variety of outside resources to complement its own internal resources. Outside consultants were never used for major strategic decisions; rather, they were hired on for specific functional assistance. Consultants were used for compensation, incentive plans, warehouse design and for specific merchandising areas (i.e. delis, bakeries, fresh fish areas).

One key consultant was Don Watt, owner–operator of the Watt Group, and in Currie's view "one of the world's great store and package designers." Watt had been instrumental over the past decade in developing the unique "look" for Loblaw. Doug Tigert/Psychographics, Clayton Research, Hayes Nedved and others were utilized for market research. Currie commented: "Market research is no substitute for using your own brain. We use market research to measure the gap between where we want to be and where the public is. We want to be green, but the public see us as purple. We try to sort out how we can get the public to see us as green. Research tells us how we're making out in relation to what we want to do."

View of the Marketplace

Currie cited several key differences between the food industry in Canada and in the United States:

1. Canadian managers' lack of success in the United States has to do with failing to recognize and account for differences in the respective cultures.

2. American consumer attitudes are different from Canadians.

3. Food retailing in the United States is a regional business.

Currie felt that choosing demographically correct market areas was important. Loblaw had certain demographic criteria that it considered essential for success.

American Management

Currie was adamant that American managers running Loblaw's United States operations *must* spend significant time living in Canada before returning to the United States to manage operations. He cited Loblaw's philosophy of parent-subsidiary relationships as being that management at the parent company must know the people in the field well. To that end, Canadian executives in the information, control and buying areas had spent time in the United States. Currie explained: "We Canadians have a terrible tendency to hasten back home. Canadians are great travellers — a mile wide, but an inch deep. We must get to know people and the surrounding geography. We know what Yonge/Finch means to Toronto, but must also know the comparable location in St. Louis."

Making such management transfers was not difficult, but Currie noted that it was much more difficult to get an American to come to Canada than vice versa.

The Chairman of National Tea Company was Sheldon Durtsche, an American who had previously been the Chief Financial Officer. Durtsche had always been based in the United States but had been with Loblaw for over 16 years. The President was Harold Seitz, an American who had worked with Currie in Toronto for 11 years before being posted back to the United States three years earlier. The United States board of directors consisted of company insiders.

Currie's philosophy on management of United States operations was clear: "We are not an investment company. You have to put your people in." Currie was proud of the achievements of these managers: "We tripled profits with this duo."

Currie felt that good management was important, since retailing was a people intensive business. Loblaw sought to employ Americans in key positions with one important caveat: "There is only one thing we must absolutely have — we need a person in the United States who is imbued with Canadian culture. If an American is running the business, they must know the Canadian psyche. For example, Harold Seitz, an American who runs the United States stores, worked with me here in Canada in the real estate area for over ten years before assuming his position in the United States. If we send a Canadian down to the United States, he must get to know the United States market intimately, and must live there after having worked for us here before going to the United States. If we Canadians went to the United States and lived there, we'd do well. Retailing is a street business. You can't run an American business by remote control, as Dylex, Grafton, Canadian Tire and Campeau have learned."

Consumer Attitudes

Currie had identified several key differences between American and Canadian consumer attitudes: American consumers are better informed and more analytical concerning products, politics and making decisions.

Regional Differences

Regional differences were very important in the United States, as evidenced by the fact that there was no national food retailer. Currie elaborated: "Food retailing in the United States is very regional — you can succeed in one market, and fail 200 miles away such as the powerful Jewel chain did in Chicago and Indianapolis. In Canada, you can make something work nationwide, but not in the United States. The United States market is too big and diverse. Each United States operation has to be run as a separate business. Business in the United States is very competitive."

United States markets were characterized by very local tastes. The same was true in Canada — "Zehrs will *never* convert to Loblaws" because of the unique tastes and attitudes of the predominantly German-ethnic consumer base in the Kitchener market area. In any Loblaw outlet, the core two-thirds of products were always the same. The non-grocery areas changed (besides fixtures and design). "You can't take the Yonge St. store to a small town on the Prairies."

Currie said that when comparing Saskatchewan to Toronto, the differences were significant, but it was still possible to operate nationally in Canada. The differences were greater when comparing Toronto to St. Louis. The regional differences could be even more significant when comparing St. Louis to Los Angeles, which made it almost impossible to operate a national chain in the United States.

One other major difference between Canadian and American retail outlets was that American stores carried a 35 percent to 50 percent bigger product line. This characteristic was driven by two factors: higher expectations of American consumers and a wider selection of products available to retailers from American suppliers.

Competition

Grocery retailing was a highly competitive industry in North America, and given that price was a major competitive factor, profit margins were very thin. Key success factors for grocery retailers were dependent upon their marketing skills and their ability to meet consumer demands in price, service and product range. Canadian food retailers were considered world class competitors, and a recent government study had revealed that Canadian sales per square metre of selling space were higher than in the United States.

Loblaw did not face any of their Canadian competitors in the markets served by their St. Louis or New Orleans divisions. Rather, they competed with the regional supermarket chains present in each market. In Currie's opinion, the United States supermarket business was less competitive today than it was six years ago largely due to the trend toward leveraged buyouts.

Structurally, Currie noted that in the United States family ownership was more predominant. There were more smaller sized units with strong family players in most markets. On the other hand, the United States supermarket industry was littered with LBOs, with most of the major chains dominated by significant debt.

Currie felt that the least efficient competitors were the ones who had been involved in the biggest LBOs. One strategy to compete against a leveraged competitor and make the highest profits was to set retail prices to the levels that would satisfy the bare cash flow of the most marginal competitor. Eventually, the vicious circle of debt would cause them to forgo critical capital expenditure decisions and make the LBO vulnerable to takeover by a market leader or lead to a corporate failure. According to Currie, "You can take out these LBOs when you want to."

One strategy to forestall the competition was a program of continuing capital investment: Capital costs are one-time, but secure the future.

The time element is always forgotten. Analysts go quarter by quarter. Einstein said the fourth dimension was time. People forget this — they think now will be forever.

Merchandising of Stores

United States retail outlets were set up the same as in Canada — stores offered the same look. The prototype store model in St. Louis was very similar to the look of the Zehrs chain based in Kitchener–Waterloo, while the Real Superstores in New Orleans were similar to the Real Canadian Superstores in western Canada.

Price

Generally, prices for comparable baskets of goods were much higher in Canada than in the United States, due in part to the effect of Canadian marketing boards on price structure. Pricing strategy differed in the St. Louis market compared to that of New Orleans because different competitors and competitive realities were faced in those markets.

Product

American consumers were used to a much wider range of product lines than Canadian consumers were used to expecting. Currie elaborated: "That is the marketplace. The variety of products is staggering. The American consumer expects it. The suppliers carry more products, the warehouses are large, the stores are bigger, the merchandising is more complicated, although the inventory control is sometimes not as sharp. Kelloggs Canada does not carry the same breadth of product line as Kelloggs USA. The same is true for suppliers like Kraft and Pillsbury."

Loblaw had observed differing degrees of success with some of its recent private label product initiatives in Canada vs. the United States:

Product	Canada	United States
President's Choice Teddy's Choice	very successful	reasonably successful

Nature's Choice & G*R*E*E*N	champions of a cause
	    best edible products:
	        cornflakes
	        peanut butter
	    best non-edible products:
	        diapers, toilet tissue
		tough to get public awareness

No Name	successful	not successful

One of the frustrations in launching the G*R*E*E*N product line in the United States was building appropriate consumer awareness. The Canadian launch was accompanied by great fanfare in Vancouver and Toronto and with national television news coverage, but this could not be duplicated in the United States — "You can't introduce a product in St. Louis and get on the CBS evening news."

Promotion

Regarding advertising, Currie noted that Loblaw used more television advertisements in the United States because Americans were not as heavy readers of newspapers as Canadians. Generally, the costs of advertising were higher in Canada than in the United States. The competition in the United States featured more price-oriented appeals as opposed to value or product-oriented appeals used in Canada.

Place/Location

The availability of quality real estate was better in the United States than in Canada. Currie thought that Canadian real estate was over-regulated and had become more controlled by developers as a result.

Merchandising/Display

Loblaw's merchandising and display were unmatched in the Canadian market by any of the large supermarket chains. This same level of expertise and sophisticated visual presentation had been transferred to the United States. American stores offered a larger assortment and choice of products; however, the merchandising and display methods were not different from Canada. American stores typically offered wider ranges of goods (i.e. flowers, card shop) than were typical in Canada.

In Currie's opinion visual presentation standards were superior in Canadian stores. The only American store that came close to Loblaw's standard was Wegmans: "Across the market, there are a few good niche players, but many are awful."

Service

There were several differences cited in service delivery to customers. The level of electronic–technological introduction was higher in the United States. According to Currie, Canadian supermarkets lacked electronic data, but offered consumers a much more pleasant shopping environment. Americans' wider use of sophisticated data allowed them to pursue greater segmentation in the markets they served.

Social–Political–Legal Differences

The United States was much more litigious, leading to higher costs of business. Currie felt that the United States political, economic and social system was more process oriented, and if you had an issue to resolve, you would get a definitive answer. This led to the United States system being better understood by all the players.

Labour Market

Currie noted the dwindling pool of available, skilled labour in major Canadian and American cities. Labour costs were higher in Canada than in the United States, with the wages/sales ratio at 15 percent in Canada vs. 12 percent in the United States.

Currie cited a more co-operative business-like approach to negotiations used by United States labour leaders in general: "They understand that workers are Loblaw employees first and union members second. They understand that businesses must be successful, and that you have to make money to survive. United States union leaders are less doctrinaire than many in Canada."

For instance, in New Orleans, the company had succeeded in obtaining a rollback in wages. The unions allowed changes to be made in their contract to make it more comparable to the non-unionized competition.

Loblaw had unions to deal with everywhere they operated in the United States and in Canada (except for a few Canadian independents). According to Currie, in the union town of St. Louis, if you were not signatory to the union agreement, you needn't bother opening your store, such was the union solidarity attitude. In his view, unionization worked best in cities where everybody was unionized. In a city like Toronto, prices in non-union stores such as Knob Hill Farms were lower because they could escape the pay scales demanded by unions. Currie elaborated on the difference in labour attitudes: "Americans have a materially better work ethic. Americans don't expect all the social services that Canadians do and they are willing to work to get them. But they expect their health coverage from their company, which Loblaw's offers."

Update

By 1988, the major restructuring of the United States operations had been completed and profits were growing consistently. Sales growth was small from 1989 to 1991; however, profits rose over 20 percent in this period reaching $41 million by the end of 1991. The company had started developing private label brands for Wal-Mart and the Jewel companies in the United States.

A company-wide fixed asset expenditure of $230 million was planned for 1992 of which 25 percent was to be spent in the United States. That figure was up from 15 percent of total expenditures in 1991. At this point in time, the United States division accounted for approximately 15 percent of the total company sales, but profits were growing at a faster rate than in Canada.

St. Louis, Missouri division

The St. Louis division, which consisted of 58 stores by 1988, opened two stores in 1991 and one in 1992. The competitive square footage was increasing in this market and the introduction of wholesale club stores with perishable goods departments had changed the competitive structure. Loblaw's retail market share dropped slightly as a result of this increased competition, although it still maintained the position of second largest retailer in the trading area.

Loblaw responded to the increased competitive pressures by reducing operating costs and improving its buying and control systems. It also added new products and departments such as video rentals, and expanded its pharmaceutical lines, which led both to greater consumer appeal and higher gross margins.

New Orleans, Louisiana division

Restructuring had left the New Orleans division with 38 stores in 1988. One new superstore was opened in 1991, and another early in 1992. The new, low price, high turnover "That Stanley" chain, a U.S. version of "no frills," was earmarked for potential expansion. Competitive pressures on margins were intense in this market as well.

Canada

Profits had increased in Canada between 1989 and 1991 by over 13 percent; however, the competition was increasing, particularly in eastern Canada. American competitors Price Club and Costco had expanded into the Canadian market, Price Club in the east and Costco largely in the west. Both had entered Canada in the mid 1980s, but became a more significant factor as they expanded, particularly into the Ontario market.

Loblaw sought to maintain and expand market share and sales both through the use of strong competitive pricing and bulk packaging on key items, and through the use of varying formats in the Ontario market. The three corporate formats included SuperCentre, Loblaw's and Zehrs, and franchised independent chains included Fortino's Supermarket, no frills, Your Independent Grocer, valu–mart, fresh–mart, MR. GROCER and Hasty Market stores.

The use of different formats allowed Loblaw to serve the varying market needs. In addition, its strategy was to operate in both the wholesale and the retail sectors to minimize exposure to shifts in the industry. This strategy was the same for both Canada and the United States, but the wholesale sector was much smaller in the United States.

Reflections on the Canadian Food Retail Industry

In reflecting on the experiences of both Loblaw and Provigo, we see large, stable, well run companies that are aggressively pursuing market share in Canada. The food retail industry as a whole in Canada tends to be dominated by a fairly small number of large, strong companies of which Loblaw and Provigo are in the numbers one and two positions respectively. Both are leaders in their field in terms of environmentally friendly and safe products, Loblaw with its Green Products and Provigo's Nutriclean designated products. As perhaps another indication of this leadership position, Richard Currie was appointed Chairman of the Food Marketing Institute in Washington D.C. in 1991 and was the first non-American to chair this association. The long term strategy of the Food Marketing Institute is to strengthen consumer trust in nutrition, health and food safety.

The breadth of items offered, particularly by Loblaw, is large by Canadian market standards, and the presentation in both these companies is strong. The traditional food retailing industry in Canada is generally on a par with, or more advanced than, that of the United States. Although product variety is generally wider in many American food stores, the Canadian companies tend to be larger, vertically integrated and technologically advanced, and to present their products in a sophisticated manner. Many American food retailers are family run.

The Canadian companies appear to have developed more retail formats to cater to the needs of their various markets. It should be noted, however, that the lowest price retail format, warehouse clubs, originated in the United States. Unlike much of the rest of the retail industry in Canada which is national, the food retailing industry tends to be more regional as the market is less homogeneous when it comes to food, perhaps forcing these companies to be more market driven, and giving them an advantage in the United States that Canadian retailers from other sectors did not enjoy.

We see in Loblaw and Provigo many of the same attributes of the successful American companies: leadership, flexibility, strong competitive response and the ability to innovate. Both are successful in the United States. It is worth noting that of the six Canadian companies that are in either the hold or growth modes in the United States, two others are also in the food industry. Swiss Chalet and Manchu Wok are both food service retailers.

PART 2

·

A DIFFERENT VIEW

CHAPTER 5

WHAT WORKED, WHAT DIDN'T

ANALYSIS AND COMPARISON OF THE CANADIAN EXPERIENCES

The cases describing the entries of Canadian retailers into the United States suggest a number of factors that are important to the success of a venture in that country. We have divided these factors into two groups in order to summarize them:

- management, or internal factors, include pre–entry preparation, choice of entry mode, and management of operations;
- market influences, or external factors, consist of consumer preferences and behaviour, regional differences, the competitive environment, resource quality and availability, and other factors.

MANAGEMENT FACTORS

A. Pre-entry Preparation

The pre-entry phase includes a number of conditions, as listed below, that should exist before Canadian companies enter the United States. However, simply meeting these criteria does not *ensure* success. Also, as the Provigo case shows, an outstanding job in pre-entry preparation does not guarantee *immediate* success. In order to avoid crippling surprises, the pre-entry phase should provide a crucial base of support, information and understanding from which to launch an entry into the United States.

1. An assessment of the company to determine whether it is adequately prepared and that specific pre-entry criteria are met:

   a. A stable organization in Canada. Stress or confusion generated by domestic expansion or significant changes may prejudice the entry and be transferred to it.

   b. A well developed organizational structure and processes, and information systems that are tailored to company needs and that can support expansion.

   c. Readily available financial and managerial resources to allocate to the foreign expansion.

   d. Full commitment by management and the board of directors at the time of entry and after the American operation is in place.

2. The existence of a well developed strategic plan for the entire company which includes expansion into the United States as part of this plan.

3. A well developed strategy for entry.

4. Pre-entry research using both in–house and external resources.

5. Comprehensive understanding of:

   a. the market to be entered in the United States and the consumers there,

   b. the relevant industry segment, and

   c. the competition.

1. Assessment of pre-entry criteria

Rapid growth can destabilize a company by straining and depleting the financial and managerial resources necessary for entry into the highly competitive markets in the United States. Mark's Work Wearhouse was continuing to expand rapidly in Canada even while it was entering the United States, resulting in a depletion of resources and a constantly changing structure and organization. Coles too had undergone major

192

growth, though being a well established company with growth occurring over a longer period of time, it was more stable than Mark's. But, like Mark's, Coles did not have the necessary management resources, nor the commitment from existing senior and middle management who were expected to run the United States division in addition to the expanding Canadian operation.

However, this effect varies depending on the structure of the company. Provigo, for example, had grown rapidly ever since its inception. But this growth was largely through acquisition, unlike Mark's Work Wearhouse or Coles, and senior executives were experienced in managing diverse companies in different markets. Therefore, both the structure of a company and use of the acquisition mode for expansion can allow for more rapid growth without necessarily resulting in destabilizing changes and depletion of management resources in the home market. However, as was seen in a number of cases such as Dylex and Canadian Tire, the acquired company needs to have strong management talent in place or it has to be put in place in short order.

Canadian Tire scores favourably on the criteria in all aspects except management commitment which was strong to start out, but ebbed as United States losses affected the earnings of the Canadian operation, and consequently the pockets and enthusiasm of those in the profit sharing program (ie. most Canadian Tire employees).

2/3. *Strategic plan and entry strategy*

The existence of a well developed strategic plan is important. A carefully developed plan along with the necessary pre-plan research should be in place before United States entry is entertained. United States entry must be either integrated into or be consistent with the goals and objectives of the company, diverging only when management has carefully considered the possible consequences. Since it requires the full commitment of managerial and financial resources, the chances are increased if it is part of the corporate strategy for which senior management takes ownership. Although the presence of a strategic plan obviously does not guarantee success, chances improve when management undertakes the necessary steps to produce such a plan. This is because strategic planning requires conducting pre-plan research, formulating overall objectives and goals, marketing and financial objectives and implementation programs. The process provides a framework within which both the Canadian and United States businesses are more likely to succeed. The process should highlight the company's strengths in its home market and should lead to an examination of whether these "key success factors" are transferable to a different market.

The entry strategy needs to be carefully thought out. Insofar as deciding on an entry strategy focusses attention on the choice of entry modes and the necessary requirements for acceptable greenfield sites or acquisition candidates, it is an essential process.

In the case of Mark's Work Wearhouse, entry was first entertained as a result of a proposal by the owner of a United States advertising firm. It was at his suggestion that the company began its inquiry into sites in the Idaho and Wyoming areas and, within three months of their first meeting, opened the first store in Pocatello, Idaho. Mark's suffered from the lack of any overall plan other than a desire to expand.

Another company that did not have a well planned entry strategy was Coles. By the mid 1960s, it had saturated the Canadian market and viewed southward expansion as a logical extension of the Canadian operation. It was assumed that the United States market was the same as the Canadian market, and the identical "cookie cutter" store expansion approach was used. Coles President Bill Ardell cited this deficiency in strategic planning as one of the most important reasons for the failure of Coles United States company.

Chateau Stores and Shoppers Drug Mart reacted to opportunities presented to them or were following the lead of other Canadian retailers heading south. Peoples Jewellers, Dylex and Grafton similarly had reached the saturation point and turned to the United States for expansion opportunities.

The apparent paradox was Canadian Tire which did have a well defined strategy. In 1977, Canadian Tire had forecast that the Canadian market would be saturated by 1986 and had planned United States entry for 1981. Management explored alternative businesses and finally decided to do what they did best, "stick to their knitting" and develop a similar type of business in the United States. Although this was probably the right decision, the implementation phase did not adequately assess the demand for this type of retail offering. Management examined alternative entry modes, deciding on acquisition, for which criteria were then established. The criteria were simple, but dealt only with the physical aspects of the acquisition candidate such as the number and size of stores and existence of auto service departments. Locations, markets and management were not evaluated closely. Thus, while management had gone through the exercise of developing a strategic plan and deciding on an entry strategy, the implementation of these decisions did not take into consideration market factors that were the major cause of their difficulty in the United States.

Even though most of the companies had reached the limits to growth in Canada and wanted to continue expanding, they did not seem to have well developed strategic plans or entry strategies in order to do this. They did, however, have well developed long term visions of growth in which the United States expansion was an integral part.

Expansion or growth are not, however, strategies. Management has to determine what a company's competitive advantage is at home and what it will be in the United States. A competitive advantage in Canada may not translate into a competitive advantage in the United States. The critical question to answer is what will it do better in the United States than its competitors can do. Unfortunately, very few of the retailers who went to the United States could boast of a competitive advantage over their American competition. More will be said on this matter later in this chapter.

4. Pre-entry research

Although thorough pre–entry research is a key to success in the United States, it can be carried out in different ways. Regardless of how the information is obtained, it must result in management's in-depth understanding of the different and highly competitive nature of the United States market. Collecting data and information is only the beginning; care must be exercised in the *interpretation* of internal and external research to ensure that the right decisions are made at this crucial stage.

The quality, type, and extent of pre–entry research varied widely among the companies. On the positive side, Grafton had decided early to use the acquisition mode consistent with their overall strategic plan for growth. Several companies were available in the United States, and they conducted a thorough analysis of each. When they were offered Seiferts (their eventual acquisition) in 1978, they first carried out an extensive financial analysis, then senior management went down to examine the business and the units. They visited every one of the 50 stores, meeting with and assessing the strengths of the store managers, the locations and the markets.

Loblaw's early foray into the United States was unsuccessful in many markets and was done without the benefit of research or in–depth assessment of acquisition candidates. Over the past dozen years, senior management has gained much more knowledge of the market through frequent travel to the United States, through employing managers who have worked in both the Canadian and American operations, and through external research on various facets of the industry and market. They used a variety of external resources to complement their own internal resources, using outside expertise for specialized functional assistance rather than for strategic decisions.

Provigo's pre–entry research was outstanding. It was spearheaded by CEO Pierre Lortie and Assistant Treasurer Pierre Jette, and combined both internal and external research. Studies were conducted assessing the United States wholesale and retail markets, performances of Canadian retailers in the United States, and success requirements for United States acquisitions. Next, studies were carried out in different markets identifying acquisition candidates and the success factors for each market. Prerequisites were established for markets and candidates, taking into account such factors as the favourable presence of LBO'd competition, fragmentation of the competition, demographic profile, management assessment, etc. The development strategies of world class food distributors were examined. For each candidate, background and financial information was collected and a potential strategy was developed. No stone was left unturned. This extensive research allowed Provigo to minimize or neutralize the substantial entry barriers, especially that of competition. This research has been key to maximizing their potential for success.

Peoples' pre-entry research prior to acquiring ownership of Zale was also extremely thorough, but entirely different. First, management had direct experience in the United States through its experience with White Jewellers. The White experience introduced them to the United States and the knowledge that it was very different from Canada, that the consumers were different, and that entry barriers existed. In 1981, Peoples purchased 20 percent of Zale's stock as an investment and was allowed three seats on the board which Peoples management held for five years until it and Swarovski International purchased all of Zale in 1986. The five year membership on Zale's board gave Peoples a rare chance to gain a deep understanding of the company, its markets, its management, its problems and opportunities so that when they acquired Zale, the strategy was already clear. Zale was considered a success until recently when a combination of a severe recession and high debt load forced the company to seek protection under Chapter 11.

As for Coles and Mark's Work Wearhouse, little pre–entry research was done. In Coles' case, Jack Cole had some prior knowledge of the United States industry from a supply point of view, but little else. Mark's did conduct some demographic and competitive research before deciding on specific store sites. They set out criteria for the sites but no research was done to establish the criteria. When the research showed that there was no concept like theirs, they assumed a market void instead of questioning why the void existed.

As noted in the previous section, Canadian Tire did carry out some pre–entry research as to the type of business to purchase in the United States, searching out acquisition candidates and eventually visiting White's stores. The bulk of the consumer research actually occurred after it had entered the United States. Canadian Tire found no company with the same five product categories under one roof in the United States and assumed this meant that its retail concept would work there.

5. Understanding the United States: markets, industry and competition

A thorough understanding of the United States market, industry and competition is critical to the success of any Canadian retailer intending to do business in the United States. Unlike the Canadian market, the American market is highly regional in nature, making it essential to research and understand each area separately. Generally, the extent of pre–entry research was proportionate to the resultant understanding of the market and performance in it. However, this was not always the case as was illustrated by the Canadian Tire situation in which interpretation of the research was misleading. Obtaining information and interpreting it correctly are two different things.

Canadian management must appreciate the extent of the differences between the Canadian and American markets. If they do not possess an intimate knowledge of the market themselves, they must hire management who do. The most preferable situation is to have management who understand both cultures and markets as was the case of both Loblaw and Peoples. Although the acquisition mode was generally more successful, there is no guarantee that the management of the acquired company understands the market. This was true in the case of Provigo's purchase of Petrinis. The California chain was essentially run by Mr. Petrini who retired when he sold the stores, leaving no strong management behind.

The Grafton case was somewhat unique in that management recognized that the market was very different and difficult. This realization lead them to place a great deal of importance on obtaining a company with knowledgeable American management who understood the market. In fact, their offer for Seiferts was conditional upon James Seifert remaining as head of the company. Thus, with an understanding of the extent of the differences, Grafton minimized the potential problems through "purchasing" management who comprehended the intricacies of retailing in the United States.

B. Entry Mode

There are powerful incentives luring retailers south of the border. According to the federal government, the combined United States–Canada market is the world's largest single market, worth $5 trillion a year. However, there are also entry barriers which vary with the entry mode chosen. From the case studies in this research, it would appear that acquisitions are the preferred mode of entry. The findings indicated that the barriers to entry are considerable at any time, but are more onerous when a greenfield mode is used. A *good* acquisition gets an entering firm around most of the barriers that proved insurmountable for the companies using greenfield operations. The most significant obstacles to greenfield entry are cost, advertising and promotion, management, supply problems, competition, locations and time frame required to reach a critical mass of stores.

Entry barriers using greenfield operations

Some of the following barriers are similar to those of a small acquisition. However, the initial time and expense associated with developing an infrastructure have already been incurred in the case of an acquisition, thus reducing the magnitude of these barriers somewhat.

Cost Although not as great up-front compared with an acquisition, the costs are generally born over a longer period of time, and do not allow for economies of scale vis à vis advertising, product cost, rents, management and overhead. Since the cost structures of American retailers were found to be lower than Canadian retailers, the cost inefficiencies resulting from greenfield entries immediately put the Canadian operation at a disadvantage. This was further exacerbated by quick reprisals by American competitors using lower prices and other tactics.

Mark's experienced severe price competition especially from the traditional and junior department stores. Coles, Dylex and Shoppers all experienced severe price competition from discounters as well. Coles, which originally occupied the low price market, was undercut by the competition who retaliated with prices so low that Coles could not hope to match them and still cover their costs. Not only did the competition buy more advantageously because of their size, but their cost structure allowed them more pricing latitude. Coles' entry mode had resulted in widespread marginal locations and a higher cost structure.

It is critical to note, however, that this strategy did not always work against the Canadian entrant. Loblaw turned the tables by choosing to compete against LBO'd companies that had high cost structures due to their high interest expense. The lesson to be learned is that managing cost structures is essential for success particularly in a highly competitive market that is characterized by fierce competitive retaliation based on pricing.

Advertising and promotion It was unanimously discovered that retailers advertised more heavily in the United States than in Canada. Television, considered too expensive for all but the largest in Canada, was a popular medium in the United States. Use of the greenfield mode automatically made major advertising uneconomical for companies with a small number of units. An example of the level of advertising characteristic of an American company entering a new market is that of Lenscrafters, a chain of optical stores that entered Canada and will be discussed in detail in a later chapter. In 1989 they opened eight stores in the Toronto area and launched a major promotional campaign which included 2,000 television spots in fall 1990.

Mark's found the requirements for advertising and promotion to be very high and difficult to contend with due to its small number of stores. Coles, having 58 stores across 24 states, could not economically justify a comprehensive advertising program in any of its markets. Shoppers Drug Mart found part of the competitive reprisal to their entry was an increase in advertising which it, having a small store base, found difficult to compete against.

Management   Understanding the market is key to success in the United States. In the case of a greenfield entry, unless management already has an understanding of the market from direct experience, it is extremely difficult for Canadians to obtain sufficient knowledge in time to be able to manage a retail operation of any significant size in the United States. Consequently, it is advisable to hire American management. However, this advice is a bit of a Catch 22. As a newcomer to the market, with a lack of access to United States management and an unwillingness, or inability, to pay the top prices that high performers command, this alternative is also unlikely to meet with success. And an important lesson learned was that not any American managers will suffice.

Mark's Work Wearhouse suffered from poor American management. Although the person who ran the United States division was an American, he was not trained or experienced as a retailer, nor did he understand the market. Coles was run from Canada by management who knew very little about the United States and in some cases had not even visited the stores. A United States office was opened for a period of about 18 months with "experienced" American management, but the situation worsened during this time. The store management was also questionable. Canadian managers were not close enough to the market to know the quality of management being hired.

Shoppers suffered from lack of good management for their franchise operations. There was a paucity of pharmacists who were also trained in franchise management, unlike the situation in Canada. Shoppers also experienced honesty problems. Dylex experienced disappointment with American management in a number of the United States ventures. Provigo inherited unsatisfactory middle managers with Petrini's. On the other hand, Peoples and Grafton avoided these problems. Peoples management had direct experience, although not successful, in the United States prior to buying Zale. Also, some of the American managers who had worked in the first acquisition returned to Canada when Peoples left the United States and contributed their knowledge and expertise to Zale operations. Zale, being the largest jeweller in the United States, had a cadre of talented managers to draw on. Grafton investigated its acquisition in excruciating detail and focussed heavily on the quality of the management in the stores.

Canadian Tire learned in White's that a poor company that has been losing money for a period of time loses its best management and has a difficult time attracting new, qualified managers.

Finally, against this backdrop of Canadian retailers having difficulty finding or attracting qualified American managers, we must note that many of the executives interviewed in this study commented that the American competition was loaded with experienced, talented managers and merchants.

Locations　Good locations are one of the most crucial prerequisites for retail success in any market whether the entry is greenfield or acquisition. A firm with a poor store base is probably doomed to fail, even if all the other elements are in place. Since the United States retail market has reached maturity, many regions are saturated and good locations are difficult to find. Management Horizons, a division of Price Waterhouse, estimated that in 1988 the United States had 40 percent more retail capacity than its population needed. This difficulty in securing prime locations is particularly real for a new, unknown company entering the market and competing with well established American retailers for the few good sites available.

In Coles' case, the company grew to 58 stores in the 20 years following their entry in 1965. During this same period, Dalton's and Walden's grew to 746 and 940 stores respectively, occupying the prime shopping centre locations. These two chains were owned by retail giants Dayton Hudson and Carter Hawley Hale which gave them substantial clout with the shopping centre developers. For the most part, Coles was offered only the marginal locations, or when a good site became available, they were forced to bid too high for it. Similarly, Mark's Work Wearhouse, Shoppers Drug Mart and Peoples (the first entry with White Jewellers) had difficulty finding good locations.

Provigo, on the other hand, used the greenfield mode to launch their discount store operation and did not experience difficulty in obtaining locations. Though the chain was small, it was profitable. The difference in this case is that the sites were in freestanding locations, not in major shopping centres. Hence, the type of site sought, the quality of its location, and the competition determine the level of difficulty in obtaining suitable sites. Although these factors are always at work, they are more difficult to overcome with a small greenfield operation.

Supply problems   Obtaining the right product at the right time and at competitive prices is a potential obstacle for greenfield operations. There is not only the initial learning process to develop the right sources, but the small size of the operation can mean a lack of buying power resulting in purchasing terms less advantageous than those received by the larger competition. Existing American retailers have built relationships with their suppliers over a period of years. Relationships do not develop overnight, particularly when a company is not important to its potential suppliers.

Coles had a United States supply base before entering the market and received good terms from the start. Later, however, as the competition surpassed it in size, Coles' terms deteriorated compared to those of Dalton's, Walden's and several other large competitors. Mark's experienced a number of supply problems. It could not obtain the same products as in Canada and could not buy as well as the competition. Although it did bring in some products from Canada, the transportation costs made this situation too expensive. Instead of pursuing a private label program, they promoted brand names which the competition could buy more cheaply.

Provigo and Loblaw did not encounter any supply problems in the United States due to their vertical structure. Their wholesale divisions bought for and supplied products to the stores. Thus, the supply barrier is partially a function of the structure of the retail company. Some control of supply is essential either through buying power or control of the source of supply.

Competition The speed and intensity of competitive reprisal by the American competition caught most retailers by surprise and is a major barrier to greenfield operation in the United States. There is little chance of entering a United States market unnoticed by the competition. They are ready to fight immediately to defend their market share. Much of the competition is indirect and may be overlooked by the greenfield entrant.

Time frame The time required to enter and reach a size to become successful in the United States using the greenfield mode is very lengthy. There is an extended strain on financial and management resources, and owners and management may become disenchanted losing enthusiasm and commitment to the venture.

Coles operated in the United States for 20 years before selling to Walden's. Many of those years it operated at a loss. Toward the end, when the Canadian division was also losing money, it placed considerable strain on management and financial resources and hastened the decision to sell the United States operation. In the case of Mark's, the early 1980s were a difficult time for the Canadian operation which was losing money in Canada as well as in the United States.

In summary, a company starting up in the United States with a greenfield operation faces substantial hurdles. It takes longer to develop sufficient critical mass and costs more than anticipated or planned for. This means that it is difficult to make advertising efficient or to maximize purchase terms with suppliers. This is often compounded by not having Canadian management in place who know the market and the difficulty of building a strong indigenous management team. The new entrant may experience extreme difficulty securing good locations in a mature, competitive market since they lack leverage with shopping centre developers. There is some indication that freestanding or strip mall locations may be easier to secure in the United States than in Canada, particularly if purchasing rather than leasing. It is worth noting that one of the most successful United States retail expansions of the 1980s was Toys R Us, which pursued a policy of purchasing freestanding locations typically located on the edge of major shopping centres. Not only did it have a strong real estate base, but it was independent of the major developers as well as tenancy constraints and rising rents.

Barriers using acquisitions

Most of the barriers discussed above also exist with the acquisition mode, but potentially to a lesser extent. However, another major obstacle exists for acquisitions, namely the availability of a suitable candidate.

Availability of a candidate   The research shows that success is unlikely if the candidate is unprofitable. If an American had not been able to turn the company around, then it is unlikely that a Canadian can. In each case where an unprofitable company was acquired, major problems or failure resulted. Canadian Tire's purchase of the money-losing White's chain ended in its sale at a large loss. When Grafton purchased La Vogue and Beverley's, both of which were losing money, through its United States chain, Seiferts, numerous problems were encountered. La Vogue took four years to turn around, and Beverley's was useful only for its locations. Thus, the first criterion for a suitable candidate should be profitability. There are a number of other general criteria which the research showed to be desirable, and which, if satisfied, could minimize problems with other entry barriers. Some of the lessons learned by executives in this research include:

- buy a sound, established and profitable company,
- consider smaller companies since they tend to be less expensive as measured by the price earnings factor,
- if affordable, buy a market leader,
- never buy a turnaround situation,
- buy a company with good management,
- ideally, purchase a company in close proximity to the Canadian operation,

- look for companies in a fragmented market, ie. where the top five competitors hold less than 60–65 percent of the market and no one is disproportionately high or greater than 20 percent, and
- choose a candidate in an economically diversified market.

Cost   Although the cost of a greenfield entry is protracted, acquisition extracts a very high price up front. A survey of sales in the United States by Provigo showed that the price paid for acquisitions varied from 15 to 35 times earnings producing an average of 20 times. Provigo's Pierre Jette observed that LBO's had driven up prices supported by the availability of junk bond financing and relatively low interest rates. Foreign buyers had also contributed to the high prices. Generally, the larger the firm, the higher the pricing. Since the junk bond market has fallen into disrepute over the past couple of years, prices have abated somewhat; however, they probably would still be significantly higher than in Canada.

In order to satisfy all or most of the prerequisites, the price is often felt to be too high for a Canadian company to gain access to the United States through acquisition. The return from the acquired company must be sufficiently high to cover interest costs in addition to providing a reasonable return over time. In an industry where the return on investment is typically in the neighbourhood of 8–12 percent of net sales, future anticipated returns do not always justify the required high expenditure. Proforma financial statements should be completed forecasting realistic returns for the acquired company so as to ensure reasonable expectations on the part of management. Failure to do so can mean disenchantment and loss of management commitment which is so crucial to success in the United States.

The Peoples case demonstrates how the high cost factor was initially overcome through innovative financing and subsequent financial planning. Through a joint venture with Swarovsky International Holding, the skill of Drexel Burnham Lambert Inc. who arranged the financing, and the use of Zale's assets, Peoples managed to purchase a leadership position in the United States market. In addition, financial targets were set high enough to cover interest costs in order to provide a reasonable return on investment. Everything seemed to be in place and under control until the lean years of 1990 and 1991 arrived and retail sales proved insufficient to produce the profit necessary to meet interest payments. Peoples experienced this same problem with its first acquisition in the United States. Dylex also had the same problem.

Management   Strong management is one of the prerequisites for a successful acquisition. For example, when Provigo purchased Petrini's, there was no strong middle or senior management except for Mr. Petrini who retired upon the sale of his company. Provigo thus had to build a retail management team having had little previous connection to the retail market. This, along with extensive renovations and the purchase of some stores from Lucky–Alpha Beta, many of which were marginal, resulted in a loss for the Petrinis chain. Dylex had the reverse problem with Brooks. Management stayed with the chain but had apparently lost their motivation as a result of the generous cash-out. Canadian Tire similarly had problems.

Advertising and promotion   The acquisition mode does not eradicate this entry barrier, but generally the acquired company is prepared for the extensive advertising and promotion expenditure required in the market and will already have a program in place. The competition may increase coverage in response to a new entrant. An instance of the acquisition mode not removing this entry barrier was in the case of Canadian Tire where White's locational base did not allow it to advertise efficiently.

Locations   Although the acquisition mode provides a company with an existing store base unlike the greenfield mode, it does not, of course, guarantee that the locations are good. Such was the experience of Canadian Tire in the acquisition of White Stores. Many of the stores were in local neighbourhoods as opposed to prime commercial malls. Some trading areas had large Hispanic populations who were not attracted by the product mix of the stores. A further hindrance to success was the insufficient concentration of stores in suburban areas to capitalize on advertising exposure. Although acquisition had allowed Canadian Tire to gain a fast foothold in the market, a substantial benefit over greenfield entry, the poor quality of the locations was a major reason for its failure.

Grafton's purchase of Seiferts, on the other hand, provided it with a good, if small, 50 store base. Management had visited every store to assess the locations and store management before purchasing the company.

Peoples purchased a huge and strong store base which required little paring. Loblaw, on the other hand, had purchased some marginal locations through the years, and was forced to close many during the last ten years.

Supply   Supply problems, often a stumbling block for greenfield entries, are generally not so for acquired companies. The acquisition of a successful company can remove this obstacle. The structure of the supply base varies by industry. For example, the food industry tends to be vertically integrated with wholesale and retail ownership under the same roof. The apparel industry is partially vertical with retailers often making purchasing arrangements to their own specifications with several independent manufacturers. Other industries may purchase directly from manufacturers' own lines.

Provigo already had a supply base (Market Wholesale) set up through its original Loeb purchase, and Loblaw started a wholesale division. The vertically integrated structure of these two companies was an advantage in the new environment; however, the benefit of this type of structure varies by industry. Zale had a manufacturing arm which was subsequently closed after it was purchased by Peoples. While many advantages exist, particularly cost and continuity of supply, the danger of owning a manufacturing division is that the retail arm can become supply-led as opposed to being market-led.

Due to the highly competitive nature of the retail apparel sector, some vertical integration is often necessary in order to differentiate the product offering from that of the competition. The retailers may not own manufacturing facilities, but would purchase product made to their own specifications from a number of different independent factories with differing capabilities.

In the food industry in the United States, suppliers and products are more numerous and lower priced than in Canada, largely due to the differences in government and marketing board mechanisms. The abundance of supply is particularly advantageous in the United States market as Americans demand a far wider variety of products than do Canadians. For the most part, goods could be bought locally within the region of operation, thereby minimizing transportation costs. This latter benefit applies to regionally concentrated companies, but is lost for those spread over a large area.

Competitiveness in the United States is an advantage from a supply point of view, typically yielding numerous sources and good prices. In situations where the supply base does not already exist or is not known, an extensive learning process, as is the case in a greenfield entry, will be required to access the market, and should be considered in the early planning stages.

Competition This most important barrier remains a very strong deterrent in both greenfield and acquisition entries. Through careful research and adherence to the acquisition prerequisites, competition may be lessened or neutralized. Various acquisition experiences illustrate different ways of dealing with the competition.

Grafton's purchase of Seiferts with its strong management and locational base lessened the potential effect of competitive reprisal. Through purchasing a leadership position in the market, Peoples dominated the competition through Zales. Provigo minimized the effect of the competition by buying in a fragmented market and occupying two positions (upscale and discount) through its two chains. Selective positioning and choice of market thus lessened the likelihood of potential competitive reprisal. Loblaw had some 800 stores in the United States in the 1970s. During their rationalization process, they withdrew from areas where they could not compete and concentrated on others where they had an advantage.

Time frame Understandably, the length of time required to achieve success in the United States is generally shorter when employing the acquisition mode than for greenfield with a significant proviso. The acquired company must be profitable or the turnaround time may be as protracted as for greenfield entry. In the Canadian Tire case, Whites, purchased in 1981, was still losing money by 1985 and was finally sold in 1986. Mark's Work Wearhouse greenfield entry and withdrawal covered approximately the same time span. Grafton and Peoples, on the other hand, purchased profitable companies and made a reasonable return right away.

C. Management of Operations

The third important internal factor determining performance in the United States market is that of managing the United States operation in terms of deciding on the level of centralization vs decentralization and the use of Canadian or American managers.

Those companies that took a largely decentralized approach to management were the most successful. This does not mean laissez-faire, however. Management involvement in all the successful companies included the senior level dealing with largely strategic issues, while the day to day operation was carried out by local management. In the case of Loblaw, Provigo, Grafton and Peoples, management was committed to the American division and was prepared to spend time and financial resources to make it work. Irving Gerstein, CEO of Peoples, spent two days per week in the United States. The CEOs of both Loblaw and Provigo visited the United States frequently and were well aware of the many differences in the market. Perhaps the least involved were the Grafton senior executives who relied heavily on the strong United States management team, particularly James Seifert, previous co-owner of their United States acquisition.

Coles and Mark's lacked sufficient senior and middle management resources and willingness to spend time in the United States. It was viewed as taking time away from the more important Canadian business. Even though this was the case, Canadian management was responsible for many of the day to day decisions.

At the middle management level, however, where Canadian managers were involved, decisions were often made with a lack of understanding of the United States market particularly on critical marketing and merchandising issues. All Coles district managers were Canadian at the outset; purchasing was done by Canadian buyers who had never seen the United States stores; merchandising methods emanated from Canada; and the advertising and promotion program (small as it was) was planned in Canada. In the case of Mark's, all the merchandising and marketing decisions were made in Calgary, and the first store was even run by a Canadian. Senior management spent very little time in the United States. Canadian Tire sent four Canadian executives to the United States to run the United States division. Later 22 Canadian dealers were sent down because they understood, and were trained in, the Canadian concept.

In breaking down the areas of centralization by function, it can be seen that the more successful companies had the fewest centralized functions. In particular, each firm that centralized the marketing and merchandising functions (ie. marketing and merchandising decisions were made in Canada) was unsuccessful. Necessary to success, however, is the consolidation of the strategic planning and financial budgeting process. In fact, these were the only two areas of integration in the case of Grafton and Peoples. Peoples' senior management were far more involved than Grafton's, but the involvement was confined generally to the strategic level.

Loblaw's Currie felt strongly that the integration of the real estate and procurement functions was a major success factor for the company. This latter is more likely to be true where the regional base is small and additional purchasing power is useful. Provigo did not find any need to centralize purchasing with their California operation so this factor appears to vary by company size and region.

Currie felt it was extremely important to Loblaw's success that American senior management were imbued with the Canadian culture as well as Canadians being knowledgeable about the United States market. As such, he put Americans in senior positions in the United States who had spent time working in the Canadian operation. Due to a lack of strong management in Provigo's United States acquisition, Bussières was forced to send two Canadian managers to the United States until they could be replaced by qualified Americans.

Peoples' senior management were highly involved in the United States operation. Gerstein led Zales through the process of restructuring and repositioning immediately after the takeover. He and two other senior executives had sat on the Zale board for five years prior to the purchase. Eventually, Canadian Tire sent an executive who was born in the United States and had significant experience there as the senior person responsible for marketing and it also hired a highly qualified American to be president of White Stores.

In summary, there are several key areas where centralization is indicated:

- strategic and financial planning.
- procurement. In some cases it is best to centralize this function so as to obtain the best terms, but this varies with the size of Canadian and United States operation, type of industry, region and knowledge of markets.
- real estate — at least some Canadian intervention is recommended.
- systems — some integration is necessary so as to facilitate the flow of information between the American and Canadian operations.

And some areas where de-centralization is indicated:

- marketing and merchandising should be left largely to indigenous management who know the market best.
- procurement should be combined only where the intricacies of the markets are understood by the buyers, and the benefits clearly outweigh the potential hazards.

Regarding the use of Canadians or Americans, the lessons seem pretty clear. It is essential that senior and middle level management understand the market. The issue really is not the nationality of the management so much as the direct experience managers have in the American market. "Bi-cultural" executives, those who have lived in both countries and who have had experience in both countries, are more likely to be successful. This assumes a high level of expertise because living and working in the two countries is not a simple substitute for expertise.

Canadian senior executives must be involved with the United States company and willing to spend sufficient time in the United States. However, it is probably preferable that Canadian middle management not be involved with the United States company on a day to day basis or in an important decision making capacity unless they meet the criteria set out above. They could be sent to the United States to develop the experience and understanding that is required of managers who manage companies that operate across national borders. Operational and most administrative tasks tend to require a close knowledge of the market and are best left to *qualified* American management who can respond to local conditions. This is especially important because of the intense and fast changing competitive environment as well as the highly distinctive nature of the different regions.

It is also important wherever possible to imbue American manage-ment with an understanding of Canadian culture as well as Canadian management with that of the United States.

Lacking individuals who fit the criteria, the development of a cross-cultural team was seen to be effective.

MARKET FACTORS

The following section describes the market influences which surfaced as being key to the success or failure of Canadian retailers in the United States.

A. Consumers

American consumers were found to be quite different from Canadians. Although it is difficult to generalize about American consumers since they vary from market to market, our research uncovered substantial agreement about several distinguishing characteristics.

- American shoppers expected and demanded a far deeper and more specialized product offering, rather than a generalized product mix.

- They tended to be more price sensitive than Canadian consumers and were generally sophisticated comparison shoppers. This was largely as a result of the intense retail competition that focussed very heavily on price. The American shopper has come to expect to be rewarded for comparison shopping.

- They tended to shop in different places than Canadians. In Canada, consumers will shop at national chains more so than at an independent. Americans shopped anywhere the deals were.

- They expected and received higher levels of service than Canadians.

- They demanded more convenience than Canadian shoppers.

- They had different tastes than Canadians, which also varied by re-gion, and tastes that changed rapidly.

- They had a stronger propensity to buy. In Canada, saving is more highly valued.
- They expected heavy retail advertising that focussed on value. In many areas, literacy levels were low requiring television instead of print advertising.

B. Regional Diversity

Many people have likened marketing in the United States to doing business in a number of different countries. Vast differences exist between the very temperate South Atlantic region, the intemperate West North Central and the Pacific Coast, for example. Not only are climatic variations pronounced, but populations vary with high concentrations of Hispanic people in some areas, African-Americans in other areas, and pockets of European and Asian ethnic groups — Germans in St. Louis and Japanese in San Francisco, to name two. The physical and demographic distinctiveness of the regions also bring other differences such as values, ethics, laws, degree of litigiousness, political leanings, customs, and merchandise requirements, all of which require an extensive learning process on the part of the retailer.

For marketing purposes, the United States is often divided into nine separate regions, namely: Pacific, Mountain, West North Central, West South Central, East North Central, East South Central, New England, Middle Atlantic, and South Atlantic. Five of the regions *each* contain a population larger than that of Canada. For the most part, retailers have been regionally concentrated with few national chains, although this is changing. This has allowed each one to focus the attention required on its own market, occupying key niche positions. The large retail conglomerates such as Allied Stores, Associated Dry Goods, Dayton–Hudson and May Corporation, to name a few, tend to own a combination of department stores and specialty stores, sometimes as many as 15 or 20, each catering to different segments of the market. The independent retailer is still the backbone of the market, making up almost 80 percent of all retail establishments and accounting for just over 50 percent of all retail sales. This includes franchises which account for 30 percent of American retail sales.

Regional diversity in terms of demographics, ethnic makeup, consumer tastes and attitudes, economic base, climate and many other factors is pervasive in the United States. As one executive noted, markets could differ dramatically in a radius of 30 miles. The existence and potential effect of this diversity should not be ignored by companies entering markets in that country. Although the regions of Canada exhibit diversity, there was felt to be a stronger similarity in the Canadian market as a whole than existed in the United States. The value systems in politics and economics in the United States were found to be more diverse than in Canada, which is generally regarded as a homogeneous market. Values varied more moving from west to east (ie. Los Angeles to New York) than moving from north to south (ie. Vancouver to Seattle).

Each region must be treated as a separate entity in terms of pre-entry research and ongoing management. A correct concept for one area could be unsuccessful in another. This was evident in Loblaw's case where it was forced out of certain markets due to intense price competition, while on the other hand it did very well in St. Louis partially due to the large German population. Loblaw turned a geographically scattered and unprofitable company into a profitable operation through developing regional "critical masses" in demographically correct markets.

Company size and critical mass

Size of the company did not necessarily dictate performance outcomes, although small companies generally had fewer financial and managerial resources to commit to major expansions. Two small companies (by United States standards) failed, while two others succeeded. Large companies also failed. However, there did seem to be a correlation between critical mass, or market concentration, and success. Although the company size may be small, as long as there is sufficient market concentration, the chances for success are increased.

Market heterogeneity led to lower sales in certain cases where there was insufficient market concentration. This was true in certain stores and regions for Coles, particularly in areas with a large Hispanic population. The impact was negative partially due to inappropriate selection and lack of regional concentration, making it difficult to cater to each market's requirements. Canadian Tire found that markets even within a few miles of each other could vary dramatically. There could be widely varying degrees of literacy, and racial, ethnic and language differences. It was also noted that in any one geographical region there were three markets at work: a national one, a regional one, and one based on local climate. One of the major drawbacks to Canadian Tire's White chain was the lack of concentration in suburban markets.

Although Grafton largely concentrated in the mid west, it found the demographics to vary considerably even within the region, particularly between large and small population centres. The large centres supported highly specialized retailers while broader assortments were acceptable in the smaller centres. Grafton managed the situation by varying their strategy by market and retreating to the smaller markets when they found their assortment to be less successful in the larger urban areas.

Mark's management noted that even in markets where the demographics were similar to those in Canada, it didn't mean that the tastes and values were the same. In fact, they were quite different when it came to styling, colour, assortment and price preferences. Both Loblaw and Provigo sought regional concentration thus enabling them to develop a strong niche market orientation focussing on their distinctive target markets.

Regional diversity can have a negative impact on performance especially on companies that are not regionally concentrated. Regional concentration allows a retailer to focus attention on the target market and develop niche marketing concepts that are demographically correct for the area. In addition, effective advertising is almost impossible without clustering stores. Regional concentration or critical mass permits developing regional leverage such as in the following areas:

- better buying power (sources are often regional),
- advertising efficiencies,
- warehouse and distribution efficiencies,
- efficiencies of regional management,
- unionization or lack of same, and
- store format development for homogeneous target market.

C. Competition

Competition is one of the most important market factors to be dealt with in entering the United States. In this mature market, the number of competitors and the speed and intensity of competitive reprisal surprised most of the Canadian retailers. All the companies found the United States competitive situation to be extremely intense and price oriented. Loblaw was forced to flee some markets where it could never be competitive. This was also one of Coles' main reasons for leaving the United States. Provigo also experienced intense competition, largely caused by new entrants to the market. However, Provigo's pre-entry planning and choice of retail concept lessened the negative impact.

The competition was not always among like companies, or intra-type competition; rather it was often inter-type, or among different types of retailers by product line. Mark's, for example, found that while no other store had the same concept, other stores carried its product lines but in more depth. Management found that it was very difficult to differentiate their offering. The consumer did not require their breadth of assortment, competitors undercut their prices, were better at advertising, and had superior service. Although in Canada the keys to their success were assortment, price, service and advertising, none of these could be implemented to advantage in the United States.

Canadian Tire also found the competition to be indirect, but extremely intensive. Unlike in Canada where Canadian Tire faced little competition, in the United states it came from unexpected areas. Its major competitors included Sears, Wal-Mart, and K Mart, who forced White Stores to have a higher than average promotional content, and to double their advertising budget from three percent to six percent of sales. White's was not successful enough to invite strong competitive reprisal, but management felt that if it had been, it would have been very intense. Typically the competition had a lower cost structure and competed hard for market share.

Because of the large size of Zale, Peoples effectively purchased a large part of the competition. Even so, management felt the United States company had to be far more competitive than in Canada. They observed that, unlike in Canada, no product was unique in the United States. If it was not already there, the competition would copy it immediately. They also noted the high degree of specialization that the large American population base supports. The retail offering had to be very clear and focussed.

All the companies that failed to react to the competition were unsuccessful. Early on, Coles had almost solely occupied the low price position in the market. However, over the years it allowed its position to be undercut by the competition. Coles hardly seemed aware of the situation and made little or no attempt to counter. Mark's did not understand that its major competition was inter-type, often in the form of department stores. Management also thought the competition was foolish to sell goods so cheaply. What Mark's management did not understand was that competitive cost structures were also lower, thus allowing competitors more pricing latitude.

In the Canadian Tire case, much of the competition was also inter-type and was very intense. In response to the competition, Canadian Tire increased their advertising from an average of three percent of sales to six percent and changed to a 40 percent television advertising content. It also reacted to the K Mart entry into the do-it-yourself market by deemphasizing some areas and expanding others. The merchandise mix was too shallow and the competition covered each product in more depth.

In the more successful companies, swift competitive action was taken where necessary. Seifert's was forced to cut prices and tried to buy from Asia in order to protect margins. In Loblaw's case, price competition was found to be very intense in most markets. In the St. Louis market it endured a five year price war before the competition gave up. Loblaw exited other markets where management felt they could not compete on a long term basis.

In summary, the following were found to be characteristics of the competitive environment in the United States:

- It is highly fragmented with proportionately fewer national chains than in Canada.
- It is far more intense and price oriented.
- It is largely based on market share.
- Retaliation is faster and more vigorous.
- Competitors fight harder for the best sources of supply, best locations through bidding up good potential sites, advertising domi-

nance, and very often for price leadership depending on the commodity.

- Product exclusivity is short-lived as the competition will copy it very quickly.

- Competition, although severe, is not taken personally. It is not unusual for companies to actively try to put competition out of business. It is all part of the game and to the naturally aggressive American mentality, not seen as unfair.

- It tends to be a very specialized, niche approach with narrower and deeper assortments, generally lower prices, margins, and cost structures than Canadian retailers.

- There is a higher service orientation than Canadian retailers have.

- There is a high percentage of promotional items and high levels of intense hard sell advertising.

D. Labour Market

The supply, quality and cost of the labour force was generally a positive factor. Retail selling was regarded more highly as a profession in the United States than it was in Canada, where it was often seen as a stepping stone to something better. Americans generally expected lower pay and fewer benefits than Canadian retail sales staff except in California.

The American work ethic appeared stronger partially due to fewer government support and benefit programs, and a higher commitment to work and achievement. Although in general retailers commented on the prevalence of an excellent work ethic, there appeared to be some regional differences. Grafton found that the work ethic was not as strong in parts of Michigan where Seifert's purchased the Beverley chain as it was in the other states in which they operated. Shoppers Drug Mart was not satisfied with the work ethic of employees in Florida.

Wages offered in the retail sector were generally lower than in Canada with the exception of California. The latter appears to be a regional aberration as Provigo found wages in California to be similar to those in Canada, but also found benefits to be higher, unions to be stronger and more demanding, particularly with respect to legal issues. In the experience of the other companies, wages and benefits were lower.

Unions, where present, were generally more conciliatory and business oriented than in Canada. California was an exception to the above, as noted. Labour in the retail food industry was highly unionized, whereas many other types of retail industries were not. The extent and strength of unions varied by region.

Peoples' senior management observed that American employees were more individualistic and operated more independently than Canadians, whereas consensus management was more important in the Canadian system. Canadians were felt to be more formal in their business dealings, typically exercising European restraint. Coles' management observed that Americans were more achievement and success oriented and willing to take more risks than Canadians.

E. Other Factors

There are a number of other elements in the American business environment that make it different from that of Canada.

Legal

In general, Canadian management found the United States to be far more litigious. While the consequences were minimal in most cases, Provigo experienced complications and additional expense with respect to employee terminations and franchise agreements. Workmen's compensation and insurance were very costly as customers and employees sued frequently for minor injuries. Shoppers Drug Mart found that equal opportunity was an issue in hiring and that this resulted in more litigation.

New entrants should be aware of the highly litigious nature of the United States market and should plan for additional time and expense. There are international legal consultants who provide specialized services and information in this area. Franchise regulations are different in the United States and should be researched well ahead of any planned entry.

Economic factors

Economic factors had a negative effect on most of the companies. While the worldwide economic slowdown of the early 1980s had an adverse effect on business generally, certain areas were particularly hard hit. The downcycle in the oil and gas industry hurt Loblaw's performance in the New Orleans area, Mark's in Utah, and Canadian Tire's White Stores, especially in Texas. Drought in Texas and the devaluation of the Mexican peso added to the woes of the White stores.

The farming communities also suffered from depressed prices such as in Idaho, where a number of the Mark's stores were located. The midwest farm economy was hard hit, the severe agricultural conditions proving very difficult for Seifert's which had 30 percent of their stores located there. The result was increased competitive pressure on prices and higher occupancy costs.

While strong growth in the California and the sunbelt markets provided Provigo and the Whites stores respectively with a good sales opportunity, it also attracted many new players resulting in intensified competition. In the future, Provigo would not seek out high growth areas, and Canadian Tire felt that the competition was too fierce.

The recession of the early 1990s severely impacted almost all retailers in the United States and Canada and drove many of them such as Peoples and Grafton into receivership.

While the findings of this research indicate that regional concentration is a key to success, the potential for negative impact of regional economic factors must be recognized. It becomes very important to choose regions and states with a diversified economic base, and to assess the competitive situation carefully before entering an area of high growth.

Political

The political situation had little perceived effect on most of the companies studied. In Coles case, the Californian tax laws provided some difficulty. Provigo found lead times to be very long in obtaining permits from the local government, and Loblaw found the political process generally better than in Canada, though somewhat lengthy. However, Allan Gotlieb, one of Canada's previous ambassadors to the

United States, believed that many Canadian firms entering the United States were very naive in their assessment of the political climate. Although his experience covered a broad industry base, not confined to retail, he stressed that success was often highly dependent upon a good understanding of the political process, employing a well connected lobbyist, and where possible, having a point of leverage with local government figures.

He noted that competitors were always trying to achieve strategic advantage through the political process. In addition, there were certain states not considered hospitable due to close alliances between competitors and key political figures.

While the findings are far from conclusive, it does appear that the political process should be assessed before entry. Gotlieb strongly recommended that Canadians intending to enter the United States should conduct a political environment study including such topics as:

- key political figures in intended state(s) of entry and their stand on pivotal issues.
- understanding of major issues, eg. unemployment, pollution, slow growth, etc.
- local attitudes.
- knowledge of the political process.
- level of competition and, where possible, their political ties.

Technological expertise

While the level of technology in the market was not mentioned as a major factor influencing performance of Canadian retailers in the United States, it is often assumed that Canadian systems are far behind those of the Americans. In the cases studied, the level of technological expertise in the United States was not found to be uniformly higher than that of Canadian companies, but varied by company and industry. However, well developed systems can provide great advantage in the United States market due to its highly segmented nature. Such systems allow for tighter inventory control which is especially important in light of the depth of assortment demanded by American consumers. In addition, they provide the mechanism for reading and responding to different local market conditions, a great advantage in this diverse and highly competitive retail environment.

Provigo in Canada had more advanced technology than its United States acquisition and a number of other companies in the California market. Loblaw's Currie felt, however, that in general, Canadian supermarkets lacked electronic data, but offered consumers a much more pleasant shopping environment. Americans' wider use of electronic data in the food industry allowed them to pursue greater segmentation in the markets they served.

Canadian Tire was very advanced technologically in the Canadian market, using robotics and computerized inventory and cataloguing. It had been their intention to transfer this technology to the United States operation. Coles and Mark's were generally at a disadvantage to the market, and in Coles case, this resulted in an inefficient inventory control system.

WHAT REALLY HAPPENED — SYSTEMS AND BARRIERS

Simple and single explanations

Observers of the retail failures and many executives who have been in these situations often explain the outcome by pointing to certain events. The reasons usually are the tangible, observable "mistakes" that are easy to see with the benefit of hindsight, but may not be so easy to see while standing in the present and looking toward the future. They are of the "what happened," "what they did wrong," "what they missed" genre of explanation. Peter Senge, in his book *The Fifth Discipline: The Art and Practice of the Learning Organization,* calls these "event explanations," or "who did what to whom." We have seen a lot of them in the reflections of executives in the cases and in our own analyses. Some of these event explanations include:

- They bought the wrong company.
- There was a recession.
- They paid too much for the company.

- The stores were in poor locations.
- They did not do research.
- Management did not understand the market.

The list could be expanded. The events on the list could also be turned around to emphasize the positive and provide reasons for a successful venture. At issue is not whether they are right or wrong for there is undoubtedly truth in them, but rather that any one or few of them taken together are probably incomplete. In addition to being partial explanations, they are static and invoke a simple cause and effect assumption. It is as if there are a set of independent, correct decisions that once they are made automatically unfold as desired. These explanations tend to take people's eyes off a larger set of relationships and behaviours that are at play.

Senge refers to "patterns of behavior explanations" as those that focus on trends and their implications. We see these as being more process oriented in that they recognize that there are other players involved, and that the act of entering another country is a dynamic, indeterminate process in which the actions of other players in the system cannot be forecast with certainty. It is particularly difficult to understand and predict responses from outside the system. Some of these pattern explanations included:

- They underestimated the competition. The competition was too tough.
- Suppliers did not provide good terms or delivery.
- The distribution systems worked against them.

Another pattern explanation, for example, might be the use of greenfield sites which put into motion a different set of dynamics than would an acquisition.

The most powerful type of explanation is the one that answers the question "What causes the pattern of behavior?"

Systemic explanation

Systemic explanations are powerful because they address "why" things happened, not just "what" happened. Throughout the book to this point we have referred to entering the United States, or markets, or regions in the United States. The challenge, in reality, is not simply to enter another country or region, but to enter an industrial system or market system in which there are established companies who have ongoing relationships with suppliers and consumers and who understand the market from first hand experience. Assimilation into this system is not something that is going to take place quickly for a new entrant. In the cases of retailers who entered the system in the United States, we saw the dynamic reaction of its members — the intense retaliation of competitors, the power of suppliers, the effect of new entrants particularly in high growth areas, and finally the differences in consumer behaviour.

Not only is there a structure of suppliers, customers and competitors in place, but there are barriers to entering this system. The barriers to

Figure 1   Industry Structure in the United States

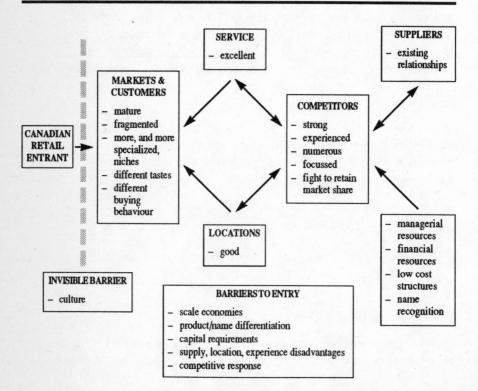

entry that were encountered in the cases in earlier chapters included the lack of economies of scale (advertising, distribution), the difficulty in establishing product, name, or image differentiation, high capital cost, and disadvantages related to acquiring supplies, locations, and knowledge or experience. This structure and system is represented in Figure 1.

What really happened to the Canadian retailers, in the authors' opinion, was:

1. The ones who met with the least success never got in place all of the necessary elements of their entries that would be required to deal with the components of the retail system in the United States.

2. For the most part, with the exception of the food retailers, they did not have a competitive advantage vis à vis their competition. There was nothing that they did better than the American retailers.

3. Many of them were operating with faulty assumptions that the United States was like Canada only larger, and that somehow in such a big, rich market it would be easier to expand and to make money. In this regard there probably was another barrier operating — *culture*. Culture, in the authors' opinion, was not so much a barrier to entry as it was a *barrier to learning!* Learning begins with the ability to see differences and we observed in the cases that a lot of differences were ignored or assumed away.

The authors also wish to note that the cases in this research have come from the retail sector and a question remains as to how applicable are the lessons learned for firms in other industries. The experiences of the Canadian retail companies appear to be consistent with those of companies from other industries and, indeed, from other countries. For example, the observations and conclusions drawn from CEOs outside the retail industry and from studies of Swedish companies entering the United States are remarkably similar to the recurring themes that have developed throughout this research.

PART 3
·
DIFFERENCES IN THE EXECUTIVE SUITE

CHAPTER 6

CULTURE:
AN INVISIBLE BARRIER?

INTRODUCTION

As neighbours sharing the same language, a common border, similar geography in many respects, a large advertising and cultural overlap through print, sound and visual media, there are obvious similarities between Canadians and Americans. In fact, unlike any other country with which Canada could be compared, the United States is probably the most similar on numerous dimensions, and there is little doubt that a "North American" culture does exist. Yet, although these two countries resemble each other more than any other two on earth, there are significant differences between them in their social and business values, behaviours, and institutions.

EXECUTIVE PERCEPTIONS OF CULTURAL DIFFERENCES

With only a few exceptions, the executives across all of the companies studied agreed that there were marked cultural differences between the United States and Canada. Moreover, when the executives' responses were analyzed, they were not based on their company's performance in the United States market. In other words, companies that had done well in the United States and those that had difficulties generally believed that the two cultures differed, and that this was potentially an invisible barrier to success in the United States market. Analyzing their responses also indicated a number of common cultural themes or patterns. The ten most common cultural differences cited by the Canadian executives who experienced the two markets are presented below. The directions of these differences are generally consistent with existing literature comparing Canadians and Americans as well as with the conventional wisdom and experience of the Canadian public.

- *Commitment to winning:* Americans were believed to have a stronger commitment to winning than Canadians.
- *Competitiveness:* Americans were seen as more competitive.
- *Work ethic/belief in hard work:* Americans were perceived to have a stronger work ethic and believed in hard work more than Canadians did.
- *Level of aggressiveness:* Americans were considered more aggressive.
- *Risk propensity:* Americans were seen as willing to take more risks.
- *Individualistic orientation:* Americans were perceived to be more individualistic than Canadians.
- *Action orientation:* Americans were believed be more action oriented.
- *Mastery/control over one's destiny:* It was perceived that Americans had a stronger belief in control over one's destiny.
- *Achievement orientation:* Americans were perceived to be more achievement oriented.
- *Attitudes toward government and authority:* Canadians were believed to hold a more positive view of government and authority than Americans.

Canadian executives found Americans extremely *committed to winning.* What this commitment meant was that Americans were prepared to do whatever was necessary to ensure that they came out on top, or to successfully stamp out their competition. The American tactics that executives felt displayed this commitment to winning included putting pressure on suppliers, which had the effect of locking their competitors (i.e. the Canadian entrant) out of resources, severe price cutting, and massive increases in advertising budgets — all of which made it very difficult for the new competitor to survive in the United States market. This came as a shock to the Canadian companies which were accustomed to being the biggest and best in Canada and to calling the shots. For example, the senior executives from Mark's Work Wearhouse commented that in Canada opening a store in a new area often meant that any other competitor would practically roll over and die. Opening in a new market in the United States was a declaration of war. Furthermore, one CEO summed it up as, "In the United States, the game is about winning. In Canada, loyalty, being nice and trying hard count. In fact, playing the game is often more important than the victory."

Similarly, the executives continually described the Americans they encountered as being intensely *competitive* — much more so than their Canadian counterparts. Indeed, Canadian executives frequently used terms of battle to describe the competitiveness of the Americans they encountered, such as, "Their arsenal was impressive," "They used every battleground they could," and "They declared war!" Executives also commented that in the United States competitiveness is a way of life — a mentality. American management is focussed on putting others out of business. The executives' recommendations were that in order to succeed in that market, you also had to develop that mindset. Yet, unlike in Canada, such competitive behaviour was not to be taken personally. Rather, it was considered a normal part of business activity. The advantage of having the capacity to keep personal self-image out of the business frame was that it made Americans open to criticism and willing to learn.

The executives described the American culture as one having a stronger *work ethic* and a strong belief that through hard work one would get ahead. The general view was that this was much stronger than in Canada because there were fewer social programs in the United States to provide the security net considered to exist in Canada.

Consistent with their rationale for why a stronger work ethic exists in the United States was the perception that Americans were more *aggressive* than Canadians. A noteworthy quote from one executive was,

"Maybe when you don't have things given to you, you become a little more aggressive to get them." In addition, one CEO commented, "The average businessman is very different. The necessity to survive in the United States breeds an aggressiveness in him. We are all products of our markets. In Canada, national retailers control the bulk of the market, so they don't need to be as aggressive. In the United States, there are proportionately fewer national retailers. This affects their behaviour...dramatically."

Similarly, the executives perceived Americans to be more *risk taking,* more entrepreneurial, more opportunistic and more willing to spend money than Canadians. Some of the executives also commented that in the United States, the government encourages risk taking more than in Canada.

Canadians were described as much more *collectivist* in orientation, as evidenced by the nationalization of Canadian industries, the level of government involvement in the economy, the vast array of social programs, and the higher level of unionization. On the other hand, Americans were perceived to be more *individualistic,* being more user-pay oriented, with individuals responsible for their own success or failure, and having deregulation, less government involvement, fewer social programs, and a much lower level of unionization.

Americans were perceived as being much more *action oriented* than Canadians, quicker to make decisions and to act on propositions or opportunities. This orientation can be seen in the cases on American companies in a later chapter. It was strongly believed that the reason for this was that they had to be.

In the United States, the executives perceived a *survival of the fittest* mentality. Americans take things into their own hands or else they will not survive. There is a deep sense of internal control or *mastery* over their own destiny. The belief underlying much of American management is that people can substantially influence their futures. By contrast, the executives perceived Canadians to more often have a sense of external control — an attitude that if they didn't do well, they could get help. Someone would bail them out.

The executives perceived Americans to be more *achievement oriented,* capitalistic, and to have a stronger desire for advancement than Canadians. Additionally, executives found the American culture to hold more negative attitudes toward government, whereas in Canada, the culture holds that Canadians have a right to government aid.

EMPLOYEE AND MANAGEMENT ATTITUDES, VALUES AND BEHAVIOURS

Several comments from executives involved in the research centred on the differences between American and Canadian employees at all levels, including management, in the retail industry.

Employees

Desire for independence

American employees were described as possessing a greater desire for independence than Canadian employees. The attitude of "I have the responsibility for this area, and I will make the decisions" prevailed among employees in the United States. In addition, there appeared to be less consensus management in the United States retail organizations, and less desire among American employees to be a part of the overall decision making process. One of the businessmen interviewed stated, "Americans like to be in charge of their own destinies — to make their own things happen. There's much more of this than in Canada." However, this perception may be a self-fulfilling prophecy. Workers may be responding to management's expectations.

American employees were also found to be much less interested in unions than Canadian employees. Unions represent a means by which employees can increase their strength or voice by banding collectively. However, the attitude among American employees was that they had more to gain by doing well themselves than in a group. In the United States, individual rather than collective achievement is the focus. Each individual is responsible for his or her own success or failure. Furthermore, the absence of a labour party or a strong union movement in the United States has meant that few Americans see themselves as belonging to a class. Class membership would conflict with the egalitarian concept guiding the American culture which suggests that individuals will have an equal opportunity to get ahead, and that advancement is based on merit.

Orientation toward work

American employees generally were found to be very hard working and much more conscientious about productivity. Several of the executives interviewed found a significant difference in the level of service provided by American employees as compared to Canadian employees. The employees in the United States were also perceived as being more aggressive. A senior executive from the Grafton Group commented, "We have women working in the United States stores making $60,000–$70,000 per year. They are very aggressive, friendly, and 'after the sale'...and they get it! I just wish we could get some of their type up here in Canada." With respect to doing business in the United States, the general advice can be summed up in a comment from one Vice President of Marketing, "If you want to go down there and compete, you have got to take on that aggressive attitude...because everyone else has it."

Reward expectations

American employees' strong positive orientation toward work created an expectation that they would be rewarded based on merit. Since they worked more independently and in a way to further themselves individually, the types of reward systems were different in the United States retail industry. Incentives appeared to be key to managing United States employees. Incentives create an atmosphere in which each employee has an equal opportunity to further him/herself, depending on amount of time and effort expended. This is interesting in that it ties in to the two basic American values — equality and achievement. All individuals are believed to begin on a level playing field with equality of opportunity. American employees learn to compete aggressively for rewards because they know they are based on merit. The connection between performing well and getting ahead appears to be much more well established in the United States than in Canada.

Strong desire for advancement

Many of the characteristics discussed so far differentiating Canadian and American employees can be explained by the stronger desire for advancement of American employees. Few adhere to any other ideology. The fact that American employees were found to be more hard working ties into this desire for advancement, as hard work is apt to reap the employee higher rewards, both monetary and otherwise. A strong desire for advancement also explains the greater desire for independence among American employees. Getting ahead usually involves individual effort and skills, as opposed to group involvement. Similarly, being involved in a union tends to mean that rewards will be based on seniority, instead of merit, and that the group will benefit as a whole, instead of the individual. Hence, the lack of interest in unions in the United States, relative to Canadian employees.

Mobility

Because each individual is driven by the prospect of advancement, this means that mobility is a must. Not surprisingly, Canadian executives doing business in the United States found that American employees were much more mobile than their Canadian counterparts. This led to the perception among Canadian executives that United States employees were, therefore, less loyal. In Canada, the assumption tends to be that if an employee works very hard and is concerned with productivity, he/she is a loyal employee. In addition, perhaps due to the perceived or actual lack of options within Canada, many employees who are interested in advancement tend to do so within a single organization. Relative to Canada, this was much less true in the United States. An employee may work hard for a particular company, but at the same time, he/she is more opportunistic. If a better opportunity is found, it appears that he/she will leave without hesitation. This behaviour is perceived by Canadian employers as a lack of employee loyalty. However, in the United States, these attitudes and behaviours are not viewed this way. Competition for jobs is commonplace and is not taken personally. Employees are responsible for their position in society. They must always act to better themselves, because others do. This creates competition for their own job which is their only means of survival. Therefore, no one sits complacently in one job for too long.

Management

In addition to the above characteristics which they shared, American managers were found to be different from Canadian managers in two major ways. First, the level of professionalism was found to be different. A senior executive from Mark's Work Wearhouse summed up the difference with the following statement, "It's simple. Everyone down there was better." Furthermore, an executive from Peoples Jewellers commented on the American executives at Zale Corporation compared to the Canadian executives at Peoples Jewellers, "Generally their skills, their experience sets, are much, much broader — not only in terms of variety but also in terms of depth of knowledge — than what you will find in Canada.... In Zale, we have a professional management group who have a higher level of management skills in whatever area they are dealing with, as well as skills to manage people and to implement things. Whereas here [in Canada]...they are good implementors, but they, by circumstances, may not have had either the educational background or the depth of experience in a variety of retail backgrounds to bring a broader perspective to the business. But this is typical of small organizations. The level of professionalism a business has is by virtue of its size."

Several executives discussed the reason for the higher level of professionalism in American retail organizations. The common theme behind their statements was the following. In the United States, there were a much greater number of people who are both highly educated and who have very diverse and strong retail backgrounds. To obtain a top level position in a large United States retail company meant that you had to be very talented, because there was a much greater number of other people vying for the same position, many of whom had similar characteristics. In Canada, there was not nearly the competition for positions within or across retail organizations. And, due to the smaller number of large organizations, retail executives were unable to be subjected to the breadth of experience executives would have in the United States market.

The second major area of difference affecting management in Canada and the United States was the higher performance expectation of American managers. The perception among the executives interviewed was that if American managers did not do what they said they would, they would be fired. In Canada, it was felt that that would not happen. In the United States, there was also much less of a security net for people who were dismissed. One company noted that the severance pay the company gave American employees when they exited from the United States market was far beyond what employees expected. Because this was standard practice in Canada, the company management had not thought to change the practice for the United States.

Because of the high performance expectation among management in the United States, American managers were far less tolerant of overhead and other expenses, and acted very aggressively in these areas. The general opinion was that to do business successfully in the United States required that Canadian retail organizations employ American management with such skills.

RELATIONSHIPS

Cultural differences also affected the nature of relationships with suppliers, with customers, with other business persons and with employees. Not recognizing this early could lead to failure. For example, the executives at Mark's Work Wearhouse entered the United States assuming that supplier relations would be the same in the United States as they had been in Canada. In Canada, Mark's Work Wearhouse had an excellent relationship with its main supplier (Levi's). Work Wearhouse was Levi's largest customer. Yet, in the United States, Mark's Work Wearhouse was treated very poorly by its suppliers. In general, the executives' comments centred on the difficulty of gaining access to suppliers and the necessity of long term relationships to build the necessary rapport. In Canada, there was a tendency to build long term relationships, even with inadequacies, because there were not a lot of suppliers. In the United States, this was not true. If you performed inadequately in the United States, the relationship was quickly severed. This was true on both sides of the relationship — buying and selling. This perceived problem with supplier relations led most executives to conclude that it was best when doing business in the United States for companies to acquire the established relationships with United States suppliers, as discussed earlier.

Because United States customers were believed to demand a great deal and have very different buying habits, such as shopping around and cherry picking specials, Canadian managers found it particularly difficult to establish loyal customers in their United States organizations.

With respect to relationships with other business persons, one executive stated, "In the United States, shaking hands on a deal is not enough. In Canada, it is. In the United States, you must sign. The business practices are very different in the United States."

Finally, relationships with employees were considerably different in the United States, where Canadian management found employees to be short term and individually focussed and not as loyal as their Canadian employees.

THE PERCEIVED CULTURAL DIFFERENCES: HOW REPRESENTATIVE ARE THEY?

Many people, including the executives interviewed in this study, have commented that cultural differences exist between Canada and the United States. Their conclusions have been based on historical analysis, observation and experience. There is little statistical research to support or contest these conclusions. However, they do have considerable face validity since they are consistent with the experience of people that have lived and worked in the two countries. When the interviews were finished, we were left with a strong feeling about the importance of cultural differences between the two countries and their impact on business. But we were also left wondering how representative the perceptions of the executives were. One could argue that perception is reality for those who had the experience and who hold the perceptions, and that these beliefs could affect the ability of Canadians to compete in the United States market — sort of a self-fulfilling prophecy.

We were interested in taking the analysis one step further to learn whether the perceived cultural differences between Canadians and Americans could be measured more objectively and, if so, what the differences were.

A questionnaire designed to measure value and attitudinal differences was mailed to the chief executive officers of the top 369 retail companies in Canada and the top 338 retail companies in the United States. A total of 271 chief executive officers responded to the survey.

180 of these were from Canada and 91 were from the United States, yielding response rates of 55 percent and 37 percent respectively. It is possible that the response rate varied by country because the Western Business School is much better known in Canada. However, there were some interesting differences in the response patterns that also contributed to the differential. Four times as many CEOs from the United States (16) either stated on the questionnaires they returned or called to say that they were too busy to fill out the survey compared with the returns from Canada (4). In addition, many more American retailers had policies prohibiting participation by their members in such surveys. One executive explained that without such a policy he would be inundated with questionnaires of all types every day. This is understandable given the size differential between the two countries, the greater number of universities and other organizations conducting survey research, and the greater propensity to do market research in the United States.

The responses were aggregated for the executives in each country and compared. The results of the survey were consistent with the information collected in the executive interviews and with the conventional wisdom and literature on Canadian–American differences. Before presenting these results, a word of caution is in order. Readers may be tempted to ascribe the differences found in this research to Canadians and Americans in general. The authors want to state that the differences found apply to retail CEOs in the United States and Canada, and possibly to the retail communities in these two countries. Although the findings may be consistent with readers' experiences outside the retail industry, generalizing to other industries and elements of society in the two countries could lead to misunderstanding without further research.

Survey Results

Some demographic characteristics

The survey categorized respondents according to age, gender and educational level. There were very few female chief executive officers in either country. Indeed, the number of female respondents in both countries was exactly the same — 3.3 percent of the total.

Particularly interesting were the results with respect to age and educational level that are presented in Tables 1 and 2. CEOs in Canada tended to be somewhat younger than CEOs in the United States. The average age of Canadian chief executive officers was 49.3, whereas it was 52.5 in the United States group. Most of the Canadian CEOs fell into the 40-49 age category, whereas most of the American CEOs fell into the 50-59 age category.

Table 1   Age Differences*
Retail Company CEOs

Age Range	Canada	United States
Under 40	19.6%	14.3%
40–49	35.6%	19.8%
50–59	27.2%	39.6%
60–65	12.8%	19.8%
Over 65	4.4%	6.6%

The differences in the averages of the two country groups are statistically significant.

In addition to the American executives being somewhat older than the Canadian executives, they also had completed a greater number of years of formal education. In Canada, the average number of years of formal school education completed was 14.6 years, whereas in the United States, it was 16.3 years. This means that Canadian CEOs had not, on average, completed the equivalent of an undergraduate university degree (13 years of secondary school in Ontario and three years for a general B.A.), whereas American CEOs had, on average, completed the equivalent of a university degree (12 years of high school and four years of university).

Table 2   Years of Education Differences*
Retail Company CEOs

Years of Education	Canada	United States
Less than 12 years	13.9%	0.0%
12–13 years	22.8%	12.1%
14–15 years	21.1%	11.0%
16–17 years	22.3%	36.3%
18 years or more	20.6%	40.7%

* The differences in the averages of the two country groups are statistically significant.

It is also interesting to note that no one among the United States respondents had completed less than 12 years of formal education. In Canada, 13.9 percent of the chief executive officers fell into this category. Moreover, 40.7 percent of the United States executives had 18 years or more education (the equivalent of a graduate degree in the United States), whereas only 20.6 percent of the Canadian chief executive officers did.

Linking these results back to earlier discussions, there is a possible relationship between the age and education differences and perceived greater level of professionalism and experience that Canadian executives ascribed to their American counterparts.

One could argue that since the top companies in each country were chosen to participate in the study, the United States companies would be significantly larger than the Canadian companies, thereby biasing the results. Therefore, United States companies with approximately ten times the sales volume would require chief executive officers with higher educational levels and who probably would be somewhat older by the time they reached this level. Although it is true that the average sales volume of the top United States companies was about ten times that of the Canadian companies, it is important to remember that the study surveyed the top level companies within each country. It also surveyed persons at the CEO level in each country.

This survey provides a snapshot of the competition and the people running these companies. It provides an indication of what the competitive milieu in American retailing is like. It could be argued that the same skills, experience and educational requirements should be necessary in top level positions of Canadian companies that wish to compete with the American companies.

Value and attitude differences

Table 3 shows the results of the survey of the various values and attitudes measured by the questionnaire. The table has three columns: (1) the value or attitude measured; (2) the conventional wisdom which is the direction of the value or attitude that observers and researchers have usually found, as well as the common stereotypes and beliefs of Canadians and Americans (held by Canadians), and the executives' perceptions from the research; (3) the survey results in terms of whether or not the conventional wisdom was supported. Statistically significant differences, meaning that they cannot be attributed to chance, were found between the respondent groups from the two countries on all of the dimensions listed below except one — aggression. A brief discussion of the various measures and the findings follows.

For many years, Americans have been described as being more achievement oriented, aggressive and risk taking than their Canadian neighbours, and the literature generally supports this conventional wisdom. This survey found significant differences for two of these three values — achievement and risk taking. The *achievement* items measure one's orientation to work and to play, while *aggression* is a measure of the degree and quality of one's interpersonal orientation. American respondents were found to be slightly more aggressive than those from Canada, but the results were not statistically significant. Therefore, contrary to the conventional wisdom, we must say that there was no difference. One reason for this is that the items measuring aggression tended to focus on physical aggression, as well as the expression of anger or disapproval. Many people use the word aggressive to mean competitive, which is a quite different meaning and very different than what was measured. Many of the achievement items were more concerned with competitiveness than were the aggression items.

Risk taking covered four aspects: physical risk taking, monetary risk

Table 3   Value and Attitude Differences
Retail Company CEOs

Value/ Attitude	Canadian Conventional Wisdom	Survey Results
1. Achievement	Americans more achievement oriented.	U.S. CEOs scored higher on achievement.
2. Aggression	Americans more aggressive.	Although the differences were in the expected direction, they were not statistically significant.
3. Risk taking	Americans more risk taking.	U.S. CEOs scored higher on risk taking.
4. Tolerance	Canadians more tolerant.	The reverse was found. U.S. CEOs scored higher and the difference was significant.
5. Protestant work ethic	Americans stronger work ethic.	U.S. CEOs scored higher on work ethic.
6. Job involvement	Americans more job involved.	U.S. CEOs scored higher.
7. Individualism	Americans more individualistic.	U.S. CEOs scored as more individualistic.
8. Masculinity	Americans more assertive and acquisitive.	U.S. CEOs scored higher on this scale.
9. Uncertainty avoidance	Canadians more uncomfortable with uncertainty and ambiguity.	U.S. CEOs scored as being more comfortable with uncertainty.
10. Power distance	Canadians more accepting of power differences in organizations.	CEOs from Canada scored higher in power distance.
11. Optimistic action orientation	Americans more optimistic and action oriented.	U.S. CEOs scored higher.
12. Cautiousness	Canadians more cautious.	CEOs from Canada scored as more cautious.

taking, social risk taking and ethical risk taking. However, monetary risk taking was more heavily weighted in the scale than the other types.

The *tolerance* dimension measured whether differences existed between executives in the United States and Canada in their tolerance for different people, points of view, culture, etc. The results indicated that the respondents from the United States were more tolerant than the Canadian executives. This may be important if interpreted in light of earlier reported findings that one of the key reasons that Canadian retail companies had difficulty in the United States was the inability to adjust, or adjust quickly enough, their Canadian pre-entry orientation and attitudes regarding the requirements to compete in the United States. When presented with a culturally different people and different market conditions, Canadian executives had difficulty adapting to those differences.

Several of the Canadian executives interviewed stated that American executives work harder and spend much more time at work than their Canadian counterparts. In addition to being described as more involved in their work, American executives were also described as working harder, providing better service, and having higher productivity levels.

This *belief in hard work* has two dimensions to it. The first is a value component. The author of the Protestant ethic measure used in this research describes a person who possesses this ideal as feeling that "personal worth results from self-sacrificing work or occupational achievement." The scale was designed to measure the strength of this value orientation. The other dimension is more behavioral and measures the degree to which a person is involved in his or her job. The authors of this measure define job involvement as "the extent to which a person's work affects his self esteem. The job involved person is one for whom paid employment plays a central part in life and who is affected personally by his or her employment circumstances."

The next four dimensions, individualism–collectivism, masculinity—femininity, uncertainty avoidance, and power distance, were developed by Geert Hofstede. For example, some norms in an *individualistic* culture include the ideas that everyone is supposed to take care of him or herself; identity based in the individual; emphasis on individual initiative and achievement; autonomy, variety and pleasure; and belief in individual decisions. In more *collectivist* cultures, the other end of this dimension, people look after members of their family, clan or organization in exchange for loyalty; identity based in the social system; emphasis on belonging to an organization; and belief in group decisions. Whereas both Canada and the United States are typically viewed as individualistic cultures relative to other cultures such as Japan or China, for example, Canada traditionally is seen as less individualistic than the United States. This belief was supported in the survey findings.

Hofstede named the *masculinity–femininity* dimension to reflect the different values generally assigned to the two genders. In highly masculine cultures, the general norms would be assertiveness and the acquisition of money and things; performance and growth; independence; decisiveness; big and fast; and excelling. In feminine cultures, people, the environment, the quality of life and interdependence are more important. Again, both Canada and the United States are usually viewed as masculine cultures, but with Canada less "masculine" than the United States. The survey's findings were consistent with this perception.

Uncertainty avoidance has to do with the extent a society feels threatened by uncertain and ambiguous situations and tries to avoid them by providing greater career stability, by establishing more formal rules and by placing belief in experts and authorities. Some of the norms associated with higher uncertainty avoidance include the avoidance of conflict and competition, need for consensus, security, and law and order. The Canadian respondents were found to score higher on uncertainty avoidance.

Power distance basically deals with societies' beliefs about human inequality and values about the exercise of power. One way to think about this dimension on a political level is in terms of egalitarianism, or beliefs about the degree to which inequality should be permitted. Views as to whether Americans or Canadians are more egalitarian are mixed. The answer may be that they are both more egalitarian, but in different ways. Americans talk about being concerned with equality of opportunity, while Canadians express more concern with equality of results. In relation to organizations, power distance would be related to concentration of authority and centralization.

CEOs from Canada scored higher on the power distance items than the CEOs from the United States, which appears consistent with the data in the cases about Canadian retailers and from numerous observers of the two countries.

The two final dimensions on which significant differences were found were *optimistic action orientation* and *cautiousness*. The optimistic action orientation factor consisted of aphorisms such as, "Better a bad decision than no decision," "Why put off until tomorrow what you can do today," "Lost time is never found again," and "He who hesitates is lost." On the other hand, the factor labelled cautiousness included items such as, "A penny saved is a penny earned," "Once bitten, twice shy," "Haste makes waste," and "There is no act more moral among men than that of rule and obedience." The American group of respondents had a higher optimistic action orientation score. The Canadian group scored higher on the cautiousness scale. Finally, it should be noted that four other orientations were measured, but that no significant differences were found between the respondents from Canada and the United States. These orientations were winning at all costs mentality, capitalistic orientation, belief in fate, and distrust of authority.

REFLECTIONS ON CULTURE

In today's global marketplace, the importance of understanding the culture of other countries is being increasingly recognized. Although not typically viewed as such, the United States represents an international market for Canadian businesses. Because of the proximity of the United States and the fact it is so familiar, Canadian executives need to be on guard not to overlook some important differences that can impact their business ventures.

It appears that culture may present an invisible barrier for Canadian companies doing business in the United States market. The results from interviews indicated this to be the case, and the survey questionnaire supported the perceptions of the Canadian executives. Five key areas of difference have been described in this and previous chapters: consumers/customers; regional diversity and market concentration; competition; employee and management values, attitudes and behaviours; and relationships.

However, Canadian executives must realize that culture, in terms of values and attitudes that influence behaviour, is not something that only the people in *another* country possess. The pervasive, but hidden, effect of the attitudes and values of their culture influence their decisions, behaviours, and management practices. Executives become accustomed to doing business in certain ways that they have learned throughout their lifetimes and careers in a particular country making it difficult to approach another culture/market differently, especially one perceived by many to be the same. As a result, the Canadian frame of reference can cause difficulty operating in the United States if assumptions are not validated and important differences not recognized.

A final, but very important, point is that although differences in culture and market factors exist between the two countries, they *alone* are not the reason Canadian retail companies experience difficulty in the United States. Rather, it is the lack of recognition of those differences, prior to entry, or not responding fast enough once there, that account for problems in performance. The differences between the United States and Canada can be managed provided Canadian companies recognize that they exist, learn what they are and how they affect business practices. However, this knowledge must be incorporated into the strategic decisions and implementation plans related to entering the United States.

PART 4

·

THE AMERICANS
ARE COMING!

CHAPTER 7

NEW FACES,
NEW IDEAS

This book is not only about Canadian retailers doing business in the United States, but also about competing in Canada amidst the influx of new competitors who are, to a great extent, American. The entry of American retailers into Canada has increased, creating more competition for market share in an already crowded marketplace. Some of the American firms have been here for many years in several cases establishing Canadian companies or operating with Canadian partners or equity, such as the Woolworth empire which owns Kinney Shoes, Footlocker, Lady Footlocker, Randy River, Willow Ridge, Karuba, Champs Sports, Canary Island, Afterthoughts/Reflections, Silk and Satin and Woolco Department Stores.

Other long term resident American retailers include such familiar names as K Mart, Sears, Pier 1, Radio Shack, Toys R US, Ethan Allen, and Eddie Bauer. More recently, however, the pace has increased with the addition of nine newcomers — Color Tile, The Gap, TJ Maxx, Price Club, Costco, Talbots (recently acquired by a Japanese company), Cole Hahn, Lenscrafters, and Tiffany's. This does not include catalogue houses such as Quill, L.L. Bean, Land's End and many others which have extended their mailing lists to include the Canadian market. Nor does it include the numerous fast food retailers, both corporate and franchised, that are so familiar.

There will likely be other arrivals as American retailers size up the opportunities in the Canadian market. After all, 55 percent of the Canadian population lies conveniently within a 600 mile band between Windsor and Quebec City along the Canada–United States border. It is rumoured, and many people are anticipating, that the giant Wal–Mart will be in Canada in the next few years.

To date, many of the American retailers have become dominant in their category in the Canadian market. Of the top ten United States specialty chains, as ranked by the National Retail Foundation, six are already in Canada, three having entered within the past two to three years. The remaining four giants, The Limited with sales of $4.6 billion, Circuit City at $2.1 billion, Marshalls at $1.9 billion and Petrie Stores at $1.2 billion, have so far not signalled their intentions.

In addition to an influx of American retailers, Canadian consumers have gone south in droves, driven by a desire for low prices, greater variety, and better service. Consumers in this shopping exodus created by both recessionary times and media exposure are experiencing the thrill of the chase in American stores, leaving Canadian retailers with empty cash registers and forcing more aggressive retailers, such as Bata and Future Shops, to respond and to advertise their guarantees that Canadians will not pay more for the same item in Canada. Management Horizons estimated in 1991 that by the year 2000, 50 percent of existing retail chains in Canada will be wiped out by heightened competition. The competition will be coming, largely, from the United States.

The Canadian retail industry has been very healthy until the last two to three years, and its major players have been extremely successful. The abruptness of the changes in the Canadian business environment, changes such as the Free Trade Agreement, cross border shopping, the influx of American retailers, a high Canadian dollar, a deep recession, and a "boomer" consumerism that has given way to a sudden lack of consumer confidence, has dealt the Canadian retail industry a severe blow. Virtually all these changes have occurred simultaneously, creating the need for a major restructuring of the industry in a very short period of time.

It is, thus, even more important now than when this research was launched that Canadian retailers not only look to the United States for expansion, but prepare for new competition in their own market. An extensive learning process by many Canadian retailers is necessary to maintain and gain market share in both the Canadian and United States markets.

The examination of experiences of the Canadian companies entering the United States that have been described in the earlier chapters provides many insights into succeeding in the United States. However, it is also critical to learn how American retailers operate, as well as how they have managed to enter into the Canadian market so successfully. As retail bankruptcies rise in Canada, and more Canadian retailers withdraw from the United States, it is imperative to learn how the American retailers function if one wants to compete in the retail big leagues with them.

THE BOMBAY COMPANY, INC.

Background

This specialty retailer of home furnishings products operated over 300 stores in the United States and Canada, and was profitable in both countries. The Canadian subsidiary accounted for about 15 percent of the total stores and 15 percent of the 1991 operating profit.

The company started in the United States as a mail order firm in 1976. Its name recalled the image of British colonial India and it offered a limited collection of English reproduction furniture and accessories. The first retail store opened in New Orleans in 1979. Robert Nourse, a Canadian, left his position as a professor of marketing at the Western Business School to join a venture capital firm in the mid 1970s, and in 1979 he bought the Canadian rights for the mail order business of The Bombay Company for $1.00 plus a royalty.

In 1980, Tandy Brands Inc. purchased the United States company and moved the headquarters to Fort Worth, Texas. By 1983 there were 13 stores in Canada and 36 in the United States. The Canadian operation was profitable; however, the United States company was losing money.

United States Turnaround

Nourse was asked to come to the United States. In 1984, he and his wife, Aagje, took over the American operation and began to remake the whole of The Bombay Company on their Canadian model. Nine of the 36 United States stores were closed in the first year, largely due to poor locations. A major reorganization took place and three other stores were added in the same year.

Growth continued at a rapid pace with 32 stores added in 1986 and a further 48 in 1987. The company planned to open 30–40 stores a year until it reached 550–600, a saturation point determined by market research that the company undertook. By mid 1991, it had reached the halfway point with over 300 stores across the United States and Canada.

Corporate Structure

In late 1990, Tandy Brands Inc. consisted of three divisions; its primary business, The Bombay Company retail chain; Alex and Ivy, a new home decor store featuring European country styles that the company was testing; and Tandy Brands Accessories, a manufacturer and marketer of men's and boys' leather products and accessories.

The accessory division was spun off in early 1991 and Tandy Brands Inc. changed its name to The Bombay Company, Inc. The company was to concentrate on specialty retail with the expansion of the chain and the development of the new Alex and Ivy concept.

The Concept

Product

The Bombay Company offered a highly specialized home furnishings assortment in an unusual manner. The product consisted of reproductions of 18th and 19th century furniture and accessories including occasional tables, desks, prints, mirrors, lamps, benches and ceramics. Danish acid-cured furniture finishes were used to resist scratches and moisture. All items were flat packed and ready to assemble, an unusual twist for traditional furniture. Each store had every item in stock which made for instant consumer gratification.

There was a constant flow of new products. Within a year, 30 percent of the store's wood items, 50 percent of the prints, and some 70 percent of all other items turned over as new designs were introduced and old ones dropped.

Suppliers

Approximately 95 percent of The Bombay Company's revenue was accounted for by proprietary products, having been designed and manufactured to the company's specifications. Two-thirds were imported from Far Eastern countries, the company maintaining an Asian office employing 20 people in Taiwan. Although some competitors have tried to copy the products, Nourse contended that they had built a source of supply that was very complex and would take years to replicate.

Price

Most items sold for less than $150, with the top price around $500. It was estimated that 60 percent of the sales were impulse purchases that were stimulated by the combination of popular price points and the sophisticated merchandise presentation.

Presentation

The stores were run as a fashion chain in so far as merchandise presentation was concerned. Layout and accessorization were changed frequently during the year: Christmas 1 (September/October); Christmas 2 (November/December); winter promotional sales (January/ February); spring decor (March/April); wedding, graduation, and Mother's and Father's Day gifts (May/June); and summer sale (July/August). Large backdrop posters were created for each "season" for in-store display and were accompanied by a new catalogue, each issue of which coincided with a new store layout.

Promotion

Promotion expenses — advertising expenditures, in-store presentation and catalogue production — were high compared to the norm. The company ran bimonthly newspaper ads in each of its markets and placed ads in shelter magazines. The catalogue was mailed to approximately one million customers seven times per year. Direct catalogue purchases, however, amounted to less than five percent of total sales.

Location strategy

Another element of the unique concept was the location strategy. Most of the stores were in malls, unusual for home furnishings stores which were generally in freestanding locations. The malls chosen tended to be in upper middle and upper income trading areas. The stores averaged 1,500 to 1,600 square feet which was much smaller than the typical home furnishings store. Optimal space requirements were rigidly adhered to in site selection so as to maximize product presentation and display.

The Market

The Bombay customer was identified through market research to be between 20 and 65 years of age, with a middle to upper middle income, and to have higher than average education. The higher than average level of education meant that these customers had the propensity and confidence to accessorize their homes.

Management

The United States office consisted largely of American management with the exception of Nourse (Canadian), his wife Aagje who was Dutch, and a German manager who ran the mail order department. The organization was essentially the same in Canada as in the United States and the proportion of women in both divisions was high, with four vice-presidents and 70 percent of the store managers being female.

In terms of business ethics, the company's stance was strict, requiring an eight page document of ethical rules to be re-signed annually by all managers.

Labour costs were found to be higher in Canada, and according to Nourse, high by any standards in the world. Nourse had to pay more in Canada for a comparable level of responsibility.

Strategic Planning

One of the key strengths of the company was the commitment to the strategic planning process. Annually, a five year plan was completed with two years of monthly data and three years of annual data. It entailed a full environmental analysis, including a competitive audit, a review of the company's own strengths and weaknesses and how they had evolved, and included the latest data available on market trends and consumer buying patterns.

The planning process began in December and was completed by the end of May. The plan was updated quarterly. Part of the staff was fully devoted to planning and updating and they constantly watched the oblique or indirect competition. Since it was a growth company, more attention had to be paid to strategic planning and Nourse felt that if they did not do it then they would not be in the leading position which they occupied.

Financial Results

The Bombay Company was profitable both in Canada and the United States. Within a little over ten years, the company had grown from one to over 300 stores, and to sales of over $139 million. Its increase in revenue and number of stores had been very high compared to other major American furniture retailers.

With expansion planned at approximately 30–40 stores per year over the 1990s, it was expected to continue to gain market share from other major furniture retailers. With no debt other than a debenture which was to be paid off within a year, the company was well positioned for growth.

The Canadian operation, however, was marginally more profitable than the United States division. At 9.1 percent and 9.9 percent respectively for the United States and Canada, the operating profit as a percentage of net sales provided a very respectable return.

Margins and Expenses

The initial marked-up price was slightly higher in Canada because of duties. Gross margin was usually the same in the two companies.

With the sale mentality predominant in both Canada and the United States, there was a concerted effort to limit the amount of revenue generated at sale prices. Key elements of the strategy included differentiated products and good marketing programs to ensure that the company maintained a high proportion of the revenue from sales at full price. According to Nourse, this was one reason why "many successful retailers in one way or another were controlling their sources of supply."

Controlling supply could be done through contracts with manufacturers, owning the manufacturer, or becoming important to key manufacturers. "If you are selling other people's brands, the market has been tending toward discount. If you want to differ by fashion or style, which really means designing it, not just repackaging, then you can get a pretty big jump ahead."

Despite generally higher labour and rent costs, expenses were actually a little lower in the Canadian operation due to the Canadian stores and leases being a little older. This situation was expected to even out in time. In general, the company ran at 0.3 head office people per store.

In terms of productivity, the average sales per square foot was $309 for 1990, and was approximately $315 for 1991. Sales per store averaged $453,000 for 1991.

The Future

Expansion

The plan of The Bombay Company was to develop a number of reasonably autonomous specialty retailers in the field of home related products. Its goal was to be a billion dollar company by the end of the decade. In a positive cash position, the company was well situated for expansion. After saturation was reached in the North American market, management would look at other international markets, and at other concepts that would be tested, refined and potentially expanded.

Quebec

Bombay entered the Quebec market in 1991 and found that the challenges were many, not the least of which was to get bilingual packaging from the Orient. The catalogue, which was to be launched when the stores were in operation, was also presenting some difficulties. New artwork for packaging for the Quebec market was estimated to cost $60,000, copy required translation, and names had to be changed. Nourse felt it was much harder entering Quebec than the other United States regions, and that they were learning a great deal from the difficulties presented by the Quebec market. If the company was successful in Quebec, he was optimistic that it would help to develop the skills to prepare for entry into a market such as Mexico where the language was again different.

Alex and Ivy

The company was testing a new home furnishings concept called Alex and Ivy. The concept was similar to the Bombay stores; however, it featured more casual country styles as opposed to Bombay's traditional English reproductions. Three test stores, greenfield sites, were located in southern California. This market was chosen since it was one in which Bombay had low penetration and test results would be clearer.

One drawback to testing a greenfield concept was the long time frame involved. Until there were twenty or twenty-five stores, Nourse contended, "You're not ready to put something on the front burner. You must know it's working well and is good enough to build forty or fifty stores. You have to know how to make a brick before you can make a wall."

An American Perspective on Various Aspects of the United States and Canadian Retail Environments

Canadian and American management

The major differences between Canadian and American management was seen as attitudinal rather than aptitude or education. Canadian managers always seemed to have someone else to blame, usually government or unions.

There was no reason for Canadians not to be as strong players as the Americans, but there was a difference in the willingness to recognize a problem, address it squarely, and deal with it. Canadians tended to twist even the smallest problem and blame it on something relating to the GST, government policy, free trade, or the incompetence of somebody else.

Americans, in contrast, felt a sense of urgency that perhaps existed in few other places to the same extent. Canadians must deal with the realities of the United States market in which situations are more often regarded as opportunities than as problems, and where a sense of urgency prevails.

Values/politics

Social values differed between Canada and the United States. However, Nourse thought the differences to be no greater than within Canada. "When coming to the United States, you just take on a dozen or so additional regional markets. The social and value structure in Texas is very different from that of Massachusetts. You must adapt."

In terms of politics, there was less government regulation in the retail industry than in other sectors. A strong lobby did exist, however, regarding a variety of issues relating to direct mail postal rates and sales tax collection, which was complex in the United States. Sales tax was levied at the community as well as state level.

United States retail structure

The retail structure was more complex in the United States. There were many configurations of mall and retail types which hardly existed in Canada and which could not afford to exist there in the same diversity. The level of diversity was probably greater than anywhere else in the world. In Germany, for example, the retail industry was legislated very closely and could only go on sale periodically during the year. Evening openings were forbidden, and laws were rigidly enforced. All this was intended to protect the small stores. In Japan, numerous laws existed to protect the small retailer from competition.

In comparison to the United States, the strong retailers in Canada were probably stronger within their own market. The United States retail industry was becoming more national and less regional, however. In mall based retailing, most of the important mall tenants were national companies such as The Gap, The Limited, Zales, and The Bombay Company. The regional department stores were being purchased and run as national stores. For example, the May Company had bought Foley's and was running it like a national chain. Nordstrom had also become a national company with stores in Washington, New Jersey, Chicago and Baltimore.

The supermarkets had continued to be regional; however, the discounters were largely national such as K Mart and Wal-Mart. A very competitive segment, office superstores had been regional but were becoming national. Specialty discounters such as Home Depot tended to be regional. Retail giant The Limited had seven concepts in one mall and could take 30 percent of the gross leasable space in a new mall.

Retailing in a United States mall was becoming more and more like theatre. It seemed that excitement was important in order to compete. The new Disney stores, for example, were a sound and light show and had really taken off.

Nourse cited the Pentagon Fashion Center in Washington as a fine example of many new retail concepts. Some Canadian centres contain "poor clones of United States stores." The new American malls tended to be general, but with highly specialized stores which were real niche players such as the Nature Company which sells the environment, The Bombay Company which is very specialized, and Norditrak Stores which sell only exercise machines.

Mall structure and the development industry

The retail structure in Canada has evolved to a very confined number of strong shopping malls and a large number of strip centres, with very little in between. This was not the case in the United States where there were many more secondary centres as well as the strong regionals and the strip malls.

In Toronto and Montreal, for example, there were a large number of malls where the average sales were over $400/square foot and, therefore, stores could open and earn a good return. In the United States, since the operating costs were generally lower, a store could make a profit at a lower sales level. The high productivity malls were comparable in both Canada and the United States. The Canadian market was more dominated by strong centres and much greater corporate concentration. This concentration of high productivity malls in the United States would be unusual.

In the United States, the average sales of a shopping centre were $140–146/square foot. Bombay did not enter many at that level. However, it was in numerous centres where the average was $180–$200/square foot and could make a very acceptable return.

Nourse indicated that startup costs were higher in Canada. Although base rents were similar, the additional expenses such as real estate and business taxes in Canada were much higher than in the United States. Add on occupancy costs in an average American centre were $7–8/square foot but would be double that in Canada at approximately $15/square foot. Much of this expense was property and business tax.

There were over 200 developers in the United States and, as such, there was a great deal of competition to obtain good retailers as tenants. This was unlike the situation in Canada where the number of developers was very small and the competition amongst retailers to obtain space in shopping malls was intense. It was not uncommon for an American developer to pay to obtain a desirable tenant. As much as $100,000 or more might go toward "build outs" for the tenant. In effect, the developer became an off balance sheet lender for the retailer.

The developers were willing to do build outs under two different circumstances: 1) they became off balance sheet lenders as previously noted, and would just charge more rent for build outs. This they only did for an established retailer who they were sure would be in business so they would obtain their payback; 2) A new mall would do build outs for retailers if it was competing to get them. For example, if a mall could confirm tenancy of such retailers as Anne Taylor, Gap, or The Bombay Company, it helped them lease the rest of the mall by creating critical mass to enhance leasing and provide a draw to consumers. The latter case was most common in new mall situations, but seldom in existing malls. Since many of the developers were suffering in the current recessionary climate, some of the build out money was expected to dry up.

On the other hand, if the mall was extremely attractive, retailers would be clamouring to get in. This was the case with Danbury Mall in Connecticut, which was the first new mall to be built there in ten years. Generally, however, the competition was the other way: "There are no barriers to access to real estate if you've got something good to show. Americans are, to some extent, entranced by things foreign — it is almost an asset!"

Nourse counselled that to get the best space, a retailer had to hire an expert: "Real estate is an information market and you need expertise and contacts." Bombay had to be extremely discriminating in order to get what it wanted. In the first year it acquired only three stores, the second year 13, the third year 39, and in 1990 it acquired 61. The first leases in Canada were all handled by Nourse.

As a result of The Bombay Company's unique concept and profitable operation it was now in a good bargaining position. It did not have to compromise on its requirements.

Preparation for entry and barriers to entry

Nourse's advice for entering the United States market was "to do your homework thoroughly before you come. Recognize what your distinctive features would be to enable you to make a living in this market." The best managers must be assigned to the United States. Often companies hire someone in the United States, but they are not really competent.

Nourse stressed that companies must have not only the managerial resources, but also the financial resources to successfully enter the

United States.

One of the most common pitfalls was to look at a market, see that there was no direct competition for a Canadian retail concept, and make the mistake of taking that concept to the United States and assuming it would work.

The United States was very seductive because everything looked similar and familiar. Though companies saw a few differences, they didn't appear to be major. Hence, they entered assuming the market was similar, and made a huge mistake. Hypermarkets, for example, were struggling because they were too general and had competition from all sides. A very thorough competitive analysis was required to "understand what you're up against."

Greenfield entry

The Bombay Company used the greenfield mode of expansion both in Canada and in the United States. With a highly specialized and unique concept, it was an asset to a mall, thus facilitating greenfield expansion. A key aspect of greenfield expansion was that it must be approached regionally. Many companies had failed because they did not begin regionally.

An American perspective on the Canadian market

Many American business executives do not understand the Canadian market and incorrectly regard it as one market of 26 million people, not as having five distinct regions. Nourse had numerous calls about the Canadian market from American retailers, many of whom were big names in the American retail industry. He felt that interest in expanding to Canada was fairly high. They were concerned with what the Canadian market was like, what the differences were, what it was like to run two companies in two countries, and what the problems were.

Reflecting on the Bombay Experience

The Bombay Company experience, along with the overview of both markets from an American point of view, provides important insights into the United States markets that help explain the different perceptions held by some of the executives of Canadian companies studied.

One of the greatest difficulties experienced by the Canadian companies in the United States, particularly those using the greenfield mode of entry, was with respect to securing good locations. It seems clear from Nourse's experience that this is a problem unless the retail offering is specialized and unique. Regarding this need to differentiate the offering, he pointed out two ways to do it — proprietary products and control of suppliers. The key is having a concept that is unique. The need to specialize and focus on a different segment of the market than your competitors is the most critical aspect in obtaining good locations because it provides differential advantage.

The Bombay Company's experience shows that the Canadian market is a much more difficult market in which to find good locations, partly because there are fewer choices and fewer developers. However, it was not a problem for the Canadian companies studied because they were large and important in Canada. They controlled their suppliers by being large.

The Bombay Company's success provides some insights into creating differential advantage and maintaining a leadership position in a highly competitive market. Its key success factors are the unique concept it has created, the complex supply network, top locations, very strong visual presentation and promotional strategy, its frequent strategic planning, and the company attitude and approach to change. These factors will be covered in more depth and compared to the Price Company and Lenscrafters cases in a summary of the keys to succeeding in the United States. They will all then be compared to the experiences of the Canadian retailers in the next chapter.

LENSCRAFTERS INTERNATIONAL INC.

The Lenscrafter Story

Lenscrafters is a 100 percent owned subsidiary of a diversified American corporation, The United States Shoe Corporation (US Shoe). In 1988, Lenscrafters entered the Canadian market and has grown to a profitable chain with over 30 stores.

US Shoe, headquartered in Cincinnati, Ohio, is a publicly traded corporation that began as a shoe manufacturer. By 1980, the company had evolved into a vertically integrated footwear manufacturer and retailer. During the 1980s, the company transformed its business focus through a series of acquisitions and startups, first through the entry into women's apparel retailing, then through the acquisition in 1984 of a small optical retailer, Lenscrafters. At the time, Lenscrafters was a chain of three stores with sales of approximately $4 million.

By 1991, US Shoe had grown to encompass 2,738 retail outlets and leased departments in the United States and abroad, and Lenscrafters was yielding the highest average operating profit as a percentage of sales of any of the US Shoe divisions. The optical retailer was a prime example of the niche retailing trend that had developed in the 1980s. It had developed its own corporate vision that focussed on the competitive advantages it wanted to give its customers and employees:

- most appreciated retail customer service,
- most convenient for customers,
- superior products,
- most engaging work environment,
- best informed and qualified associates,
- known for superior optometric patient care and service,
- most distinctive and effective marketing programs,

- most efficient purchaser and producer, and
- superior autonomy and access to capital by producing outstanding financial results for the corporation.

The Lenscrafters retail concept featured a one stop, one hour approach to being outfitted for eyewear. Each Lenscrafters store had the following: dispensing optician, full service laboratory for grinding lenses, and flexible hours geared to consumer traffic patterns (ie. not necessarily 9–5, Monday to Friday).

Additionally, Lenscrafters leased space next to its stores to independent optometrists who performed eye examinations. The one hour service was highly effective, with a 95 percent delivery rate. High levels of customer satisfaction resulted from Lenscrafters' focus on quality, value and customer service.

Lenscrafters USA was founded in 1983 by former Procter & Gamble (P & G) executives who exploited a new concept for the retailing of optical wear. Another chain of stores had pioneered the super-optical concept before Lenscrafters, but it was Lenscrafters that took it to national prominence. Initially, all Lenscrafters' locations were in the United States midwest region. In its first year of operations, Lenscrafters opened three stores, hired 12 employees and built the operation to $4 million in sales. In 1984, US Shoe purchased the super-optical store concept by acquiring 100 percent ownership of the fledgling Lenscrafters.

In 1985, Bannus Hudson left P & G to join Lenscrafters, and in 1987 became Lenscrafters Chief Executive Officer. His goal was to build a $1 billion company by 1993, without sacrificing any entrepreneurial spirit in getting there. In 1990, Hudson was made President and Chief Executive Officer of US Shoe.

With the purchase of Lenscrafters, US Shoe management took an active role in the management of the company. Their financial resources, retail experience and unique inventory management systems were a strong resource for Lenscrafters.

By 1990, the company had grown to 409 super-optical stores which represented more than a third of all optical superstores in the United States. Lenscrafters had led the expansion of the superstore concept, which now accounted for roughly ten percent of the total United States optical sales of $10 billion. Lenscrafters sales of $580 million gave it an approximate 5.8 percent market share. In 1991, Lenscrafters was aiming to increase market share and boost productivity with a series of measures, including refocussing on high profit locations, formal sales training to increase customer satisfaction, tying management bonuses to customer satisfaction ratings, and new product and display initiatives.

John McArthur, President of Lenscrafters Canada, attributed the American company's success to several factors. First, it had been a pioneer of the super-optical concept in an industry that had not featured tough competition previously. Second, it was built on midwest values that genuinely cared about people and had evolved into a company that was not just another New York retailer. For instance, company values encouraged employees to make every decision in the customer's favour. According to Hudson, "We don't worry what it will cost, or the irrationality of the customer. We never criticize an employee's decision if it is in the customer's favour — we may train that associate to act differently next time, however."

Lenscrafters had ten core values that were central to the company's founding principles of decentralized management and empowered associates (as Lenscrafters referred to its employees):

1. nurture individuals,
2. build on people's strengths,
3. accept mistakes,
4. promote team players,
5. push ideas,

6. each store a separate business,
7. plan for the 21st century,
8. demand highest quality,
9. constantly improve,
10. have fun.

Empowerment was crucial to understanding Lenscrafters' approach to its employees. According to David Browne, CEO of Lenscrafters USA, "We walk like we talk. With clear direction and ample tools to do the job, good people will do the right thing and do it better than you could ever dictate, mandate, or prescribe policy for. We try to minimize policy and procedure, but optimize understanding of what is expected and optimize the values with which we expect people to operate.

"We want people to push ideas, and in connection with pushing ideas, we want people to know it's o.k. to accept mistakes. If we're not having mistakes, we're not pushing enough ideas. It's o.k. to fail in our [corporate] culture as long as you learn from it. It's o.k. to try ideas and have something not work, as long as you learn from it and the company learns from it.

"We don't want to make the same mistake 15 times, but accepting mistakes is important. It removes fear. It encourages innovation. There's a lot of room for folks to tailor-market, to tailor-merchandise, to tailor their operation's approach."

Lenscrafters USA offered a range of employee motivation programs. Horizon Club was a program that honoured employees with outstanding examples of customer service through nominations submitted by managers. Each year the company also had a national Lab Olympics in which winners received Super Bowl styled rings with diamonds, plus a $1,000 bonus.

Expansion strategy

Lenscrafters USA had grown and expanded through a regional retail strategy beginning in the midwest that had targeted primary markets. By 1991, Lenscrafters had covered virtually all the primary markets in the United States and were now seeking growth in three ways: increased penetration of United States markets, different eyewear retail concepts, and expansion abroad.

Lenscrafters pursued increased penetration through entering secondary markets or by putting more stores into certain urban markets (ie. downtown or suburb penetration). Lenscrafters now looked at secondary markets with a service area population as small as 150,000 people and had adjusted the size and formulations of its store concepts. It was estimated that an additional 300 stores could be added to the network. As a result of this strategy, there were now few holes remaining in the United States national network.

The different retail eyewear concept that was now being tested in the United States was a low price, down market eyewear chain called Sight & Save. Sight & Save sold prescription eyeglasses for $40, but did not offer one hour service. The test currently involved three stores, and early results were good.

Lenscrafters had also expanded to two countries outside the United States and by July 1991, the Canadian chain numbered 30 stores, while the UK chain, launched in 1990, totalled five stores. To facilitate this expansion abroad, in 1988 Lenscrafters had formed an International Division headquartered in Cincinnati.

Lenscrafters in Canada

Pre-entry preparation

In 1987, Lenscrafters USA first considered entering the Canadian market. According to McArthur, the "slightly precipitous" entry decision was motivated in part by the start-up of a competing eyewear retailer, EyeMasters. The private, American owned EyeMasters had opened a store in Vancouver that was a virtual clone of the Lenscrafters concept.

The most important factor supporting Lenscrafter's entry into Canada was its strategy to expand internationally. The Canadian entry was rationalized as a low cost/low risk approach to test Lenscrafters' concept outside the United States. It also offered the advantage of proximity.

Pre-entry research included several usage and attitude studies conducted by telephone in Calgary and Toronto. These studies found a Canadian optical consumer that was more educated about product options than Americans, and concluded that the one hour service delivery would be a new concept in Canada.

It was decided that a greenfield entry would be used since there were no super-optical acquisition opportunities in Canada. Once the decision was taken, a series of lease commitments were made concurrently, involving the opening of six to eight stores. These initial store openings were watched closely, with monthly tracking. In situations where the new store was able to attract doctors to practise next to the store, the results were as good as in the United States; where doctors resisted Lenscrafters, the stores were not as successful.

Tom Kremer, who was Operations Director of the Canadian division from 1988 to 1991, noted that Lenscrafters was in a strong position coming into Canada: "We had operated in 45 states with a couple of hundred units before we came up here. We had lots of experience to draw on."

Barriers to entry

One major entry barrier that was underestimated by the American decision makers was the enormous hurdle involved in establishing relationships with Canadian optometrists who were a relatively tight community. Optometrists were crucial to the company's success since Lenscrafters needed prescriptions to sell glasses. They found that the Canadian associations and colleges were extremely uncomfortable with their concept and perceived their arrival as an unwanted increase in competition. In direct contrast, there were waiting lists and competitive selection criteria to become a doctor associated with Lenscrafters in markets where Lenscrafters had been involved for a long time (eg. Ohio).

Lenscrafters responded by gradually convincing the optometrists that Lenscrafters stood for quality and that it did not want to interfere in the delivery or quality of examinations. However, obtaining an audience with optometrists, especially at any professional gatherings, was difficult if not impossible.

Lenscrafters had a small competitive disadvantage in this regard because, although all optical firms were confronted by the same difficulties, the competition, such as Hakim or Standard Optical, had an enormous head start in establishing relationships and credibility.

Kremer thought the Canadian optical community vis à vis its American counterpart was "more political and closely regulated — a tighter group with fewer rebels." He said it took a rebel optometrist to join ranks with Lenscrafters, which was considered "commercial optometry" in the schools. Canada as a whole closely resembled the most incredibly strict states of the United States.

Another entry barrier was the relatively closed development industry, which made finding locations difficult since Lenscrafters had chosen to enter Canada with a greenfield strategy. In the beginning, when the company was new and unknown, securing appropriate locations was a challenge. They were also searching for larger space (4,000 to 5,000 sq. ft.) than was typically the norm for Canadian retailers. In March 1988, Lenscrafters opened its first Canadian store in Calgary in South Centre Mall, a major regional mall.

Other start-up challenges

In entering the Canadian market, Lenscrafters had to learn about a different culture. Although the United States and Canada shared similar media, products, food and restaurants, Lenscrafters found there were some major differences. To understand consumers better, Kremer compared Canadian markets to American ones. For instance, he likened Edmonton and Calgary to the Denver and Seattle markets, or Toronto to Chicago, and looked for what worked best in these similar markets.

The start-up was not without its difficulties. There was a learning curve involved, especially around the balancing of the best concepts and programs developed in the United States with the need to address market characteristics in Canada and, specifically, allowing the Canadian Lenscrafters division to operate with relative autonomy.

Expectations versus early results

By July 1991, Lenscrafters had grown to become the largest optical superstore chain in Canada, with 30 stores. The number of stores had been cut back slightly from plan, but that was largely due to the economic recession of 1990–91.

Regarding profitability, an important milestone had recently been achieved. The 1990 US Shoe annual report stated that "the group incurred lower, but continued losses in the Canadian operation." However, by July 1991 the Canadian stores as a whole were now profitable. Initial expectations had been for "immediate profits, but there had been an underestimation of the impact of moving into another country."

Comparing Canada to California

In terms of approximate market size and uniqueness, the entry in 1988 was similar to the California entry in 1985. For each market, it had taken roughly three years to reach profitability, although California was significantly more profitable with its larger scale of operations.

Kremer felt that specialized regional markets led to American companies being more successful coming into a new market like Canada — "we're used to playing to different rules in different regional markets. In Canada, you play by California rules when you talk workforce rules."

Philosophy

Organizationally, Lenscrafters management style was patterned after Procter & Gamble, where two of its founders came from. A significant number of current Lenscrafters executives were ex-P&G, and elements of the P&G culture existed throughout Lenscrafters USA: strategic product development, careful marketing planning, rigorous research and consumer testing. Lenscrafters USA featured centralized management for procurement, advertising and finance that was based in Cincinnati, but marketing and merchandising functions were decentralized.

Canadian management

The Toronto headquarters of Lenscrafters Canada had been set up to parallel the traditional organizational design of the Cincinnati head office. The only new position created was Director of Professional Development which was a special post created in Canada to recruit and manage relationships with doctors, to develop group vision care programs for employers and manage relationships with third party providers (ie. government).

In March 1988, the initial management team was hired by the Vice-President International, and consisted of six Canadians and three Americans. Although American managers were part of the initial team, the intention from the beginning was to develop an all-Canadian management team.

McArthur was hired by Lenscrafters as president of the Canadian subsidiary in the summer of 1988. Shortly after joining Lenscrafters, McArthur determined that he would have to restructure his management team. In the initial hiring, the skill levels and appropriate salaries required for the management positions had been underestimated. Over the next two and a half years, McArthur restructured his Canadian-hired management support team, and by early 1991, McArthur had hired managers qualified to "manage their piece of the business." This was important because the Canadian office operated autonomously from Cincinnati in many areas. Operations, marketing, human resources and purchasing all had to be tailored to the Canadian market.

All Canadian directors had spent an orientation and training period in the United States, although the length of time varied for each.

McArthur himself had spent three months, while other directors had only spent a brief amount of time there. McArthur described his executive team as a tightly knit group.

Reporting relationships with head office

Occasional challenges had arisen over the issue of Canadian autonomy; however, these were mostly attributed to Lenscrafters history of operating centrally from Cincinnati. McArthur likened Lenscrafters Canada to a freestanding operation: "The United States company is an incredible success story, but you can't simply cookie-cutter the formula." Capital was allocated to the divisions, including Canada, through a negotiation process that took into account ability to fund and persuasiveness of appeal.

Kremer described the Lenscrafters strategic planning process as constant. Strategic plans were developed upwards, and were reviewed quarterly while operational plans were reviewed monthly. The marketing plan was developed annually for sales and spending, but could be altered over the course of the year. Variances against plan were determined monthly, and adjustments in expenditures or promotion were made accordingly.

Comparing Operations in Canada and the United States

The product

Lenscrafters had radically changed the traditional approach to optical retailing in many ways by pioneering the super-optical concept that allowed for one stop shopping. Lenscrafters had introduced the concept of one hour turnaround that included on site fitting, lens fabrication and receipt of finished glasses. They had ingrained this benefit in consumers' consciousness by advertising heavily to pull in customers, instead of the traditional opticians' reliance on walk in trade and optometrist recommendations. They carried approximately 3,500 stock keeping units.

Lenscrafters accommodated sales surges (ie. a heavy rush of consumers at lunch hour or on Saturdays) by designing a flexible scheduling system to expand capacity when necessary. Even though only half of all customers returned back within the hour, Lenscrafters carefully monitored the one hour delivery promise, and was able to achieve one hour turnaround 95 percent of the time. The one hour promise did not include out of stock items. Lenscrafters was also developing a new scheduling system based on tracked traffic patterns.

Suppliers

McArthur felt there was not much of a difference between Canada and the United States when comparing the cost of goods sold. Although Canadian net costs of merchandise in the store were slightly higher, most of the difference was accounted for by different tax structures. Return policies, terms of credit (days), and discounts available varied according to supplier and to the size of deal, but were not different from similarly sized deals from suppliers in the United States.

Lenscrafters Canada did *not* buy through the United States buying group because it was more cost effective and efficient to buy independently in Canada. Despite lower economies of scale, Lenscrafters Canada was still able to obtain near United States prices by leveraging on being part of a large United States company, while maintaining flexibility. Suppliers drop shipped to the stores in Canada, allowing for just in time inventory management.

Lenscrafters put great value on maintaining close relationships with its suppliers. They worked them hard, placed huge expectations on them, but also wanted them to profit from their association. To show its appreciation, Lenscrafters held a Vendors' Day celebration every year in Cincinnati that involved upfront studies on delivery and product quality, and culminated in a major awards ceremony for Vendor Of The Year. At the Vendors' Day presentations, Lenscrafters shared with their suppliers various corporate information relating to needs analysis and upcoming plans.

More deals tended to be closed with a handshake and without signatures in Canada compared to the United States. It was felt, though, that the vendor networks were not as advanced as in the United States probably due to the small size of the Canadian market.

Systems

When Lenscrafters entered Canada, it used the same inventory control system as in the United States. However, Canadian suppliers used bar coding for their products, and Lenscrafters Canada adapted their management information systems to accept the Canadian bar codes. This enhancement proved so successful that the Canadian model was recently introduced to the United States.

Advertising and promotion

Lenscrafters invested heavily in advertising. McArthur estimated that in Canada and the United States, 12–15 percent of the sales dollar went into marketing costs (which included media costs, research, overheads and coupon redemptions), which far outstripped Canadian competitors who on average spent considerably less on advertising. Of the Canadian competition, EyeMasters fluctuated in its advertising intensity (heavy at times), while numerous other competitors advertised significantly.

Advertising was heavily focussed on television, radio and newspaper. There was limited use of magazines, transit (worked in Toronto on subway stations near locations but failed miserably in Atlanta), direct mail and billboards. Lenscrafters had been very successful in its use of coupon value packs.

In Canada Lenscrafters had used a combination of United States and made in Canada advertising. In the United States, Lenscrafters had greater flexibility to obtain full discounts year round using ad hoc media buys, whereas in Canada, they had to buy their media on a 52 week commitment to obtain volume discounts.

Employee motivation and compensation

One key to Lenscrafters success was its corporate mission statement that placed great emphasis on making sales happen by developing team players: "In our business, it takes a team of people to make a sale." The Lenscrafters concept meant that for one sale, a customer might come into contact and deal with six different people (greeter, frame stylist, initial dispensing optician, laboratory technician, cashier, different fitting optician).

Central to motivating employees was empowering field management, many of whom, in turn, successfully empowered employees. McArthur observed that "Americans run with empowerment. A retail career is looked upon as a profession. In the United States, store managers see themselves as budding entrepreneurs." McArthur had found that Canadian store managers reacted positively to additional responsibility and authority via empowerment.

There were many differences between Canada and the U.S. in dealing with employees. As McArthur noted, " In the United States, you can let anyone go for whatever reason. In Canada, you need more time to counsel people toward improvement before getting them out of the company."

McArthur found wage levels between Canada and the United States relatively comparable when comparing similar cities. For instance, sales associates and lab technicians were paid $7 to $8 per hour in both countries. In the end, after income tax and statutory deductions, Canadians had less take home pay.

There were differences between Canada and the United States in the kinds of benefits offered. In Canada, employees were covered by various provincial health programs, whereas in the United States, Lenscrafters paid for employee health insurance. In this area, costs were much higher in the United States.

Employee motivation programs were offered in both countries; however, in some cases, there was less reaction to them in Canada than in the United States. McArthur found that Canadians responded better to length of service acknowledgement.

Management had found employee sales contests to be less popular in Canada, although contests in March 1991 had electrified the company. McArthur was unsure whether this success was the result of tough times or three years of repeated sales contests finally taking effect.

One major area of compensation that differed between Canada and the United States was commission sales and bonus systems. In the United States, employees were motivated by a myriad of compensation systems. In most United States retailers, sales commissions were the norm. In addition, Lenscrafters United States used a spiff incentive system under which, for example, an employee might receive a monetary incentive (say $1) for the sale of a particular product. In Canada, the bonus system that had been derived shared bonuses with all employees based on overall store performance.

Lenscrafters Canada's unique store-shared bonus system was being closely watched by Cincinnati management who strongly believed in the merit of individual incentives. At present, Lenscrafters United States was considering implementing a consistent United States wide policy of pooling spiffs or bonuses, largely for the same reason as that found in Canada, namely dissatisfaction from backroom lab technicians.

McArthur was pleased that on a recent company survey of Canadian and American associates, the Canadians scored higher on every scale such as customer satisfaction and one hour delivery. He commented, "We've taken all of what is best in the American hero culture and Canadianized it some." Examples of an un-Canadian business environment were evident — dress down day every pay day at the corporate office and promotional T-shirts worn by all. For some new Canadian executives, used to more conservatism in the business culture, it took time to acclimatize to American organizational values that were more frank in stating issues and more expressive in terms of support.

To ensure the Lenscrafters philosophy on customer service style was met, Canadian store management went through training in the United States.

Productivity

The three productivity measures that McArthur watched very closely were the delivery of the one hour promise (slightly higher in Canada), labour productivity, and sales/margins. In comparing overall productivity between Canada and the United States, McArthur found rough similarity except for selling, general and administrative costs, which, when taken together, were 15 percent higher in Canada. The major differences were in rents and head office expense, which were significantly higher in Canada. Cost of goods sold and marketing costs were slightly higher as well, all leading to lower profits and return on investment for the Canadian operation compared to the American group. If the higher Canadian corporate office expense was netted out, and comparable stores compared (ie. three years, same size, same market/product mix), the profits would be the same except for the higher occupancy costs in Canada.

Stock turned over about twice a year. In Canada, markdowns were taken on a periodic basis and were used to adjust inventory levels. Markdowns were 30 to 40 percent greater in the United States because there was more of a discount mentality.

Canadian senior management participated in a bonus system that was very similar to the Lenscrafters United States formula. Bonuses, which ranged between 5 to 25 percent of net salary, were based on a combination of profitability, return on assets, and the achievement of individual objectives (not consumer satisfaction).

Canadian Expansion Strategy

Lenscrafters Canada had followed the same basic expansion approach as in the US — primary markets first, secondary markets second; Lenscrafters originally thought that the company could build 50 to 60 stores across Canada (roughly 10 percent of the United States number of stores) before reaching saturation. In Canada, once past large metropolitan markets, there was a lack of appropriately sized markets. McArthur estimated that by 1995 the window on further expansion will have been closed either by Lenscrafters or the competition, and he hoped to have the Sight & Save concept introduced before then.

Consumers: Demographics, Attitudes and Behaviour

McArthur and the members of his management team all agreed that the Canadian market was more fashion forward than the American market, and therefore the Canadian merchandise mix had been tailored to include more high fashion product. When Lenscrafters first opened in Canada, the Canadian stores were stocked with inventory similar to the United States. This product mix did not sell well and it was changed to suit the market. Kremer thought that Canadians approached eyewear purchases from more of a product quality standpoint.

Kremer thought that overall, Americans were much harder to please, and were heavily influenced by price because they went to low price retailers where they were not going to get service. Canadians, on the other hand, seem to factor in those trade offs more and were willing to pay for quality service.

One very important demographic trend affecting Lenscrafters was North America's rapidly aging population. By the age of 35, roughly 80 percent of adults required some sort of corrective eyewear.

Market Research

Lenscrafters commissioned a great amount of market research in both markets. For instance, American consumer satisfaction was constantly tracked via mail in cards (more than 20,000 responses were processed each month), a procedure that was now being tested in Canada.

This consumer tracking was indicative of a company that was obsessed with the consumer and their behaviour — for example, all advertising was thoroughly researched and tested with consumers in focus groups before being used in a marketing campaign.

Competition

Competitive optical retailing trends in the United States market were toward one hour service, two for one promotions, and cut rate prices. The first two trends were also found in Canada. In McArthur's opinion, the United States market was more intensely competitive than Canada's. In Canada, only five chains competed in the super-optical segment, and Lenscrafters was the largest super-optical chain in Canada.

In both Canada and the United States, the merchandising department made price comparisons every six months. Lenscrafters strategy was to maintain its prices at about the mid range of the market. It responded to competitive actions by increasing its marketing expenditure (through advertising, couponing, promotion, etc.).

In both Canada and the United States, it was the responsibility of everyone in the company to watch the competition and forward intelligence to central management. Every store subscribed to all newspapers in its market area. The marketing director would plan a strategy and defence was immediate. Instead of responding to competition by cutting prices, Lenscrafters main responses included coupons or special offers such as a second pair at a fixed price (eg. $50). Lenscrafters also differentiated itself by delivering more post sale service. Another unique marketing strategy was that Lenscrafters made heavy use of internally generated advertising to pull the consumer into the store. Lenscrafters advertising had also created a consumer expectation for one hour service that had not existed before.

Part of Lenscrafters motivation in entering Canada was to defend its unique concept which was being cloned by EyeMasters. Lenscrafters employed heavy advertising in Canada to create awareness and pull in consumer demand, and spent on total marketing costs (media, research, overheads, coupons) in the 15 percent of sales range.

Cross Border Variable Comparison

A major cross border variable was the higher level of taxation in Canada. However, eyewear had been exempted from the seven percent Goods and Services Tax introduced in 1991.

McArthur felt there were major differences between Canada and the United States regarding real estate: "In the United States, retailers call the tune — the only time you have influence in Canada is in bad times." By 1990–91, with the recession, Canada was now a buyer's market and developers were courting Lenscrafters aggressively. Part of that was also attributable to Lenscrafters heavy advertising reputation which made the store a destination and pulled traffic to malls.

Post-Entry Hindsight

One important lesson that Lenscrafters had learned from the Canadian example, and was now applying to the UK entry, was to fully understand the market before entering and to put more emphasis on upfront study. Looking back on Lenscrafters successful entry into the Canadian market, McArthur assessed the obstacles overcome and successes of the Lenscrafters experience. The company overcame:

- the initial hiring of an inappropriately experienced management team;
- the initial failure to recognize the fashion forward nature of Canadians; once recognized, Lenscrafters had to adjust inventory levels;

- the underestimation of the power of Canadian optometrists and their resistance to the new concept;
- the expense of Canadian retail real estate, but especially during entry which occurred at the height of the boom years of 1988 and 1989 and resulted in expensive lease agreements.

The successes were:

- Lenscrafters successfully met the cloned concept challenge from EyeMasters;
- American head office management recognized the need to develop a separate and increasingly autonomous Canadian management team;
- approximately three years after entry, the Canadian subsidiary was profitable.

Key Success Factors

The most important reasons for Lenscrafters successful entry into Canada were: 1) its achieving the key success factors that had led it to success in the United States, ie. fast one hour service, product quality and customer satisfaction, and competitive pricing; 2) realizing the uniqueness of the Canadian market and adapting to it; 3) overcoming major barriers in establishing relationships with optometrists and developers.

Reflecting on the Lenscrafters Experience

Again, in the Lenscrafters case as well as that of The Bombay Company, was the realization of the major differences between the Canadian and American markets. These differences ranged from the unexpected barriers found in Canada such as the closed optometrist community, to differences in consumer tastes (surprisingly more fashion forward in Canada), costs, level of competition, and the development industry. Like the Bombay experience, the Lenscrafters experience also dispelled the myths regarding the Canadian perception of the United States development industry — "In the U.S. retail calls the shots."

The keys to creating differential advantage, like Bombay, involved a unique concept, very strong promotion, and differentiation through product and service. Bombay's product was more proprietary than was Lenscrafters. However, Lenscrafters put a greater emphasis on promotion and service to set them apart. Strategic planning was also continuous like Bombay.

The strong emphasis on company philosophy and values in Lenscrafters, the development of a company culture, and the empowerment of employees compares very closely to the Price Club story which follows. These elements are central to their success along with the ability to change quickly which is seen in all the American companies. It is not that American companies do not make mistakes entering Canada, they do; but they seem to have recognized the differences and corrected them quickly.

THE PRICE COMPANY CANADA

The Price Company, founded by Sol and Robert Price in the United States in 1976, had grown to 51 warehouses with sales of $6.6 billion by 1991. It was highly profitable, posting a 1991 net income of $134.1 million. In 1986, it expanded into Canada through a joint venture with Steinberg's. Within two and a half years, the Canadian operation had turned a profit. Since then, the company has opened 12 warehouses with sales of approximately $1.5 billion by 1991. In October 1990, the Price Company increased its ownership in Price Club Canada from 50 percent to 100 percent.

Company Beginnings

In the early 1970s, Fed Mart, a retail company, was founded by Sol Price and other investors. It was not oriented to selling to small and medium sized businesses. The company went public in the late 1960s. The controlling financial interest was sold to a German investor in 1975. Sol Price and his son, Robert, remained on the board after the sale for six months, at which time their employment was terminated by the majority owner. It was shortly thereafter, in 1976, that the Price Company was formed.

The Prices had observed that there were many wholesalers and intermediaries who were making a lot of money selling to small businesses. Large firms, on the other hand, could go direct to the manufacturers, thus obtaining better prices. Their concept was to obtain very low prices through buying and selling in bulk, thereby cutting out the middlemen, and selling competitively to the small and medium sized firms.

In 1976, they took over an old industrial building in San Diego, in which airplane engines had been manufactured, and opened the first Price Club. It was run strictly as a business membership club at first; however, about two months later, membership was opened to government and public utility employees. Sales were poor and they lost money the first year. Results improved in the second year. The company was modelled partly after the European cash and carry warehouses except that they were retail and Price Club was wholesale. Essentially, it was a totally new concept in the North American market.

By 1982–83, they were doing very well and had opened 11 units. Then clones began appearing in the marketplace, such as Pace Membership Warehouse (owned by K Mart), Sam's Wholesale Club (a division of Wal–Mart Stores) and Costco.

The United States Company

Despite the competition from newcomers to the market, the Price Company continued to do well and grew from its California base. Early growth was centred in the west and eastern expansion followed several years later.

Organization

The company was divided into an eastern and western division, each having its own president and separate organizations. It was essentially run as two companies, with the only centralized functions being accounting, EDP and legal. By the late 1980s, Sol Price was less active in the company, and chairman Robert Price was trying to remove himself from the day to day operations.

There were separate buying and real estate offices for the eastern and western operations, each having sufficient buying power to obtain the best prices. President of the Canadian Price Club operation, Pierre Mignault, observed that the Price Club was in constant motion, always trying new products, services or methods. If a program did not work, it would be dropped, and they were on to something else. They were untraditional, change was extremely rapid, but not at the expense of their employees, whom they protected.

Presentation

Physically, the clubs used a prototypical warehouse format containing between 96,000 and 135,000 square feet of floor space. The floor plan allowed for high operating efficiency. Members could push flatbed carts or large basket style shopping carts through the wide aisles selecting products for business or personal use, or for resale. Merchandise was generally offered in case, carton, or multiple pack quantity, or in single, jumbo sized packages, and was displayed and stored in packing cartons on pallets and steel racks.

Location

Since shoppers were attracted to the Price Club due to its low wholesale prices and brand name goods, the clubs did not need to be located on prime commercial real estate. Instead, they could locate in areas with lower property costs than traditional retailers. By 1988, the company operated 39 facilities, 36 of which it owned, one was leased, and two were owned buildings on leased land. By the end of 1990, 12 more outlets were opened, with eight planned for the following two years. The owned properties ranged from nine to 17 acres. In addition to owning most of its own sites, The Price Company had an interest in several real estate and shopping centre developments, from which it received lease revenue.

The cost of opening a new warehouse facility was generally estimated at $8 to $19 million. These costs were lower if existing warehouses or similar buildings could be purchased or refurbished. Initial inventories were typically financed by trade payables, ie. goods were purchased on terms allowing for sufficient sales in the interim from which to pay suppliers.

Since warehouse clubs required a huge sales volume in order to survive, they could only be located in markets with a minimum population of 400,000 people, and at least 20,000 small or medium sized businesses within a 15 kilometre radius.

Membership

The Price Club facilities were open only to members, of which there were two types: Business and Gold Star. Businesses with a resale license or any other proof of business could become business members by paying an annual $25 membership fee. Two other cardholders could be designated by paying an additional $10 per person. Gold Star memberships were available to government and public utility employees and certain large private employment groups for a fee of $25 per employee, with an additional spouse card, if desired, for $10.

Product

The Price Company sold a wide variety of products and services, many of which were brand name goods; however, the selection within each category was very limited. For example, customers might be offered only two brands of tires, and canned pears came only in one size and were sold by the dozen. In retail there is a rule that 20 percent of the items produce 80 percent of the sales. The warehouse club strategy was to carry only the top selling items in huge quantities, purchasing direct from the manufacturer and trucked directly to the selling floor. This meant that a warehouse store might carry approximately 3,000 to 3,500 items, compared to a K Mart which could stock up to 80,000 items.

In terms of sales mix by broad category, sundries (sundries, health and beauty aids, office supplies, tobacco and candy) accounted for approximately 33 percent of total sales, food for 27 percent, housewares for 19 percent, with hardlines, softgoods and liquor making up the balance. The foregoing did not include other operations such as optical, pharmacy, gasoline, tire installation and food cart sales.

Purchasing

Company buyers and re-order specialists from each division purchased almost all of the merchandise directly from the manufacturer. There was detailed direction and controls, along with extensive sales information, to guide buyers in their selection of product, much of which came from local suppliers.

Operation

The strategy of the company was to keep expenses and margins low, turn over the merchandise rapidly, and invest any excess cash in the money market. On average, inventory turned over 19 times per year and sales averaged $110 to $120 million per warehouse per year. Cost of goods sold as a percentage of net sales was 91.1 percent in 1990 for the total company, with a selling, general and administrative expense of 7.47 percent. Rental cost of 0.8 percent was included in the cost of goods sold. Gross and net profit were 8.9 percent and 1.42 percent respectively.

The company had grown rapidly and was highly profitable, net income per share almost doubling from $1.25 in 1986 to $2.47 in 1990. During the same five year period, revenues grew from $2.6 billion to $5.4 billion.

Employees

The Price Club was a major employer, employing between 300 and 500 part and full time personnel in each outlet. It was the company's policy to pay close to the highest prevailing wages and benefits in the community. For each of the outlets in California, Maryland, New York, Connecticut, and New Jersey, the company had entered into labour contracts with locals of the International Brotherhood of Teamsters, Chauffeurs, Warehousemen, and Helpers of America.

Competition

As with any good concept, it was bound to be copied, and during the mid 1980s several other companies expanded into the warehouse club business, including Costco, which was co-founded by an ex vice-president of Price Club in 1983. As of 1991, Costco had 70 warehouses, including nine in Canada.

By early 1991, there were a total of 400 warehouse clubs operated by five major corporations in the United States. The North American industry leader, with 177 outlets, was Sam's Wholesale Club, a division of Wal–Mart stores. The second largest operator, with 78 outlets, was Pace Membership Warehouse Inc., a division of K Mart Corp. Neither Sam's nor Pace had Canadian expansion plans at the time this case was written.

Entry into the Canadian Market

In 1984, Irving Ludmer, CEO of Steinberg's, approached Sol Price to form a joint venture in Canada. Price, at the time, was not interested in pursuing a joint venture. Shortly thereafter, Ludmer hired Pierre Mignault, then a general manager at the Bay, to look after new ventures for Steinberg. Mignault subsequently was sent to re-open negotiations with Sol Price, and five months later a deal was struck to form a 50/50 joint venture.

Thus in 1985, Price Club Canada was created, and was run by Mignault as a separate company, independent of both Steinberg's and The Price Company United States. A board of directors was appointed consisting of Arnold Steinberg and Irving Ludmer, another member of the Steinberg organization, Sol and Robert Price, and a Canadian attorney.

The new company was run independently, but was able to benefit from the different organizations. According to Mignault, Steinberg's did not understand the Price Club business; however, it had a large real estate division that was critical in the search for locations. Its legal department was also helpful in dealing with this concept which was new to the Canadian market.

The aim was to clone the American concept in Canada. Mignault spent a lot of time in the United States learning the systems, organization and methods of management. He took their electronic data processing system and Canadianized it over a period of about six months. Price Club United States had a different philosophy on people than most Canadian organizations, allowing far more freedom and participation for executives.

The United States company had a management stock ownership program. Taking its cue from the United States, the Canadian company devised a stock option plan, giving ten percent of the company to management. It was complicated by the fact that Price Club Canada was a private firm owned by two public companies. Despite this difficulty, an innovative plan was developed, which Mignault felt created a real sense of ownership and entrepreneurship, though management did not have to risk their money. Imbued in American management was the thinking that they could be successful together.

Price Club Canada

In November 1986, approximately one year after the Canadian company had been created, the first store was opened in a leased building in the south shore area of Montreal. The first year was very difficult, so much so that the continued existence of the company was brought into question. The turnaround came in the second year. They opened more stores in Montreal, Quebec City, Mississauga, Vaughan (north of Toronto), Ottawa, Kitchener, London, and two in Vancouver. Generally, where the concept was known, the stores gained quick success; however, other markets proved somewhat more difficult.

Thus, in five years, the company had grown from one to 12 warehouse units, and from one to 4,500 employees. According to Mignault, they were now in a rest period and not planning to open further stores until 1992. The rapid growth had been exciting and somewhat scary, and management wanted to ensure that the philosophy was entrenched in the company before the next expansion.

From the time of incorporation in 1985 until the first store was opened in 1986, the company had operated on the original investment from Steinberg's and Price Company. It was very lean, with primitive office space, but the new company never went back for additional funds, and within two and a half years from inception (one and a half years from first store opening) it had turned a profit.

Sale of Steinberg share of Price Club Canada Inc.

In 1989, Socanev Inc. of Montreal with the backing of the Caisse de Dépôt et Placement du Québec, purchased Steinberg's. It was a leveraged buy out, with CASC, the company formed to buy Steinberg's, paying $17 million for a firm worth over $1 billion. There was thus a large debt, and assets were sold off, including three of the four restaurant chains, Miracle Food Mart and the 50 percent share in Price Club Canada Inc.

In the original joint venture agreement between Steinberg and Price Club, all cash was to remain in the new company since they wanted it to grow. If either party wished to sell, the other had first option to buy. To the new Steinberg owner in a high debt situation, Price Club was not an asset, as no cash could be taken out. Hence, in mid 1990, CASC (Corporation d'Acquisition Socanav–Caisse Inc.) decided to sell its half interest to Price Club U.S. for $57.5 million. The only portion remaining in Canadian hands was the ten percent owned by Price Club Canada employees.

Relationship of Canadian and American companies

Although the company ownership changed, very little else did. The board remained the same, headed by Mignault (four directors were Canadians and two were Americans). Board meetings were held four times per year and were often organized around a warehouse opening, or in San Diego. In addition, Mignault tried to interact with the American management other than at board meetings.

Organization

Price Club Canada was organized into many separate companies — as many as 15 to 20 corporations. The company was decentralized in many areas, with few functions such as accounting, some buying and EDP being controlled centrally. Some products were sourced for the whole company from head office, while many were bought at the store level from local market sources in order to cater to the individual trading area tastes and requirements. Each warehouse had a membership manager, responsible for recruiting members in the trading area, personnel manager for the outlet, and administration manager responsible for all store administration and payroll.

The company concept was to push authority as low as possible, thereby giving the power to those at the lowest level. For example, each stocker would take total control of his or her section. Mignault noted that generally there were fewer layers of management in the United States and that there was a trend to cut layering. It meant that employers were closer to their employees. On the other hand, he felt, Canadian managers sit in an ivory tower not visible to and not relating to their staff. He felt that labour in the United States was generally more "rah rah pro company than in Canada — it's in their blood."

Locations

By the end of 1991, Price Club had grown to 12 outlets in Canada: five each in Ontario and Quebec and two in Vancouver. Essentially the same location requirements existed for the Canadian company as for the American — a minimum population of 400,000 people and at least 20,000 small or medium sized businesses within a 15 kilometre radius. With a population only a tenth of that of the United States, expansion opportunities were limited in Canada.

The Price Club had concentrated primarily on the eastern markets, while its rival, Costco, had started in western Canada, growing to eight units by 1991. With three Costco units, and the recent addition of two Price Club outlets in Vancouver, the saturation point had almost been reached for that market. Costco was beginning to move east and was locating in the Toronto market in 1992. The competition for locations in the major markets would soon heat up.

It was company policy, as in the United States, to own the sites and buildings wherever possible. However, the real estate was owned separately by Price Club Real Estate, which in turn leased it to the warehouses. By mid 1991, Price Club Canada owned approximately half of its sites, all financed from the Canadian company earnings. Management intended to increase ownership as sites and capital became available. Leasing was regarded as a short term strategy that might save some money in the early years of operation but would cost more in the long term as rents escalated. Since their profit margins were so small, it was particularly important to control costs in the long term, as an increase in occupancy costs could make the difference between profit and loss.

The United States company had revenue from its real estate developments, but the Canadian company had not yet reached that stage. As the opportunity arose, Price Club Canada intended to buy tracts of land, develop them into shopping centres or office buildings, and lease them out.

Entry barriers

One of the major problems encountered was finding sites in Toronto. The land was owned and controlled by a small number of people who were extremely wealthy. Mignault noted that, due to capital gains taxes, if they sold their land, they did not stand to make much money. He had found Ontario to be over governed, and the many layers of government were extremely complicated. The Golden Horseshoe area had grown very rapidly and the city had decided on uses for particular tracts of land, leaving little or no flexibility and making it extremely difficult for companies such as the Price Club to do business.

Architecture was the first stumbling block, since the cities/municipalities preferred upscale, attractive office buildings, as opposed to factory, retail or warehouse structures. Mignault described the attitude of the politicians as snobbish. Although a Price Club warehouse brought many advantages to its trading area, creating as many as 400 to 500 jobs, buying from local businesses and providing surrounding companies with low priced goods, they were effectively kept out of the market. For five years it had been trying to get into the Toronto market, but had to overcome major obstacles.

Another barrier was zoning. Since Price Club did not fit the retail zoning category, it was forced to apply for spot zoning through the Ontario Municipal Board. For example, if the existing zoning was commercial, but allowed only the sale of groceries, then a minor amendment was required since Price Club sold hard lines as well. Public hearings had to be held and the local merchants such as Loblaw, Bonanza, and A & P could, and did, oppose the amendment. A long drawn out process, including going to council, Ontario Municipal Board Hearings, and city studies, all proved a formidable barrier.

This process, strong opposition from competitors, and the unwillingness of the politicians to deal with them had effectively kept Price Club out of most of the prime Toronto locations for five years. Finally the company was receiving some co-operation from the city of Scarborough. Mignault noted that when the Price Club expanded in the United States, the governments and municipalities quickly recognized that the new store format required new zoning, and regulations were changed accordingly.

Presentation

Like the American parent company, the Canadian Price Club outlets were the same warehouse format ranging from 96,000 to 135,000 square feet of floor space. Although there were standards that had to be adhered to, the floor plan changed constantly. As long as two major aisles and three sectors were maintained, it was up to each warehouse manager to arrange the merchandise within the sectors as he/she chose. Fixturing/racking was similar to that in the United States, and goods were displayed and stored in packing cartons on pallets and steel racks.

Product

The types of products carried were similar in both markets with a limited choice of brands and sizes available in each product category. The sales breakdown by category in Canada differed somewhat from that of the United States, largely due to differences in supply and the ability of buyers to exploit some areas better than others, thus creating different strengths in the assortment. The most significant difference in sales mix was the proportion of food sales, which was approximately five to six percent higher in Canada.

Consumers

Mignault noted that the American consumer, on average, had much higher discretionary income, and that their life style, on a same salary basis, was much better in the United States. He also felt that Canadian consumers were becoming more price sensitive than they used to be, more like their American counterparts. The Price Club experience and research had shown that the higher the consumer income, the more price sensitive they were!

Purchasing

Almost all the products were sourced in Canada, with only five to ten percent imported, largely from the United States. Sourcing was done on a store by store basis, as well as nationally. In order to adapt to the different markets, there was a buying team in each city, Montreal, Toronto, and Vancouver. Since the stock turnover was so rapid, turning 21 times per year in Canada, compared to 19 times in the United States, it was difficult to deal with foreign merchandise.

Approximately five percent of the products were bought on the grey market for the Canadian stores. As Mignault pointed out, "In Europe there are no boundaries to selling, and we may have to change our thinking in this market as we move to a global economy. Many products which are manufactured can be sold in most countries and are CSA approved." Companies generally have sales reps in each country and price disparities do occur. The market will eventually even out these differences.

According to Mignault, a lot of buying was done at the local level in the United States as well. There had been little liaison between the Canadian and American buyers in the start-up stage; however, by 1991 they were beginning to meet on a regular basis.

Prices

Mignault felt that prices were higher in Canada for several reasons. Higher taxation at every level was one of the major factors. He also thought that due to the United States being a much more competitive market, suppliers prices were lower. In Canada, there was a perception that higher prices added prestige to a line and that suppliers often gouged the retailer.

Using the example of a Toshiba TV that sold for United States $600–$699, the same television was priced at C$1,400–$1,500 in Canada. Since Toshiba was purchased outside North America, and transportation costs from Japan to Los Angeles or Vancouver were approximately the same, the major difference was the lower markup taken by the manufacturer in the United States. While acknowledging differences in levels of taxation and other costs between Canada and the United States, he attributed the major price differences to suppliers.

Competition

Price Club regarded everybody as a competitor, with the primary players being wholesalers and cash and carry stores. As in the United States, Costco was a major competitor being the largest other warehouse operator in Canada. It was run out of Seattle and had a buying office in Canada. Unlike the Price Club, however, much of the merchandise was brought in from the United States.

Canadian wholesalers found competition from the Price Club to be very tough, and in the beginning, Mignault received many threatening calls from other wholesalers as Price Club was selling below their cost. A few, particularly in the Quebec market, were so upset that they threatened Mignault if he did not raise prices.

The Price Club promise was to have the best price, but it would not sell below cost. In order to live up to their promise, competitive prices were checked *every day*. This was extremely important in order to retain credibility with the small and medium sized businesses. If competitive prices on an item were less than their cost, then a sign on the item would tell the customer that it could be purchased for less at the competition.

Employee incentives

Price Club Canada was not unionized. They paid among the highest wages for staff in the industry and offered a benefit package second to none. One of the key benefits was the opportunity for growth within the company. Employees started from the bottom and worked up and did better than if they had come in from outside. Rapid company growth led to the creation of many good job opportunities.

Managers were well compensated. For example, a warehouse manager had a base salary of $70,000 plus a 30 to 35 percent bonus and an attractive stock option plan. If the company performed well, it would be extremely lucrative for the employees. The stock option plan was similar to that in the United States. However, the American company was planning to adopt parts of the Canadian plan which it regarded as superior. Bonuses were based on profit. Management budgeted on a quarterly basis and were paid bonuses twice a year based on achieving their quarterly profit plans. Canadian salaries were quite close to those in the United States company. One of the main differences was that they started lower in the United States and rose more quickly, whereas they started higher in Canada and rose more slowly.

The American company had discontinued the bonus system except for the warehouse manager, but based on the success in Canada, American management was thinking of reinstituting it. Mignault noted that the Americans were very quick to change and adapt, while the Canadians were much more conservative and set in their ways. It took much longer and required far more persuasion to change anything in Canada and the decision making tended to be more democratic. In the United States, for example, when a decision was made not to provide cars to management, it was simply instituted and accepted. Management and staff were more accepting all round.

The distance between senior management and labour compensation tended to be smaller in the Price Club than was the norm in the United States. In relation to the hourly wage earners, Robert Price's salary was 13:1, whereas the average American CEO to labour ratio was approximately 80:1. This same figure was not available for the Canadian market, but is presumed to be significantly lower than in the United States. Mignault felt it was representative of the company philosophy in Canada, and in the United States, that there was not a great distance between senior management and labour, in line with the American trend to cut layering.

There was an egalitarian, casual and no frills atmosphere not only in the stores but in the head office. Staff, including Mignault, were casually dressed, and meetings took place in utilitarian offices. Everything was geared toward keeping costs low, and the warehouse environment was evident from the selling floor to the senior management offices.

Advertising

On the day before each warehouse was opened, Price Club advertised in the local newspaper. Other than this announcement, there was no advertising since it would add to operating costs. It did publish its own newspaper five times per year telling about new programs, products and services, and company news. This was available in the stores for customers and employees.

Membership

Membership was key to the Price Club operation, and was run in a similar manner in both the countries. Sales could be quite accurately forecast based on the number of club memberships. The renewal rate was thus very important and was similar in both countries for both the business and individual members. Each store had a membership manager who was in charge of marketing to the local community to maintain/increase membership. Catalogues were sent to businesses inviting them to come see the warehouse.

Company wide, there were approximately 1.1 million business members and 1.8 million Gold Star or Privilege members, as they are called in Canada, having a total of six million membership cards. In Canada, approximately two-thirds of the sales were from business members, the balance coming from Privilege members. The United States company was slightly different. Some members referred to the Price Club as the "$300 Club" because they could not make a trip to the Price Club without spending at least $300.

Financial results

Since the Canadian company was a wholly owned subsidiary, all financial data was consolidated with the American parent. The Canadian company's sales were approximately $1.5 billion and the total company's sales $6.6 billion in 1991. Net income was approximately 1.2 percent of net sales in Canada compared to 2.4 percent for the total company. Although reaching profitability within a year and a half of opening the first Canadian store, Price Club Canada still had a slightly lower profit rate than the American operation due to higher costs incurred in Canada. Return on equity for the overall company was approximately 45 percent.

Occupancy costs were the major difference in the higher Canadian expenses. Since the United States company owned most of their properties, the rents charged to the stores were very low. Although almost half the properties were owned in Canada, the balance were leased, resulting in higher occupancy costs.

Head office expense was another area where the Canadian costs were higher since there were fewer units over which to spread the cost. The difference in salaries between Canada and the United States, as a percent of sales, was minimal. Expenses controlled by the warehouses were a little lower in the United States as they were slightly more efficient. Promotion and advertising expenses were low and approximately the same in both countries.

Since surplus cash from trade payables was invested in short term securities, the decrease in interest rates in 1991 and 1992 was negatively affecting the return on equity. Efforts were being made to turn inventory faster in order to improve the return on equity.

Strategic and sales planning

The Price Club did not believe in long term financial forecasts, as was evidenced by Robert Price's statement in the 1990 annual report, "As you know it is not our practice to predict what future sales and earnings will be. There are many uncertainties in the nation's economy and no one can be sure how all of these factors will affect merchandise sales." Of the same opinion, the Canadian company did two year financial and real estate forecasts. For the most part, however, while not neglecting the two year forecast, management planned on a quarterly basis. The United States divisions had been favourably impressed with this method of planning and were modelling their forecasting on the Canadian system. Although their previous planning methods had been successful, they were very adaptable, always looking to improve on existing procedures.

Mignault was not in favour of the incessant forecasting done by the major specialty and department stores. He did not believe that retailers should lose money nine months out of 12 and make all their money during the last three months of the year.

Future expansion

The Price Club was considering expansion through joint ventures in other markets such as Europe. It had already formed a 50/50 joint venture with a Mexican company that was the second largest retailer in Mexico and was opening a warehouse there in the fall of 1991. Mignault was on the board of the new venture, which in many ways resembled the start-up in Canada. Unlike the Canadian situation, however, many of the products were sourced from the United States.

Mignault saw many advantages to joint ventures when entering a new country. It was important to know the legislation and nature of a new market, and this was best accomplished by a joint venture with indigenous management. Using Canadians in Canada, and Mexicans in Mexico, helped the operations to be successful, since there were so many elements that differed from the United States.

In his view, the Americans were also helpful in Canada. They taught the new management the company philosophy and how the operation worked. The interaction between the two resulted in a superior operation than if either had attempted it separately.

Management's View of the Key Success Factors of American Retailers in Canada

Mignault saw the main ingredient of American success as being their dynamic, quick attitude. Americans don't necessarily work harder, but they are very positive and creative. The American dream still exists in the United States and they are committed to achieving it. In addition, the American retailers are closer to and more focussed on the customer.

Reflecting on the Price Club Experience

There were several factors that paved the way for success in Canada.

1. The uniqueness of the concept which was new to the Canadian market. Due to its low cost format, Price Club could offer prices which were lower than virtually all its competitors in a market where few dis-

count formats existed.

2. The timing was good as the market was becoming very price conscious with the onset of the recession.

3. In management's view, the joint venture was a key, giving the new company access to American expertise, operating information, and management philosophies, as well as to strong knowledge and understanding of the Canadian market.

4. The de-centralized structure allowed each outlet to cater to its local market.

5. The dynamic, quick and positive attitude of the parent organization.

The strong corporate culture and uniqueness of concept are reminiscent of the other American companies. Finally, it is worth commenting that in the same way it helped Price Club enter Canada, joint venturing may be a vehicle to help Canadian companies enter the United States.

CHAPTER 8

MARCHING TO
DIFFERENT DRUMMERS

The American retail environment is perhaps the most fiercely competitive in the world. Not only is the degree of competition higher, as illustrated by Canadian experiences in the United States, but the actual amount of competition is greater. In Canada the enclosed mall retail space was 12.2 square feet per capita in 1990. The comparable number in the United States was 18.2 square feet, almost 50 percent higher.

Americans revel in success. Competition is warlike, with the attitude succinctly stated by Kevin Gordon of Best Buy in Minneapolis who remarked, "Think about the worst thing your competition could do to you, then do it to them first." This is the environment American retailers compete in day in and day out. How do they fight the never ending battle for market share? Competing in this type of environment gives American companies an edge. It is critical for Canadian retailers that would like to enter the United States, or that are facing competition from American retailers in Canada, to understand how the American retailers operate.

SURVIVAL TACTICS:
CREATING COMPETITIVE ADVANTAGE

The research has identified a number of ways that successful American retailers create competitive advantage. Each of the companies studied were market leaders and all adhered to the following fundamentals for success: unique concept, ability to change quickly, a company philosophy or set of values, strong presentation, a strong, complex supply network, strategic planning, service excellence, operational efficiency, and quick competitive response. These are not the only reasons for their success but they tend to have developed these attributes and methods for creating advantage.

Concept

This study shows that highly specialized and unique retail formats tend to be the most successful in the United States while a general offering is likely doomed to failure. The Bombay Company, for example, created its distinctive concept by providing a unique home fashion accessory assortment in a non-traditional mall setting and by using the traditional seasons of the fashion apparel industry on which to base their in-store and catalogue promotional calendar. The complex supply network and product exclusivity allowed it to realize good margins while remaining competitively priced and ultimately led to the ability to offer good value to its customers. Another unique concept was that of the Price Club which was the originator of the warehouse club format.

In the case of Lenscrafters, although it was not the first to create the super-optical concept, it was responsible for developing and growing it across the country and was among the first to implement one hour optical service. Another distinctive concept is that of The Gap. A strong design team, six week merchandise cycle, large clean store format, outstanding promotion and exemplary service all combine to create a unique offering.

Two Canadian companies now may be getting it right also. On the apparel front, Dylex's California based Wet Seal is an example of a highly specialized, unique format. It caters to the fashion forward, female junior market through introducing new products into the stores on a *daily* basis. Canadian Tire's Auto Source entry is a specialized concept unlike its first venture into the United States.

Market Orientation

The American retailers are close to the market and focus on delivering what the consumer wants. Top management spends time on the selling floor talking to staff and customers in order to keep themselves informed and ensure that company direction is in line with what they heard on a first hand basis. Millard Drexler, president of The Gap, for example, has many informal meetings with middle management and sales associates, asking them for their opinions on new designs, advertising and many other facets of the business. In general, the ability of American senior management to listen to customers and staff, along with conducting market research, gives the companies a strong market orientation. Since the United States consumers buying habits change very rapidly, it is critical to have a strong market orientation.

Attitude Toward Change

The American retailers studied were market leaders. Numerous companies have tried to emulate their concepts, some with success, but others without. These companies must defend their positions by constantly changing and improving. Change is necessary in all facets of the retail operation to maintain or gain market share. From merchandise presentation and product assortment, to service and operating efficiency, the successful companies are in a constant state of change which American management appears to embrace. By Canadian standards, they might be accused of being flighty; but this willingness to try something, abandon it if it doesn't work, and try something else is central to their success.

In each of these companies the authors discovered a willingness to adapt to situations and changes in whatever way was necessary to be successful and more efficient. American management always seemed to be searching for better ways and would adapt new methods and integrate them into their own systems. For example, the United States divisions of Lenscrafters and Price Club were quick to recognize and adapt certain systems which their new Canadian companies had developed. In the case of Lenscrafters, the United States divisions were considering implementing a United States wide policy of pooling spiffs or bonuses based on the Canadian company's example. By the same token, Price Club

United States had been impressed with the Canadian company's method of planning and was modelling its forecasting system on it, even though its planning methods were successful.

Experimentation with new concepts and new markets is important for a retailer to be successful in the United States. The Bombay Company was experimenting with the Alex and Ivy concept, was actively considering the European market, had recently entered the Quebec market, and had plans to enter Mexico.

Company Culture and Philosophy

The ability of these companies to change may have some roots in the different social fabric of the United States described in the earlier chapter on culture. However, the companies' culture, their philosophies and values which were entrenched in the organization, supported and encouraged change. It is within this framework that change was promoted and took place. This nebulous element is the heart and soul of a company; it provides the stability while everything else is changing.

Company culture is central to providing excellent service and — that overused phrase — employee empowerment. A company with a strong culture exudes enthusiasm and dynamism. Perhaps the best and most concrete example is that of Lenscrafters. It has ten core values that are central to the company's founding principles of decentralized management and empowered employees. These values are posted in every office and store so that employees are constantly reminded of them. The goal is to optimize the understanding of what is expected and the values within which people are expected to work. In addition, they remove fear which opposes change. It is interesting to note, however, how words and actions can differ. Although Lenscrafters has a value of teamwork, its compensation system of commissions and spiffs was individually oriented. Adopting the Canadian system of shared bonuses based on store performance (a more collective solution) was a move in the direction of having the administrative systems of the company support its espoused values.

Pierre Mignault, president of the Price Club, also stressed the importance of company philosophy. It was the Price Club culture, which he learned from the United States company and had the task of translating and entrenching in the Canadian company, that he felt was so important to the success of the company. In fact, expansion was temporarily slowed to ensure that the company philosophy was properly in place before further stores were opened.

Corporate culture starts at the top and must permeate the organization. It has to do with leadership — some of the great purveyors of corporate culture include the legendary Sam Walton, founder of Wal–Mart; the Fisher family and Millard Drexler, respectively the founders and president of The Gap; David Browne, president of Lenscrafters; and Sol and Robert Price, founders of the Price Company, to name a few.

Service Excellence

A commitment to service must also start at the top of the organization. It is a leadership issue. Each of the companies studied delivered service in a different way, but they all clearly articulated it as part of their culture.

Although Price Club is classified as a self-service retailer, it provides service in a different manner than having sales help on the selling floor. Since their customer's prime motivation is value for the money, Price Club satisfies this demand in every way possible, hence serving the customer well. One of the most valuable services it offers is the fact that it conducts price checks of the competition on a *daily* basis to ensure that its price is the lowest. If it is not, then Price Club will lower its price, unless below cost in which case a sign will be placed on the item advising customers where they can buy it more cheaply. This promotes credibility and customer loyalty and is a valued service.

Lenscrafters core values are key to their provision of excellent service. Managers instruct employees to make every decision in the customer's favour. Customer satisfaction is tracked constantly by mail in cards. Numerous employee motivation programs also stimulate service excellence. Through the use of performance measurements they can audit the delivery of the one hour promise and ensure that standards remain high.

The Gap's service is also exemplary with extremely attentive and knowledgeable sales staff. They chose, for the most part, not to use employee incentives, but rather all their sales associates go through a Gap training program. Bombay's in-store service is also good; however, one of the key services it offers is selling virtually all its items in knock-down form, so that customers can have the immediate gratification of taking home their purchase with them. This is unusual in home furnishings retail where many items have to be ordered and delivered.

In each of these cases, the sales staff have pride in their company, and management appreciates and is willing to support their staff.

Strategic Planning

The dedication to, and frequency of, strategic planning is generally regarded as an integral part of business in the United States. It is a key survival tactic that American companies use to compete. The more leading edge the company, the more the process is necessary to remain at the head of the pack. The Bombay Company, for example, is constantly changing to maintain its advantage. A major five year plan is completed annually and updated quarterly by people on staff whose sole job it is to plan.

Planning tended to be shorter term and more frequent, as market conditions change so rapidly in the United States. Price Club updated its strategic plan twice a year. Among other aspects, strategic planning forces management to do a competitive and market review on a regular basis. For the American retailers it is the company philosophy which sets the direction while the strategic plan maps the journey.

Competitive Response

One of the most important survival tactics is immediate competitive response. Since the market is intensely competitive, it is critical to respond to competitive actions. Price, of course, is one of the key issues, but competitive response also takes the form of amount of media exposure.

With respect to price competition, Price Club, as mentioned earlier, undertakes daily price checks and matches any discrepancy immediately. Since most of their products are known brands, they can be easily compared. Lenscrafters, on the other hand, attempts to differentiate its offering enough that prices cannot easily be compared. It competes more on a market exposure basis. Every store sends in copies of the competition's ads to head office and it is their policy to defend immediately in each market. In some cases, when management knows ahead of time, they respond *before* their competitors' ads have appeared.

The Bombay Company also attempts to avoid price competition by differentiating its product, largely by designing their own lines and obtaining exclusivity on as many items as possible. The Gap also designs all its own lines and no longer carry Levis, once a major part of its assortment, in order to avoid price competition and defend its margins. Both The Bombay Company and The Gap advertise heavily, the former through seven catalogues per year plus various magazine and newspaper ads, and The Gap through its familiar and extremely successful "individuals of style" campaign. When The Gap's personality ads began to be copied, management developed a new campaign, again always differentiating itself.

This proactive strategy, combining immediate competitive response and differentiating the product and promotional offering, is a fundamental reason for the American retailers' success and, by the same token, a lack of response on the part of many of the Canadian companies was one of the main reasons for their difficulties.

Supply

The development of a strong supply network that cannot be easily replicated is one of the key success factors in the highly competitive United States retail environment. Successful American retailers have a number of choices in terms of merchandise strategy, one of which is to sell brand name products at low margins, another is to sell proprietary products often carrying higher margins. In order to be successful at the latter, goods had to be obtained on an exclusive basis and/or made to company specifications and designs.

Designs are copied very quickly. Hence, one must stay ahead of the market either by constantly introducing new designs, or developing items that are not easily imitated, or some combination of the two. The Bombay Company, for example, uses a combination of these methods to retain its edge. It developed a complex network of sources in Far Eastern countries and designed 95 percent of its products themselves. The constant introduction of new items into the stores, changing layout, presentation, and accessorization seven times a year, is unheard of in the home fashion business.

The Gap also uses a similar strategy. It has developed a complex supply network of over 300 suppliers, many of whom are in the Orient. Virtually all their products are made to their specifications, and colour and style stories are changed every six weeks in the stores. Neither The Gap nor The Bombay Company stand still long enough for the competition to catch up.

If neither of these merchandise strategies is employed, it is easier for the competition to emulate the product assortment, and the differential advantage diminishes. Thus, a different tactic must be employed to gain competitive advantage. Dylex's Wet Seal chain in California is an example of a mixed strategy — it sells brand name, junior clothing at reasonable, but not low prices. In order to compensate for not having the lowest prices, it changes its assortment more quickly.

The American retailers tend to view and treat their suppliers as partners. They involve them in the business, giving them information which will, in turn, improve the supplier's ability to serve the retailer. Lenscrafters, for example, placed great demands on suppliers, but also wanted them to profit from their association. They held a Vendors' Day celebration every year in which they shared corporate information and which culminated in an awards ceremony for Vendor of the Year.

Presentation

Visual presentation is extremely important in the United States, especially in mall retailing where it provides another way of creating a differential advantage and attracting the customer. It is somewhat less critical in discount retailing. Mall retailing is, however, becoming more and more like theatre, and the excitement is needed to compete.

Exciting presentation is one of the chief ways in which Wet Seal achieves distinction. Through the incorporation of large music and video walls and concert quality sound systems, management has found that the visual and auditory excitement attracted customers into their stores and kept them shopping longer. No two stores are the same as the design concept is always evolving and changing.

Other successful retailers are capitalizing on exciting presentation to captivate their audiences. Great American retail institutions such as Tiffany's have used store and window designs for years to differentiate themselves. Tiffany's was the first to transform windows into self enclosed theatrical worlds to encourage fun, fantasy and drama in retailing. In the United States, the drama had to change constantly in order to keep ahead of the competition.

Operating Efficiency

A high level of operating efficiency is key to enable retailers to both conduct and withstand price wars. They are constantly reviewing their organizations and experimenting with new methods in the quest to reduce costs.

Because Price Club's raison d'etre is to provide good value, every part of its organization is geared toward keeping expenses and margins low. The no frills warehouse concept is evident from the executive offices to the selling floor. Everything is kept to a minimum. From the low number of stock keeping units on the floor to the absence of advertising, everything is geared to operating efficiently and cheaply. Selling, general and administrative expenses are approximately 7.5 percent of net sales, allowing for a gross margin of just under nine percent — remarkably low figures compared to traditional retailers, many of whose selling, general and administrative expenses would be in the 25 to 30 percent range and higher.

The large size of the United States market permits economies of scale, particularly with respect to head office expenses that can be spread over a larger number of stores. According to Standard and Poor's calculations, The Limited, Petrie Stores, The Gap and TJX (all apparel retailers) have averaged a 15 percent selling, general and administrative expense over the past five years. Wal-Mart's SGA, at close to 16 percent, allows it to work on an overall gross margin of 22 percent.

A brief comparative summary of a number of the observed cost differences between Canadian and American retailers and the two countries is presented below. The following are generalizations only and may vary with retail format, commodity, and by individual retailer.

Costs	Canada	United States
Selling, general and administrative expenses	significantly higher in Canadian companies both in Canada and United States	generally lower in American companies both sides of the border
Senior management compensation	lower in Canadian companies	higher in United States
Middle management compensation	generally higher in Canada in relation to responsibility	somewhat lower in United States
Sales staff	varies from similar to more costly in Canada	similar to less costly in United States, varies by region: for example, California costs are similar to Canada
Employee benefits	generally more offered in Canada	generally fewer offered by United States companies
Employee health insurance	company costs lower	company costs higher
Margins/mark-ups	generally higher in Canadian companies	significantly lower
Head office expense	higher in Canada	lower partly due to larger store base
Rent	when comparing like malls, base rents are similar in both markets; however, additional charges are often twice as expensive in Canada	
Advertising	Canadian retailers spend less	United States companies often spend twice as much as a percentage of net sales
Presentation	Canadian retailers tend to be less creative and sophisticated, except for the food retailers	more innovative, dramatic, and scientific
Store sizes	generally smaller	generally larger

Costs	Canada	United States
Competitive response	slower	immediate
Planning	less frequent	constant and comprehensive
Service	Canadian companies generally underperform compared to United States retailers	
Employee incentives and commissions	more widely used in the United States than in Canada	
Employee training	less extensive in Canada	more extensive at all levels of management and staff
Retail formats	fewer	more retail formats in United States with more emphasis on discount sector

These observations are made largely from the perspective of the American companies and serve both to confirm and augment those identified previously by the Canadian companies.

OTHER FACTORS INFLUENCING SUCCESS IN CANADA

How is it that American retailers can enter a market that, as has been illustrated throughout this research, is different from their own, yet have a virtual 100 percent success rate while Canadians, on the other hand, have fared so badly in the United States? There is no lack of outstanding managers in the Canadian companies. The answer to this question is obviously complex, involving many variables; but there are several factors which have emerged over the course of this research and must be taken into consideration when addressing this issue.

Maturity of the United States versus the Canadian Retail Industry

In the authors' opinion, with the exception of the traditional food retailers, the United States retail industry is approximately five to ten years ahead of the Canadian retail industry in terms of its life cycle. This is due, in large part, to the highly competitive nature of the United States market which has forced the industry to evolve more quickly.

For the past ten years, United States retailers have been trending down market in terms of their retail concepts, catering to a more price sensitive and demanding customer. While the 1980s saw the emergence of many low price concepts, such as power centres (malls made up of large superstore type retailers), manufacturers outlet malls, warehouse stores, catalogue showrooms, and commodity superstores in the United States, Canadian merchants were trending up market with more boutiques and designer collections geared toward the name conscious Canadian consumer. For example, by the end of the 1980s in the United States, the discount store segment had grown to become the largest retail channel for apparel sales. In Canada, this segment accounts for only a small proportion of apparel sales. By 1991, there were 275 discount outlet centres in the United States compared to three in Canada.

With the recession, Canadian consumers began to take on many of the characteristics of their neighbours. What American retailers achieved in ten years, Canadian firms will have to achieve in a fraction of the time in order to survive and compete effectively both in the United States and Canada. It is critical that they develop an improved attitude to change and studying the United States market is, in many ways, an opportunity to see what may be in store for Canada.

Adapting to the Market

Both Lenscrafters and the Price Club have adapted their systems, products, buying, and incentive programs to suit the different demands of the Canadian market. They have brought the American company philosophies and translated them to work in this environment.

Management and Financial Resources

Almost all the American entrants into Canada have tended to be extremely large, billion dollar plus companies with abundant managerial and financial resources. Many of these companies have the capacity to open the equivalent of a large Canadian chain in the space of a year, thereby gaining a major share of the market in a short period of time. Wal–Mart, for example, has opened 150 to 200 new stores in *each* of the last three years. Although this by no means guarantees success, the Canadian companies that have succeeded in the United States have tended to be the larger ones with more resources. These greater resources provide the ability to withstand losses for a longer time in the Canadian market than Canadian companies might be able to in the United States.

Overcoming Barriers to the Canadian Market

As we've seen in the early chapters of this book, there are barriers to entering the United States such as problems finding good locations, the high price of acquisitions, the intensity of the competition, regional differences, and the list goes on. Despite the fact that American retailers have had such success in the Canadian market, it has not been achieved without overcoming some major barriers to this market.

Locations

Virtually all the American companies had problems securing good locations in Canada. The Canadian development industry, by comparison, is smaller and less competitive than that of the United States, with more power concentrated in a few hands. Both Lenscrafters and The Gap had difficulty finding prime mall space larger than the standard 2,000 to 3,000 square feet generally found in Canadian malls. In addition, although they were exceptionally large and successful companies in the United States, their worth still had to be proven to the imperious Canadian developers.

Although the recession had changed this situation for Canadian and American retailers alike over the past 18 to 24 months, the Canadian development market was still less competitive than in the United States.

Price Club experienced great difficulties obtaining locations in the Ontario market. However, Price Club persisted in its attempts to enter the Toronto market in particular. Its eventual success stirred up what was a fairly closed market resulting in supermarket price wars, to the delight of Toronto consumers. In May 1992, it was reported that Price Club was facing the same process over again, only this time in Niagara Falls, where it was being forced to fight in the courts and city councils. A representative of a traditional food retailer was quoted as saying that all they (the other retailers) wanted was a level playing field. Daniel Langevin, Price Club's marketing director, was quoted as saying, "They'll object to anything — it doesn't matter what we ask for. They are just objecting to competition."

Costs

Although it comes as little surprise to Canadians, the United States companies found the cost of doing business in Canada unexpectedly high. Rent and land expenses are higher in many Canadian markets, common area maintenance charges are often double what they would be in comparable United States malls, and are largely made up of various business and municipal taxes. Management, labour, and head office expenses are often higher as well, as experienced by The Bombay Company and Lenscrafters. The latter found that it had to pay higher salaries in Canada for positions comparable to the United States, and had underestimated the cost of management when the Canadian division was established. Likewise, The Bombay Company found that a buyer purchasing for 40 stores in Canada commanded a similar salary as his/her counterpart in the United States who bought for 250 stores.

Size of the market

The relatively small size of the Canadian market spread over an extended geographic area created more difficulty with respect to scale of operations and resulted in higher head office expenses as a percentage of net sales. This is a factor well known to Canadian business, but is often not fully considered by companies entering this market. In addition to paying higher rent and land costs, both Price Club and Lenscrafters had higher head office expenses in Canada and felt there was little chance they could ever be as profitable as their United States operations.

Despite the smaller scale, and contrary to the other experiences, The Bombay Company is marginally more profitable in Canada than in the United States due to a slightly different merchandise mix, and the fact that their leases are somewhat older in Canada. This situation is expected to change over the next few years as leases come up for renewal.

Government

Highly complicated and slow government process was felt to be a severe barrier to entry for the Price Club with respect to their locations as noted earlier. Sunday shopping was also a major issue with respect to Price Club in particular, but affected the other retailers as well. Being forced to close on Sundays in most parts of Canada, when United States regulations left this decision largely up to the individual shopkeeper, was a distinct disadvantage. Price Club had argued that it was not a retailer, but rather a wholesaler, and as such, could legally remain open to their members on Sunday. The Ontario court, however, ruled this invalid, forcing it to close. The company was made to close in Quebec also.

Closed business community

The American companies were all confronted, to some extent, with the challenge of penetrating what they found to be a relatively closed business community. However, Lenscrafters had the most difficult time, as their success was dependent upon their acceptance by the optical community. In addition, market regulations varied from region to region, and were especially difficult to understand in Quebec.

Competition

The competition was found to be different in Canada from that of the United States, varying from little reaction to unexpected retaliation. It was a barrier in some cases, but generally not nearly to the extent that it was for Canadian companies entering the United States

A recipient of particularly vehement competition was Price Club which effectively undersold most of the wholesalers. In response to this new competition, some wholesalers threatened Pierre Mignault if he did not raise his prices.

The other unusual competitive response experienced by the Price Club was being kept out of the Toronto market. Although part of this was due to cumbersome government bureaucracy, it was exacerbated by competitors voicing complaints through the public hearing process, thereby further stalling their entry. Total commitment and perseverance over a five year period finally paid off.

In the case of Lenscrafters, its direct major competition was another American super-optical firm, EyeMasters, along with Canadian Hakim. Standard Optical, the largest chain in Toronto, did not offer much resistance. Competitive reaction was largely aimed against EyeMasters from the beginning, since it had forced Lenscrafters to enter Canada earlier than intended. Competition was intense for sites and advertising exposure. Instead of competing largely on price, Lenscrafters concentrated on advertising exposure, the one hour delivery promise, and after sales service. All employees were instructed to watch the competition and forward intelligence to the central office daily, and they defended immediately.

The Bombay Company has little or no direct competition in the Canadian market. There are attempts to copy its product look, but no one has combined all the elements to create the same concept. The Bombay Company's strategy has not been so much to react to competition but, rather, never to let it catch up. If it is ahead in the United States, it is almost automatically ahead in Canada.

The Gap concept has no true direct competition in the Canadian market, but there are a number of firms which compete for parts of its market, just as there are many more in the United States. The profile of Canadian competitors was unexpected by Gap management, insofar as it was heavily concentrated in the middle market. In the United States, competition was more specialized, focussing on a narrower market segment and occupying specific niches. Here, everyone was the same. Everyone went on sale and cut their own throats. It had been The Gap's strategy to sell at full price with a few selected items on sale at the back of the store for 10 and 15 percent off, as good retailing principals dictated. They were not prepared for the myriad of 50 to 70 percent off signs which appeared *before Christmas.*

Summary

Although the two major entry barriers, cost and location, exist for both the Canadian and the United States markets, the underlying reasons are different. The United States companies overcame the locational barriers in Canada in a fairly short period of time and were, by and large, very stringent in their site selection criteria. The higher costs in Canada have remained a disadvantage for two of the three of the American entrants we studied, but profitability has not eluded them.

The balance of the barriers between the two markets are quite different, the Canadian being more indirect in nature, while the American retailers, having come from an intensely competitive environment, were used to and prepared for quick competitive response and action. They were not, however, accustomed to some of the indirect tactics, of which they were the target.

Due to a lack of suitable candidates, among other reasons, few American retail entrants into Canada have used the acquisition mode. Canadian entry barriers are not as onerous as those experienced when moving south into a more competitive market. In addition, the United States companies are used to expanding quickly using the greenfield mode in order to gain market share.

American companies such as Wal-Mart are masters of gaining market share quickly through greenfield expansion. Good acquisition opportunities have been limited in the Canadian market in the past; however, this situation may change with the large number of ailing Canadian retailers, or it may simply make greenfield expansion easier.

DIFFERENCES BETWEEN CANADIAN AND AMERICAN RETAILERS

We have encountered many differences between Canadian and American retailers and their home markets. These observations have allowed us to identify both tangible and intangible factors. The tangible are more obvious and concrete such as differences in cost structure, service delivery, incentive and commission programs, employee training, strategic and financial planning, presentation tactics and implementation, store size, competitive response, pricing, retail formats, advertising and promotion. The intangible differences are also key to the success of the American retailers. These factors are difficult to quantify, but in order to obtain high operating efficiencies, service excellence, and many of the other positive attributes, it is necessary that these elements be in place. If they are only partly there, then part of the equation will be missing. One of the invisible differences between Canadian and American companies is company culture. As stated by Jeff Wells, vice-president of human resources for Toys R Us, an American retailer, "Culture is one of the key ingredients that drives our success and expansion. This makes culture one of the most critical ingredients to success and is, I believe, the ultimate competitive advantage that a successful retailer has."

In summarizing the differences between the Canadian and American retailers, it is instructive to start with the ways in which the American retailers approached the Canadian market.

Pre-entry

The American companies all met the pre-entry criteria previously found to be important for the Canadian companies entering the United States. They all had well developed organizations, readily available financial and managerial resources, and management commitment. Although the organizations could be classified as stable in one sense, ie. firmly established, they were in constant motion insofar as new systems, management incentives, products and services were concerned. Management embraced change on an ongoing basis.

Each had a well developed strategic plan which was constantly reviewed, revised and acted upon. Many of the Canadian companies that had difficulties in the United States placed little or no emphasis on strategic planning.

The prior understanding of the Canadian market, the relevant industry, and the competition on the part of the United States entrants varied. In the case of The Bombay Company, Price Club and Lenscrafters, each had a Canadian president who understood the Canadian market, making prior research less critical. Each, however, was bringing a new concept into the market, and as such, was operating in uncharted waters.

Thus, for all the companies, the American parent had a strong organization with a well developed sense of direction, and the concepts were all new to the Canadian market. The successful Canadian companies had the same attributes; however, they generally purchased existing companies in the United States. It appeared that prior research into the Canadian market was not as critical for American entrants, possibly due to this market being behind the United States in terms of its life cycle. If their ideas had worked in the more advanced American market, then their chances of success were good in Canada.

Management of the Canadian Operation

Centralization vs decentralization

All the American companies were decentralized, setting up Canadian head offices which directed the Canadian operations in a relatively autonomous manner. However, they were all centralized insofar as strategic and financial planning were concerned, and largely autonomous with respect to all the other functions. Each company adapted United States programs to meet the requirements of the Canadian market, although they tended to start off using as much of the United States concept as possible.

Advertising came from the United States wherever possible, especially in the case of The Gap and Lenscrafters. Both The Gap and The Bombay Company had very similar merchandise assortments in their Canadian and United States operations, but both were refined over time to suit the Canadian market. Lenscrafters had started with an assortment similar to the United States, but quickly found that the Canadian market was more fashion forward than their United States mid west base.

Thus, while involvement at the senior management level between the Canadian and American companies is a critical success factor, a fairly high level of decentralization maximizes the degree to which indigenous management can react to local conditions in both Canada and the United States.

Canadian and American culture mix

The American companies all administered their Canadian operation from a Canadian office. The Gap, perhaps, has the fewest functions performed in Canada, and is the only case in our study in which an American is running the Canadian operation. Price Club (a joint venture to start), Lenscrafters, and The Bombay Company all have Canadian CEOs, although in the latter case, Nourse lives in the United States. Virtually all the management in the Canadian offices are Canadian.

By and large, the management and staff of the American entrants into Canada are all imbued with the corporate culture, company philosophy and values. The Canadian management teams, for the most part, have been "Americanized" and thus understand both cultures. The tendency, especially in the case of the Price Club and Lenscrafters, has been to take the best from both cultures and combine them to create something which is better than either one is separately.

For example, Lenscrafters Canadian division adapted a company incentive program which had been running in the United States. The individual competitiveness of the program did not appeal to Canadian staff when it was tested, as it was viewed as unfair to those who could not directly affect sales. Thus, it was changed to promote a team effort, and it became an extremely successful program, which may be adopted company wide. They have also developed a high service image, one which is superior to that in the United States as illustrated in a recent survey of American and Canadian associates where Canadians scored higher on every scale!

The Gap, which employs Canadian staff in its stores, has managed to create an outstanding, high service profile, uncommon in the Canadian market. They have a training program called Gap Act, which every sales associate must complete. Unlike many other American retailers, they do not use a myriad of incentives and commissions.

Culture mix advantages are evident at the Price Club where management layering (ie. the number of layers of management) is less than that of a typical Canadian retailer, making for a better relationship between staff and senior management. Greater management appreciation of staff is evident. In addition, the philosophy of maximizing staff self esteem through pushing power down to the lowest level possible has an advantageous effect on productivity.

Management Attitude and Philosophy

Management attitudes and philosophy seemed to differ between the Canadian and the American companies. The American firms were more casual, both in dress and actions, appeared less traditional, and more open to change and innovation. They also had flatter organizations.

Innovation

One of the most critical elements of Canadian competitiveness, as noted earlier, is the need for forward orientation, ie. innovation. This is something which is clearly promoted in American society and entrenched in company philosophy. Americans were ready to act quickly and decisively when the situation warranted it. Mignault, president of Price Club Canada, noted that American management decisions were made in a less democratic manner than in Canada. They were simply instituted and accepted. There was an open mindedness in the American management prior to making their decision and a free flow of ideas down, and perhaps even more importantly, up the organization.

Management attitude toward service

It is a common observation that American retailers generally have a better service image than do Canadian retailers. A commonly held belief is that Canadian employees are, in some way, inferior to those in the United States. In fact, it was one of the perceptions of Canadian executives operating in the United States that Canadians did not regard retail sales as a profession, but as a stepping stone to something better.

However, the American entrants who have excellent service are employing Canadian sales staff. It appears that the traditional Canadian attitude toward retail sales can be overcome if management values are such that they show appreciation for their staff, they encourage innovation, authority is pushed to the lowest level possible, and management are truly committed to the provision of service.

Company culture

Canadian companies, with the exception of Peoples Jewellers, generally did not talk about company philosophy and core values. A corporate mission statement was usually the extent of Canadian company philosophy. Possibly the greater emphasis in the United States on strategic planning led to the development and evolution of a corporate philosophy. Price Club placed a major emphasis on company philosophy. As illustrated earlier, Lenscrafters philosophy is central to company success. It is a set of core company values which provides an environment favourable to change.

Leadership

Outstanding leadership was demonstrated in many of the Canadian and American companies. There seemed to be less distance between the American CEOs and their employees. They tended to put into practice the inverted pyramid theory which places the customer at the top of the organization, sales staff next, and so on down to the management and CEO whose ultimate job it is to serve the customer.

This leads to a closer and more conciliatory relationship between management and staff in American companies. Even though there is greater disparity between the compensation of senior management in the United States and that of their hourly paid employees, labour relations are better than in Canada, where the compensation gap is not as wide. Appreciation speaks loudly.

Empowerment of employees in the organization was used more often in the American companies. Staff were given goals and guidelines, and power (loosely defined as the ability to make decisions) was pushed down to the lowest level possible.

Understanding of the new market

An understanding of the Canadian market was just as critical to the American companies and, except for The Gap, they covered this issue by hiring Canadians experienced in the retail industry to head up their Canadian operations. The challenge was more to learn about the American culture and philosophy and apply it in Canada.

Since competition is more intense in the United States, and market segmentation and specialization are pivotal to success, a prior understanding of the intricacies of the local market is even more important there. Pre-entry research is key, and the interpretation is critical.

Approach to new market resources

As a general rule, management tends to react to resource bases from their previous experience, rather than from the point of view of the new market. The retail cost structures in the United States tend to be lower than in Canada. Canadian companies that lacked an understanding of the American market tended to be unable to maximize the advantage of the lower United States cost base with respect to supply, labour and locations, and tended to undernegotiate based on their Canadian experience.

The American firms, on the other hand, were entering a more expensive market. This probably resulted in more intense negotiating insofar as locations and rent were concerned. However, where they expected to pay American prices, based on their American experience, they received less than they bargained for. In terms of management, for example, Lenscrafters hired Canadian managers at the same price as those in the United States and later found that they were too junior and had to replace them. In general, however, the United States companies dealt with the Canadian labour base effectively, with employees in both Lenscrafters and The Gap providing service which is superior to the norm in the Canadian market. Although the United States companies also reacted based on their previous experience, moving into a more expensive market negated the problem of under-negotiation.

Employee Costs

From the perspective of the American companies, the wage differential for sales staff between Canada and the United States was not of major significance. Price Club pays among the highest wages in the industry on both sides of the border, and employee benefit programs are comparable and generous. Lenscrafters found that the differences lay in the kinds of benefits offered. The provincial health plans are a great asset in Canada as Lenscrafters paid for employee health insurance, the costs of which are much lower in Canada than the United States. The work ethic of Canadian employees was regarded by Canadian executives as being somewhat lower than in the United States. Despite this somewhat unfavourable comparison, it did not appear to have a negative effect on the performance of the American retailers in Canada.

CANADIAN RETAILERS LEARNING TO DO BUSINESS IN THE UNITED STATES

We are now seeing signs of Canadian companies learning to adapt to the American environment, particularly in the case of Dylex's Wet Seal and Canadian Tire. Both companies have drawn on the experience from their past ventures, and are approaching the United States in a different and measured way. They have both demonstrated the ability to change and to adapt to local market conditions, providing them with a differential advantage. This willingness to take a risk and to experiment with new ideas is critical to the survival of Canadian retailers. The following describes Canadian Tire's and Dylex's new ventures and approaches.

Auto Source: Canadian Tire Two Years Later

When Dean Groussman arrived at Canadian Tire, the conventional wisdom was that the company had reached full maturity in Canada and that it would have to look for other opportunities to invest in on either side of the border so that expansion could take place. However, two things happened at that time that turned management's philosophy away from making a major investment or acquisition in the United States market. First, they discovered that through increasing their investment levels in Canada there was a substantial horizon of opportunity left within Canada to expand the existing businesses. Second, no existing enterprises could be identified that Canadian Tire management wanted to purchase or that they felt were valued appropriately.

Thinking, therefore, of what kind of business they might want to get into, the executives decided that the automotive business in the United States was a good business to consider. In looking at the market, they saw that it was very fragmented and with no one dominant player; it was huge (over $108 billion in sales annually); and there were a number of opportunities for entry. At the same time, in the pre-entry research, Canadian Tire management looked at major retailing concepts as well as changes taking place in retailing concepts in the United States market. From this research, they decided to pursue a combined concept of auto parts and accessories, and service. Many companies had parts and accessories but no service while others had service, but no parts and accessories. Canadian Tire saw an opportunity to combine both.

The next step involved recruiting people from the United States to run the new business. Approximately ten months were spent in preparation, during which Canadian Tire took its time with the selection process. It recruited people with a tremendous depth of retail experience in the United States. The president selected had an extensive background in the automotive service business and other key executives chosen similarly had excellent capabilities in the U.S. retail market. These people were asked to look at Canadian Tire's new concept and further refine it based on their experience and know-how.

Their finding was that the "warehouse" concept of retailing, which involved shipping directly to the stores, had become popular, as had a high impact, high volume, high merchandise display approach to retailing which was being done with category killers. Category killers involved taking certain categories of goods, such as office supplies, fitness goods, and sporting goods, and making a major presentation of them in the stores. No one, however, had yet made use of such approaches in the automotive business. Canadian Tire decided to use the warehouse concept in their Auto Source stores.

Canadian Tire planned to open a few stores under the Auto Source name. Management had a general notion of the location in which they wanted to open, feeling that it should be an area that was geographically and climatically similar to what they knew in Canada so that they could better understand the market they planned to enter. In particular, they were interested in the North Central United States. Research on this area indicated that it had similar kinds of winters to Canada and people had similar kinds of problems with their automobiles. Management also learned that this area had no direct or indirect competition which was critical because they wanted to test their new concept while holding as many other factors constant as possible.

Once the concept was refined, Canadian Tire's executives finally decided to establish two greenfield operations in Indianapolis, Indiana in July and August, 1991. This city was chosen because it had a growing economic base and economic stability. In the fall, another Auto Source store was opened in Dayton, Ohio. Each of the three stores was approximately 40,000 square feet of automotive retail parts and accessories, plus 24 service bays and a couple of fast lube bays. The markets served were both retail and wholesale customers.

Although no formal figures were provided, performance results for the three operations met Canadian Tire's plans and expectations for the year. An additional five stores were being opened in 1992 in the North Central United States. Some of the locations had been selected, but others had not. It was known that all of the locations would be in the general vicinity of Indianapolis.

When reflecting on the early, positive performance results of the Auto Source stores, Canadian Tire management stated that the strength of Canadian Tire's business in Canada was an asset because it had a very good reputation with vendors and suppliers. Also, the president and vice-presidents chosen for the U.S. company had excellent connections with United States vendors. Similarly, the Canadian president (at the time), Dean Groussman, was an American who understood both the Canadian business and the U.S. market.

In the future, Canadian Tire plans to respond to the new market by taking five percent out of its operating costs, boosting productivity levels through systems and logistics development, increasing quality in their stores, and matching good locations (within 15 miles of 95 percent of the population) with service, price, and quality. In addition, some of the ideas from the United States such as the All Out Retail concept and the Category Killer concept have been imported to Canada. Whereas a traditional store at Canadian Tire had 60 percent storage and 40 percent retail space, now the stores are being reorganized to have 20 percent storage and 80 percent retail. Although the amount of merchandise has not changed, there are a number of advantages to this layout: (1) stronger presentation of merchandise; (2) it keeps the staff out of the back room and on the floor to serve customers; (3) it decreases handling by receiving right onto the floor; and (4) it ensures higher level of in-stock. As a result, not only do the stores look good, but management creates a more competitive business.

An earlier recommendation of this book was that greenfield operations should be avoided. Yet, Canadian Tire has now entered the U.S. market via a greenfield operation and appears to be succeeding. Why? There are several factors that differentiate Canadian Tire's second entrance into the United States market from the other less successful companies.

1. Dean Groussman is an American and is familiar with both Canadian Tire and the U.S. retail business. He also managed Canadian Tire's first exit from the United States and is therefore aware of the lessons learned from that first experience.

2. Canadian Tire selected excellent management with a depth of knowledge and experience in the U.S. and in automotive in particular.

3. Canadian Tire focussed on automotive parts, accessories and service — that aspect identified as being most appropriate and the only one that was profitable the first time they entered the United States. It had a distinct, specialized concept, unlike its first entry.

4. Canadian Tire management did not attempt to transfer the Canadian Tire concept or formula. Instead, they researched the market to determine what was most appropriate and started a new business quite separate from the Canadian business. In addition, they checked out and refined their concept using experienced American managers, rather than assuming that they knew the market or could manage the business in the U.S.

5. Considerable time was spent in preparation for entry. Not only were American managers used in collecting and interpreting information gathered, but also Dean Groussman's background and experience were useful in this regard.

6. Unlike other Canadian retailers who used a greenfield site, Canadian Tire was ensured of a well-established supplier network to source its products prior to entry. This was accomplished in two ways. First, Canadian Tire had a good reputation with suppliers from its business in Canada. Second, the president and other executives selected to run the U.S. operation had well-established relationships with vendors and suppliers that were used to the benefit of the Auto Source stores.

At this point the reader might ask, "Does this suggest that greenfield operations can therefore work in the U.S.?" The answer is, perhaps, if done correctly. The Canadian operation must guarantee before entering the U.S. market that it has significant clout to allow it to command an excellent supplier network and store locations. As well, it has to have a concept that fits well in the the market. However, although Canadian Tire's Auto Source stores appear to be doing well, it is important to remember that opening a few stores often does not bring forth the type of competitor retaliation that a greater number of stores can. Perhaps as the five new stores are opened in 1992, a clearer picture of their performance may be assessed.

Finally, regarding greenfield entries in general, management needs the patience and perseverance to grow the chain along with the commitment to support it, or the decisiveness to close it and cut their losses if it looks like the chain won't make it.

Wet Seal

With Wet Seal, Dylex purchased a company already operating in the United States that had developed a niche and that was important to its suppliers. A competent team combining the talents of an American merchant and a Canadian operating executive was assembled and seemed to be leading the company well.

Dylex, through its Suzy Shier division, purchased a 78 percent interest in Wet Seal, an 18 store women's wear chain located in southern California. Suzy Shier management had identified Wet Seal as a relatively inexpensive company that had a good name in the southern California market, although it was not particularly well run at the time. Little pre-entry research went into the decision to purchase Wet Seal. David Posluns, Chief Financial Officer of Dylex, felt it was really more a method of gaining good locations, taking into account a name and a market segment that was somewhat analogous to Suzy Shier's — the young junior.

The acquisition also gave Suzy Shier the chance to explore trends first hand in the California market which is the eighth largest market in the world. Co-general manager Irving Teitelbaum was quoted at the time as saying, "By purchasing a small chain at a fair price, we saw an opportunity to approach the United States market in a measured and controlled manner."

Shortly after the purchase, a Canadian executive from Suzy Shier, Ken Chilvers, was sent to southern California as president to bring Wet Seal's organization up to Suzy Shier's standards. He had a reputation for being personable, efficient and organized. The merchandising situation was also under review and a search was started for a merchant who knew the marketplace. Kathy Bronstein, who was part of a team operating a chain in the southern United States, was recruited as Executive Vice-President and General Merchandise Manager to join Chilvers.

Essentially, Wet Seal was an autonomous company, with the exception of accounting since it was consolidated with Suzy Shier, in which Dylex was the major shareholder. From time to time the merchants took buying trips with Suzy Shier buying staff, but there were no integrated functions.

The stores were large (approximately 5,000 sq.ft.) with high ceilings. Videos were used extensively in their displays, creating an exciting, youthful environment. Posluns felt that Wet Seal hit the junior market better than anyone else, which is the reason it was successful. It had considerable merchandising strength and it sourced locally. The buying organization was strong, knew its market and executed well in the highly competitive California market, according to Posluns. The company did not advertise except when required to by store leases.

In addition to the uniqueness of the store environment, Wet Seal approached the seasons differently. Instead of "chasing the seasons," it sold summer clothing year round with very little seasonal merchandise. Most other retailers, particularly the national chains, bought for all regions spanning diverse climatic conditions which necessitated seasonal merchandise change.

Virtually all Wet Seal merchandise came from local California sources and was 70 to 80 percent nationally branded. Part of its strength, being in a very fashion forward business, was having the new merchandise first before their competitors. The company's importance in the market to local suppliers put it in a position of power in terms of demanding new merchandise first. Dedication to freshness and newness was extremely important in serving its market. Merchandise was shipped to the stores on an almost daily basis. No store-wide sales were held and markdowns were taken regularly to effect a rapid liquidation of slow moving inventory. The first markdown was generally 50 percent. Unsold merchandise was shipped to the company's two clearance centres.

Wet Seal's competitive strategy was its ability as a niche retailer to attack the national chains on the fringes through highly focussed, regional product assortments. If the national chains were to design by region, they would lose some of their economies of scale. It was felt that the strength of the buying team was keeping the company aware of the competitive changes in the market. Buying from local sources also added to management's knowledge of the competitive marketplace.

In Posluns' estimation, President Ken Chilvers' major strengths lay in operations, as well as in motivating people, and Kathy Bronstein was an outstanding merchant. He noted that at a time when most retailers were chasing the aging consumer and moving up to target the 25 to 45 age group, Wet Seal remained committed to the junior market.

Store for store, sales increased by 25 percent in 1985. By 1987, the chain had grown to 45 stores and by 1990, there were over 90 stores in California, Arizona, Nevada, Hawaii and Florida. Sales were in excess of $75 million and operating profit was very high. The company was beginning to test market in the north to assess potential future growth opportunities. Sales and net income increased dramatically for the three years 1989–1991.

According to Posluns, Chilvers and Bronstein developed the chain to what it was with the help and direction of executives at Dylex and Suzy Shier. The latter, 50.1 percent owned by Dylex, funded the growth of Wet Seal. As Posluns recounted, "They took over the chain with 18 stores and put in a strong Canadian operations person and brought in an excellent American merchant. For a number of years they toyed with the mix until it hit what it was they wanted. They developed a beautiful store that targeted the market perfectly and stuck to their vision. They bought superbly well and developed a phenomenal merchandising pool of talent. All of the facets of operation were executed to such a professional degree that they started to capture a huge market share. Sales productivity and profit grew to the point where they were able to have 80 or 90 stores. The need for capital became so great they needed to go public. They went public at a very high multiple and are now opening in Florida and other regions. This success has shaped Dylex's policy toward the United States."

At the time of writing, if the balance of the stock held was sold, the annualized return on total investment would be in excess of 70 percent per annum (over the seven years 1985–1991) which translates into approximately a $55 million return.

Why does Wet Seal seem to be on the track to success? In Posluns' view, the most important reasons are the following:

1. Excellent management consisting of a Canadian CEO and an American Vice-President.

2. A strong regional niche approach.

3. Outstanding buying.

4. Sufficient local market importance to obtain merchandise first.

5. Commitment to the junior market when others had abandoned this segment.

6. Commitment to summer merchandise all year round as opposed to chasing the seasons as the national chains do.

PART 5

·

CONCLUSIONS

CHAPTER 9

LEARNING TO
PLAY THE GAME

INTRODUCTION

From the information assembled to date about the experiences of Canadian retailers in the United States, a number of fundamental factors have been identified that are critical to success in that market. At this point, it might seem logical to provide a strategic agenda or comprehensive checklist for doing business in the United States. For example, such an agenda for entering the United States would include the following points:

1. Develop an overall strategic plan for the company which integrates the United States entry. Clearly identify the company's target customers and financial and market objectives.

2. Assess the Canadian company with respect to the criteria required for United States entry. These pre-entry criteria are:

    a. Stable organization in Canada.

    b. Well-developed organizational structure, processes and systems.

    c. Readily available financial and managerial resources.

    d. Full management commitment.

3. Develop and implement a research agenda.

4. Develop an entry strategy, chose an entry mode and plan implementation.

This checklist represents fundamental requirements that a business should consider when doing business in any location. Although a lack of adherence to these fundamental requirements was a problem in some of the cases, not having such an agenda was only part of the reason that the retailers had difficulties. A more extensive strategic agenda for entry into the United States market could be presented, and a number of checklists and do's and don'ts have already been provided, but one more would be of little value to those interested in understanding how to actually compete there.

The United States could be thought of as a big chess board and entry into its retail markets as a game of chess. Researchers have shown that novices and grandmasters see chess boards differently as the following quote indicates: "The information that the master picks up from the chess board determines not only where he will move his pieces but where he will move his eyes. Observations show that a good chess player's eye movements are closely related to the structure of the position on the board; he looks at crucial pieces and crucial squares. He quite literally sees the position differently — more adequately and comprehensively — than a novice or non-player would. Of course, even the non-player sees a great deal: the chessmen are of carved ivory, the knight resembles a horse, the pieces are (perhaps) arrayed with a certain geometrical regularity.... The differences among these perceivers are not matters of truth and error but of noticing more rather than less. The information that specifies the proper move is available in the light sampled by the [novice] as by the master, but only the master is equipped to pick it up."

To finish with this analogy, the findings reported in this book suggests that, although the "chessboards" look the same, there are American and Canadian variations of chess and that it is critical to understand the different rules, relationships between the pieces and the skills of the players in order to notice the right things. The problem with checklists is that they essentially only describe the chessboard and the rules, but not the intricacies of the game. Having a well thought out agenda of activities is important. Knowing *what* to do is the first step, but knowing *how* to do it is the second step in learning the game in new market environments.

The problems experienced in the United States had deeper roots in a number of assumptions or myths that may have created barriers to learning and that prevented the Canadian companies from either considering the fundamentals and/or executing them properly. For example, consider point number three on the above list. It is crucial that companies develop and implement a research agenda. Although many of the retailers did conduct research, they may not have collected the right information or, if they did collect the right information, they either discounted its importance or interpreted it from a Canadian perspective and set of experiences.

The fundamentals must be carried out with a clear understanding of the new market. This understanding provides the ability to ask the right questions and to properly interpret the answers. Therefore, the authors believe that the added value of this chapter comes not from listing generalities, but in describing some of the assumptions that misled Canadian retailers and some suggestions for overcoming these barriers to learning.

MYTHS THAT MISLEAD

These assumptions were some of the underlying beliefs about the United States that were held by many Canadian decision makers in the retail companies — their mental maps, or pre-conceived ideas, of the United States and what it would be like to do business there.

Success

This could be stated as "success in Canada is a predictor of success in the United States." This common myth was the belief that because the retail concept worked in Canada, and because the companies were important and well known in Canada, the retail concepts could easily be transferred to, and the important relationships easily established in, the United States. This was evident in a number of the cases, but Mark Blumes probably expressed it most succinctly when reflecting on his attitude at the time his company entered the United States: "We thought we couldn't be beaten. Our concept was better than Canadian Tire, but not quite as good as McDonald's."

Some executives believed that their retail concept was so powerful that it could overcome any competition, even with disadvantages such as secondary locations. Executives must understand that no matter how effective their company's retail concept or formula is in the Canadian market, it may not be appropriate for the United States. To determine whether it is appropriate requires research by those who understand the United States retail market, prior to the decision to enter.

Canadian retailers believed that they could extrapolate from their own past history, culture and experiences in Canada when entering the United States. However, in this new market, they found they could no longer do this. Instead, the environment they faced was very different, and their experiences from the past were no longer providing useful guidelines. The old rules no longer applied, and what was required to learn the new rules was an attitude of inquisitiveness and sensitivity that many did not develop soon enough. Believing in one's invincibility based on one's success in Canada can be very costly.

Size and Certainty

This is a modern Canadian variation of the old theme "the streets are paved with gold in the United States" or "You can make more money by mistake in the United States than you can on purpose in Canada." This myth simultaneously conveys a sense of enormous wealth and ease, or certainty, in obtaining one's share of the riches. After all, the belief is that it is there for the taking. The size and assumed accessibility of this market are like a soporific, a drug that induces sleep. In the case of Canadian businesses they induced a sense of satisfaction, leading to carelessness and, often, disaster. Realizing that the United States retail market is astronomically larger than the Canadian market leads to dreams like "if we could just get one percent, we could make it," and the subsequent assumption that this probably would not be very difficult to do.

There is most likely another assumption related to the one about size that creates problems, which is the myth of "the American market." In reality, as we have seen throughout this book, there is no such thing as *the* American market. Rather, there are many regional markets each with its own distinct characteristics, and a series of retail industry systems that must be entered.

Similarity

This is the commonly held, but erroneous, assumption that "the United States is just like Canada, only larger." Learning begins with the ability to see differences, and this projected similarity interfered with learning about the markets, the regions, the consumers and the competition. For example, it was often believed that Americans were just like Canadians, sharing a similar language, culture, values, tastes and business practices. Yet it was precisely the fact that these two countries probably are more similar than any other two that masked some fundamental differences. Consumers were different; there were more competitors and they reacted differently than in Canada (even the small ones); the indirect competition was often missed.

There may also be an important corollary: "what you see may not be what you get." First, with respect to competition in the United States, companies were surprised to find out that just because they didn't see it did not mean it was not there (indirect competition). And, with respect to market niches, when they thought they had seen one, it did not necessarily exist (again, due in part to indirect competition).

Proximity

The proximity of the United States to Canada contributed to the belief that because it is close it must be easier to do business there than in countries that are further away geographically. The view was that the United States was simply the southern extension of Canada, or that it was just Canada's backyard. Given the assumption of similarity and a belief in Canada that "ties run north and south," regions of the United States that were contiguous to Canadian regions, in some cases, were organized as part of those Canadian districts. This assumption may also have been at work in the comment expressed in one of the cases: "If we can sell to a market 3,000 miles west, there's no reason we can't sell to a market 90 miles south."

Strategy for Entry

Some companies adopted a strategy for entry that could be labeled "naive incrementalism," or a "naive start small and grow" strategy. Several executives expressed the view that they could start small and grow, open quietly in remote areas, and test markets and learn without attracting the attention of competitors. This turned out to be a myth that cost some companies a considerable amount. The question is whether their espoused strategy of incrementalism was for the sake of learning, or rather was it a strategy to avoid or minimize financial risk. Because the operations tended to be small, they may not have been thought of as a major strategic decision, nor given full commitment in terms of financial or managerial resources. As a result, they were not given the chance to grow successfully.

In addition, the executives may not have realized that by entering the United States incrementally, they were only delaying facing the harsh reality of United States competition. Often United States competitors will only respond once an organization gets big enough that it begins to be a threat. Therefore, doing well with one or two stores can lead to a false sense of success.

The other problem with a naive incrementalism strategy was that it often led companies to believe that they could grow out of their problems with just a little more of an investment in a few stores to spread the overhead or with a distribution centre. When the small size of some of the Canadian retailers' United States operations posed difficulties, there was a tendency for management to believe that by getting somewhat bigger they could solve these problems. It really did not solve the basic problems and only contributed to more cost. It is very difficult to build a small operation to a size to compete successfully in the United States market without a very large investment and/or a long period of time. If Canadian companies want to become big in the United States, they must think in such terms from the beginning.

Naive incrementalism is very different from the strategies chosen by Dylex and Canadian Tire (the most recent ventures) with their Wet Seal and Auto Source companies in the United States. Although these ventures are small, they were the result of a strategy of "informed incrementalism." That is, these companies appear to have chosen an appropriate specialized concept for the United States market that they are starting small and hoping to grow. They have carefully thought out these operations and they appear to have the full support of management. The management teams are prepared to pull out of the United States market if they are not successful, and are open to learning how to change the ventures, if necessary. Informed incrementalism may be a successful strategy provided companies are clear as to their objectives for their United States operation from the beginning. If they want to grow to a large size in the United States market, they must be prepared to commit considerable time and resources to making this happen using this strategy.

The Saturated Canadian Market

This could be characterized by the statement "there are no opportunities left in Canada." Most of the companies in this study entered the United States because executives believed that the Canadian market was saturated and that limits to growth had been realized. It is interesting to note, however, that Coles found new opportunities after re-examining the Canadian market. And, how is it that the Price Club and Lenscrafters found niches in the Canadian market? Is it that the market is saturated or is it, more likely, that opportunity exists for new ideas, concepts, and retail formats and that the market is really only saturated with old ideas. Similarly, Canadian Tire believed that its market had reached saturation, yet has now found that it has at least another five years of opportunity to expand its existing businesses in Canada. Canadian Tire has also found room for new ideas gained from its most recent entrance into the United States market that are being applied successfully in Canada.

American Competition

It has been said so often that it is becoming a truism — American retailers are more competitive than Canadian retailers. The danger is that this could lead to the belief that Canadians cannot compete which is not the message that the authors wish to leave the reader. Canadian retailers can compete, but they will have to change their way of thinking and operating. This is happening with retailers like Canadian Tire, Dylex, Bata Shoes and Future Shops, but more need to learn the way to play the new game.

OVERCOMING THE BARRIERS TO LEARNING

It is evident from the above discussion that assumptions held by Canadian retailers about doing business in the United States market may have contributed to various performance problems there. In order to overcome these barriers, it is important to follow an appropriate process in making decisions regarding entering a new market — the United States or other country — as executives go about completing the activities set forth on their strategic agenda. This research indicates that when the decision making process is faulty, the results often are fatal. How do companies overcome the barriers during this process?

Treat the United States as a Foreign Market

Executives should pay attention to the market and cultural differences between Canada and the United States as they affect several aspects of doing business in the United States. In fact, it is strongly suggested that executives consider the United States as a foreign market, and treat their decisions as they would in approaching any other foreign market. Executives should not assume that the two markets are the same, or that companies within each can be managed in the same way. When decision makers start with the assumption that the two markets are not the same, they are more likely to take the appropriate steps toward entering the United States.

Test Assumptions and Perceptions Prior to Entry

The success of the decision making process relies on the accuracy of information and the knowledge of those making the decisions. The most important part of a company's pre-entry orientation is the perceptions and assumptions of the executive team because they act as a base from which all of the decisions regarding the United States venture are made. If the pre-entry aspect of the decision making process is faulty, the remainder of the process is unlikely to be effective.

The decision makers' initial perceptions and assumptions also affect their ability to learn from experience in a new market and to respond to this information. Strong beliefs about the similarity of the two markets or the power of a concept can contribute to the difficulty of adjusting when faced with conflicting information. There comes a time when it is necessary to revise one's basic assumptions and perceptions, rather than continue to alter operating decisions in a way that only supports the initial position.

Why is it so difficult to accurately understand the United States prior to entry? Perhaps one reason has to do with the on-the-surface similarities between the two countries. However, another reason has to do with the effect on decision makers of their own culture. Executives are socialized relative to the larger society or culture in which they are raised. Their culture strongly influences and, in many cases, determines their perceptions and interpretations of the world around them. Executives from Canada become accustomed to doing business in ways that they have learned throughout their lifetimes. These mental maps, or filters, of the way to conduct business are firmly embedded and often reinforced by success, making it difficult to approach another culture or market in a different way unless one has direct experience in that market or culture.

However, the challenge is not to eliminate the Canadian frames of reference, but rather to learn to complement them with others that are appropriate to the decisions being made. The real challenge is to encourage diversity of input and flexibility of response. This means that executives from the other culture, or executives who have had direct and relevant experience in the market, must be made part of the decision making process.

Develop an Appropriate Structure for Decision Making

One of the key means by which executives can test their assumptions and perceptions about the United States market is by developing and utilizing an effective structure for decision making. However, although many organizations state that they make major strategic decisions in teams, the authors found that, with respect to the decision to enter the United States market, the team structure was not used effectively. Rather, the decision to enter was often made by the chief executive officer who then involved other executives to confirm the decision and/or implement it. There was also a tendency within several companies for the top management team involved with the United States venture to concur with the views of the chief executive officer about the United States market, and about the ability of the Canadian organization to enter that market.

This lack of critical, or objective, thinking has been called groupthink. Groupthink can be a major threat to effective decision making. It emerges when members of the management team are highly cohesive, somewhat isolated from events or new markets, and there is pressure to maintain consistent thinking. The chief executive officer's initial perceptions were key in determining the effectiveness of the remainder of the decision making process. In companies where the CEO understood or had knowledge of the United States market, this knowledge was incorporated into effective decisions for the venture.

This implies that it is risky to allow only one person to make a decision of such magnitude. For this type of strategic decision, group participation seems essential. Diversity of opinion could be advantageous in such decisions to ensure that all of the pros and cons are analyzed. No one person necessarily has all the knowledge necessary to make an effective decision. Therefore, the decision to enter the United States market should be made by a management team. It is beneficial if members of the group have varied backgrounds and different functional expertise to ensure a variety of perspectives are brought to bear. And, it follows that, if individual contributions are necessary, it is important that a climate be created which encourages innovative ideas, risk taking and honest discussion.

Create Positive Team Dynamics during Decision Making Process

This lack of objective thinking, or groupthink dynamic, means that the organization does not benefit from individual contributions to the decision making process. In order to overcome this barrier, chief executive officers should be aware that they may behave in ways that are not always conducive to getting subordinates to discuss their ideas frankly. They should find the time to uncover, through careful observation and questioning, their impact on others. The aim is to make their colleagues more flexible in dealing with them.

To maximize individual contributions, the role of the CEO is to establish, build and maintain an effective decision making network. This requires exploring how the group presently functions. To do this, group members should be asked how to make the group more effective, and how to alter conditions leading to group ineffectiveness. Team members should be encouraged to play devil's advocate to avoid the perils of everyone thinking alike. All assumptions and biases should be stated and made explicit. Team members should be encouraged to challenge perceptual biases and present diverse opinions, and these challenges and dissenting opinions must be considered for the decision making process to be effective. Overall, the CEO must encourage open discussion, dissent, and opposition to prevent groupthink and to ensure continual learning and adaptation.

However, often individual team members have difficulty making changes to team interaction on their own. If the top management team dynamics cannot be improved to promote effective decision making processes, the company may have to hire a qualified and objective person from outside of the company to facilitate discussions.

Commitment to do Business in the United States

Executives should make clear their reason for entering the United States market. The reason should not be to expand the Canadian concept to a bigger market because, in many cases, the Canadian concept cannot be transferred to the United States. Therefore, the decision to enter the United States should be made because the company's executives are committed to doing business there.

In addition to entering the United States market for the right reason, it is also important that the Canadian management have a strong commitment to succeeding in that market from the outset. The decision to enter the United States market should be viewed as a major strategic decision of priority to the Canadian company. To ensure commitment to this decision, it is important that the decision to enter the United States is initiated from within the company, rather than by outsiders. Canadian executives must be prepared to commit the necessary financial and managerial resources to the United States venture. They must realize that it will take a lot of both since there appears to be a longer time line to success in the United States requiring a substantial financial resource commitment. In the words of Mark Blumes, "You have to have a passion to be there and to succeed. You have to be prepared to put your heart and soul into it." John Kron, from Canadian Tire, stated, "If you're going to go down there, you have to go down there for keeps — 100 percent."

Avoid Undo Time Pressure on the Decision to Enter the United States

It is vital that Canadian companies take the time necessary to prepare themselves. The pre-entry aspect of the decision making process is crucial to long term success in the United States. Once there, executives have little or no time to study the market, as the focus must be on competing in it.

Correct Interpretation is Key

An interesting and important observation of the study was that gathering information about a market does not necessarily lead to knowledge of that market unless the information is interpreted correctly. It seemed that the only way that Canadian companies were assured of gathering the right information, and accurately interpreting it, was either from having executives in Canada who had already learned from having had experience in the United States, or by having qualified American managers as part of the team. The nationality of the executives is not the key, but their having direct experience in the market is critical.

It appears that to gain the capacity necessary to compete in the United States market, Canadian companies should hire management talent experienced in the target market. These people should have an understanding of the targeted consumers, the competition, the competitive intensity of the supplier situation, and regional differences, among other factors. Canadian companies considering transferring, or modifying, a Canadian concept for the United States must make sure that someone experienced in the target market investigates the appropriateness of the concept.

Managing Operations in the United States Market

The ideal structure for managing the United States operation appears to be a combination of Canadian and American management. It is best to have American management experienced in the target retail market, making the day to day operating decisions for the venture in order to ensure that they fit with that market. They are the best qualified to diagnose problems and to determine solutions. It is also important that they have substantial input into the strategic decisions. Moreover, the decentralization of many of the organizational functions is critical to ensure that the decisions made are most appropriate for the United States market. Successful companies in the study often ensured that very talented United States management was in place within the United States operation prior to acquiring it, and they believed that this was key to their success in the United States market.

These recommendations do not preclude the involvement of Canadian management in United States decisions. The role of the Canadian top management team is to achieve integration and control of the United States operation, to establish the framework for making decisions, to manage the decision making process, and to offer a fresh perspective to further ensure that the decisions made for the United States venture are good ones. Control can be achieved in a variety of ways such as involving the Canadian board of directors and management. However, all decisions should incorporate the input of those experienced with the United States market. The major implication of this is that Canadian executives must ensure that they choose United States management that they have trust in.

Set Specific, but Realistic Goals

Not surprisingly, all of the executives indicated that they had expected their United States operations to be successful. However, what differed among them was whether or not their expectations for the United States venture were developed, via the appropriate decision making process, into specific goals. Setting financial goals was particularly effective.

There are three advantages to setting specific goals prior to entry. First, the process requires the top executive team members to think through the requirements for success, in terms of the time, money and effort necessary. Provided that it is done realistically, the process alone could lead to a better decision about whether or not a Canadian company should enter the United States. Second, the process can lead to a greater commitment toward achieving the goals set. Commitment to succeeding in the United States market was discussed earlier as crucial to success. Finally, goals provide a standard for measuring how the operation is doing. When people know what they are aiming toward, they can more easily monitor their progress, or lack thereof. Without any specific goals, it is very difficult to assess where the company should be. If specific goals are set, people understand when they are off track — the distance from the target acts as a signal pointing to problems — a built-in feedback mechanism to management, calling into question previous decisions and assumptions.

Develop the Ability to Learn

A final recommendation is that those making the decisions for the United States operation must develop the ability to learn about the United States. Learning has to do with increasing one's knowledge and understanding. The ability to learn is critical at all times and not just before and at the time of entry. During the pre-entry phase, Canadian management must understand that there are differences between Canada and the United States and they must learn about what these differences are from those who have knowledge of them. This learning must be incorporated into the initial strategic decisions made for the United States operation.

During the entry phase, decision makers must be open to learning from their mistakes and open to reassessing their initial perceptions and assumptions upon which their decisions were based. Finally, ongoing learning is required during the post-entry phase. Because conditions are always changing, it is important that decision makers continue to learn about the United States market and incorporate this learning into the strategic decision making process. Therefore, the more effectively a company's decision makers learn, the more likely they are to continue operating successfully in the United States market. They need to have a willingness to try something, abandon it if it does not work and try something else. This was seen to be one of the competitive advantages of the American companies coming to Canada.

Learning is more likely to occur under conditions where error is tolerated, assumptions are testable, and key aspects of information are not missing. Thus, it is vital to identify and check the assumptions of decision makers prior to entry, because their assumptions often seriously limited the effectiveness of their entry decisions. Since assumptions are often subjective and hard to identify, it is a good idea to use an objective person from outside the decision making process to help decision makers to identify them. To facilitate this process, management consultants can be used. In particular, United States consultants, experienced in target retail markets, can provide the information necessary to assess the United States market.

Figure 1 summarizes the above recommendations. What is particularly noteworthy is the importance of the decision making process and the decisions made prior to entry. The analysis suggests that if the pre-entry decision making process, and the decisions made during this process, are appropriate for entering the United States market, the chances for success in the United States market are enhanced considerably. On the other hand, if they are inappropriate, the chances for success are greatly hindered.

Figure 1   Effective Decision Making Processes

1. Accurate Perceptions and Assumptions About the United States

   • Canadian and U.S. retail markets are very different in terms of attitudes, values and business practices.

   • Organizations in the U.S. must be managed differently from those in Canada.

2. Decision to Enter the United States

   • A desire to do business in the United States versus just expand the Canadian concept.

   • Initiated from within the company.

   • Made by a team with varied backgrounds who are encouraged to critically analyze the decision.

- Canadian concept and ways of doing business may be inappropriate for the United States. Canadian concept probably is not invincible.

- Top executive team must have strong desire to enter and succeed in the U.S. and be willing to commit money and time of key management.

- Top executive team must view decision to enter as major strategic decision and must be focussed on and committed to it.

3. Increase Understanding of U.S. Operation and Target Retail Market

- Acquire or hire top management talent with knowledge, understanding of U.S. operation and experience in target retail market.

- Research conducted must be designed and interpreted with those with experience in, and an understanding of, United States retail market.

4. Decisions Made for United States Operation

- Must incorporate knowledge of United States market so that they fit with that market (ie. strategy chosen must be appropriate, as well as all other decisions made for United States operation).

- Day to day decisions should be made by (or with significant input from) Americans with experience in and knowledge of United States retail market.

- Strategic and other decisions should be made (i) by Canadians and Americans jointly, (ii) by Canadians with significant input from Americans or (iii) by Americans and approved by Canadians.

5. Set Goals for United States Operation

- Set specific, realistic goals for United States operation. Financial goals are very important.

6. Ability to Learn About the Market While Operating In It

- Feedback into perceptions, assumptions and knowledge of market must be accurate, and must be incorporated into decisions for United States venture quickly for survival/success in the United States to be possible.

In closing, let us reflect on our objectives when writing this book. We began by asking the questions: "Why can't some of Canada's biggest and best retailers succeed in the United States?", "What explained the performance differentials?" and "How could the potential for success be increased for future entries?" In attempting to answer these questions, we have outlined the experiences of several Canadian and American companies. In-depth analyses led to a number of insights and lessons learned. We have also presented less obvious, yet very important explanations such as the lack of recognition of cultural differences, misleading myths and faulty assumptions, and barriers in companies' decision making processes that have impeded the performance of Canadian companies in the U.S. market. From these, it is clear that the problems in doing business in the United States have far deeper roots than may have originally been imagined. The aim of this book was to improve the effectiveness and success rate of Canadian companies in the U.S. market. It is the authors' hope that, through careful consideration of the findings of this book, this objective will be met.

SOURCES

Chapter 1

p. 14   Mark's Work Wearhouse case study written by Terry Hildebrand and edited by Henry Lane.

p. 32   Coles Bookstores Limited case information taken from *Coles U.S. Market Strategic Analysis and Opportunities Research,* Management Horizons, April 15, 1986.

p. 46   Shoppers Drug Mart case information obtained from an interview with David Bloom, Chairman and CEO, the 1990 Annual Report, and Imasco news releases dated June 25 and September 17, 1990. The complete report of the interview with David Bloom can be found in *An Investigation of Canadian Retailers Entering and Adapting to the U.S. Market,* Terry A. Hildebrand, unpublished Ph.D. dissertation, School of Business Administration, The University of Western Ontario, June, 1989.

Chapter 2

p. 59   Canadian Tire Corporation case study written by Terry Hildebrand, edited by Henry Lane and updated by Shawna O'Grady.

p. 60   "profits during the 1980-81 period" from Tigert, Don, research report prepared for Burns Fry Ltd., April, 1982.

p. 61   "Canadian Tire had succeeded" from Baetz, Mark C. and Troschke, Ralph, *Strategic Management: Canadian Cases* (Homewood, Il.: Richard D. Irwin, 1987).

p. 62   "The system's key components...retail outlets" from Tigert, Don, *op. cit.*

p. 67   Market characteristics of the sunbelt states from Tigert, Don, *op. cit.*

p. 68   "Retail analysts identified two potential problems...company-owned and operated" from Baetz and Troschke, *op. cit.*

p. 70   Strategy to turn White's around from Baetz and Troschke, *op. cit.*

Chapter 3

p. 113 Peoples Jewellers Limited case study written by Terry Hildebrand, edited by Henry Lane and updated by Shawna O'Grady.

p. 120 "In many ways it was this exposure" from Self, Nancy, investment report prepared for Burns Fry Ltd., 1987.

p. 138 Grafton Group three years later information from The Blue Box of CBS stock reports, February 1990, August 1990, March 1991, September 1991 and March 1992; the 1990 Annual Report; the *London Free Press,* February 11, 1992; and *The Globe and Mail,* May 12, 1992.

Chapter 4

p. 152 "Lortie believed that it was imperative" from Lortie, Pierre, "Growing in the United States Market: Temptation or Obligation," December 9, 1986.

p. 154 Pierre Jette provided senior management with detailed studies and information in his document "Corporate Development Value Added Acquisition Strategies for the Nineties," February, 1989.

Chapter 5

p. 191 The analytic framework used in this chapter adapted in part from Hildebrand, Terry, *An Investigation of Canadian Retailers Entering and Adapting to the U.S. Market,* unpublished Ph.D. dissertation, School of Business Administration, The University of Western Ontario, June, 1989.

p. 222 The three levels of explanation adapted from Senge, Peter, *The Fifth Discipline: The Art and Practice of the Learning Organization* (New York: Doubleday, 1990).

Chapter 6

p. 242 For more detailed information on achievement and aggression, see Jackson, D., *Personality Research Form Manual,* 3rd edition (New York: Research Psychologists Press, 1984).

p. 244 For more detailed information on risk taking and tolerance, see Jackson, D., *Jackson Personality Inventory* (New York: Research Psychologists Press, 1976).

p. 244 "personal worth results from self-sacrificing work," Cook, J.D., et al., *The Experience of Work: A Compendium and Review of 249 Measures and Their Use* (New York: Academic Press, 1981) p. 142.

p. 244 "the extent to which a person's work affects his self esteem," *Ibid.,* p. 117.

p. 244 "The next four dimensions" from Hofstede, Geert, *Culture's Consequences: International Differences in Work-Related Values* (Beverly Hills, CA: Sage Publications, 1980).

Chapter 7
p. 268 David Browne quoted in *Industry Week,* September 3, 1990.

Chapter 8
p. 301 Kevin Gordon quoted by Morris Saffer in address to The Retail Advertising Conference, Chicago, 1991.

p. 318 Jeff Wells quoted in *Inside Retailing,* Lebhar-Friedman Inc., January 7, 1991.

Chapter 9
p. 336 "The information that the master picks up" from Neisser, U., *Cognition and Reality* (San Francisco, CA: Freeman & Co., 1976) pp. 180-181.

ABOUT THE AUTHORS

Wendy Evans, President of Evans and Company since 1986, has 20 years of industry experience spanning both the retail and wholesale sectors. Working for companies in both the department store and chain store field, she acquired expertise in areas ranging from strategic and financial planning to merchandising, purchasing, and expansion research. She now provides marketing, research and management services to a wide variety of clients including some of Canada's best known retailers, and is a member of the Research Faculty at Ryerson Polytechnical Institute.

Henry Lane is the Donald F. Hunter Professor of International Business (a Maclean Hunter endowment), School of Business, University of Western Ontario, and the Program Manager of the "Doing Business in The U.S." program at the National Centre for Management Research and Development. Dr. Lane received his DBA in Organizational Behaviour from the Harvard Business School; he teaches International Business and Organizational Change and Renewal at Western.

Shawna O'Grady is Assistant Professor of Management and Organizational Behaviour, School of Business Administration, Queen's University. Dr. O'Grady has a B. Comm. and MIR from Queen's University and a PhD from the School of Business, University of Western Ontario. Her primary interest is in strategic decision making and the Canada/U.S. international market where she helps companies to improve their competitiveness.

Terry Hildebrand is a partner of TRIAD Management Consultants, specializing in the design and implementation of strategic change and creating customer-focussed organizations. Dr. Hildebrand received her PhD in Organizational Behaviour from the School of Business, University of Western Ontario.